WEBER'S GREATEST HITS

JAMIE PURVIANCE

PHOTOGRAPHY BY RAY KACHATORIAN

HOUGHTON MIFFLIN HARCOURT
BOSTON • NEW YORK • 2017

CONTENTS

FOREWORD

The other day, I was staring at the bookcase in my office, which is loaded with Weber cookbooks. As I leafed through some of them published as far back as the 1970s, I paused to think about a question I'm often asked: how did Weber get into the cookbook business?

I would like to respond that we crafted a strategic plan for producing cookbooks and then executed it flawlessly. But the truth is, we became cookbook publishers almost by accident.

In 1952, George Stephen invented the Weber Kettle Grill. He was working for Weber Brothers Metal Works at the time, so our company has always been in the business of bending and welding metal. Back then, the Weber charcoal kettle grill was far from a success. People would look at its unusual shape and wonder why it was a grill with a lid and why anyone would pay the outrageous price—for the 1950s—of fifty dollars for it. To overcome that resistance, George put on live demonstrations of his charcoal kettle at retail stores, showing interested shoppers that his invention could grill steaks without flare-ups and roast turkeys without a rotisserie.

As sales took off, Weber kettle owners began requesting recipes and cooking instructions for all kinds of meats and seafood. George, along with friends and family, put together a small cookbook that sold for fifty cents. He was amazed at how often it had to be reprinted. And that's how our cookbook business got started.

I joined the company in 1971, and folks who wanted to be better grillers were still regularly using those little paperback cookbooks from the 1950s. I remember a recipe for back ribs that mistakenly called for the direct heat method of grilling. One of my early jobs was managing customer service, and I got an earful from grillers who burned their ribs following our flawed instructions. That experience convinced me that Weber had to become more than a grill manufacturer. We had to teach the art of covered grilling, and we had to make sure our instructions and recipes were flawless. Looking back, it's clear that we didn't have a strategic plan for publishing. But what we did have were Weber owners who showed us the way by buying our little paperback cookbooks.

I'm not a publisher or an author. I'm a grill salesman. I quickly discovered that producing

a cookbook with great recipes, beautiful photography, and clearly written, helpful tips and techniques was beyond my capabilities. Thank goodness I met an experienced publisher, Susan Maruyama, who led me to a terrific author, Jamie Purviance. I knew what Weber owners wanted in cookbooks, and Susan and Jamie had the knowledge and experience to make those cookbooks happen.

The rest, as they say, is history. Jamie has developed thousands of recipes using Weber grills and accessories. He has tested and retested each recipe with meticulous dedication, making sure that backyard chefs will be successful the first time they try any dish. Over the years, we have discovered scores of grilling tips and techniques that are now a hallmark of our books, and we have learned to bring our recipes and instructions to life with great photographs. There is nothing like a picture to help folks select a recipe and then duplicate the results for their family and friends.

I'm happy to report that we've sold literally millions of cookbooks all over the world, and that they've even been translated into ten languages. Many grillers have several of our cookbooks, and over the years, they have asked us to identify our favorite recipes. That got us thinking, and we decided to get to work putting together a single cookbook that would celebrate the best of the best.

We've done just that in *Weber's Greatest Hits*. We polled Weber cookbook owners and Weber employees, including the chefs from our restaurants and grill academies, and asked them to select their favorite recipes. It was a tough task, and Jamie had the final say on which recipes made the cut. What you'll find in these pages is indeed the best of our best.

I am sure *Weber's Greatest Hits* will be my go-to cookbook when I am eager to delight my family with a great meal. I'll bet it will become a well-worn favorite on your cookbook shelf, too.

Happy grilling,

Mike Kempster

Mike Kempster
EXECUTIVE BOARD MEMBER
AND BRAND GODFATHER

INTRODUCTION

When Weber decided to publish this collection of greatest hits, I immediately felt the weight of responsibility down to my bones. The term *greatest hits* took me back to my youth and the vinyl albums and box sets that made indelible impressions on me and millions of other music fans. I carried my prized collection from one college dorm room to another, from each new apartment to the next, and then to my first house. Even though I have since replaced all of that vinyl with digital versions, I can't imagine ever letting go of the iconic songs of my favorite artists.

I knew this cookbook had to deliver the best of Weber in the same way that my beloved records delivered the best of a band or an artist. That's a tall order, for sure. How do you choose the recipes? How can you be certain that each recipe is worthy of being part of such an ambitious title? The short answer is, you ask. You ask the people who regularly grill from the cookbooks Weber has published over the past couple of decades. They will tell you which recipes stand out as the best of the best. And they did just that.

Our survey of Weber cookbook owners revealed that taste is crucial (obviously), but it is not he only consideration. A lot of people feel strongly about the ease of preparation, too. Their comments about recipes such as Zesty Garlic Shrimp (page 38) and Corn on the Cob with Basil-Parmesan Butter (page 258) make clear that simplicity often matters as much as taste. Another factor is creativity. Weber fans aren't interested in bizarre innovations, but they do appreciate twists on familiar ideas. That's why this book features recipes such as Ginger Porterhouse Steaks with Roasted Sesame Salt (page 104), Charred Asparagus with Basil-Lime Dipping Sauce (page 268), and Chile-Rubbed Chicken with Jicama, Avocado, and Orange Salsa (page 197). These recipes are unique without being weird.

Reasonable people can—and will—disagree about the final selections here. Not surprisingly, even my Weber colleagues engaged in some heated debates about which recipes to include. It seems that everyone has a few must-haves. We did agree, however, that this book must deliver the features that are part of every Weber cookbook. That means brand-new photography of real food made from the actual recipes. We don't tolerate any fake food-styling maneuvers. We also insist on giving you plenty of insights into how to be a better griller. My Top Ten Tips for Grilling Greatness (page 10) is a valuable collection in and of itself. Follow those tips and you will be among the best grillers in your neighborhood. If you want to step up your game even more, check out my Top Five Tips for Grilling Like an Expert (page 20).

In the past two decades, Weber has developed well over 2,500 recipes to cover a huge range of grilling possibilities and occasions. But we know that sometimes all you want are the favorites. Sometimes you want to know for sure that everyone will love the food. This is the book for those times—when nothing but the best will do.

TOP TEN TIPS FOR
GRILLING GREATNESS

 PREHEAT THE GRILL. What happens when the food hits the grate can sometimes separate a good griller from a great griller. If the grate is cold, the food can stick, which means it will never have a decent chance of searing properly or developing awesome grill marks. So, even if a recipe calls for medium or low heat, always preheat the grate on high first. Open the grill lid, fire up the charcoal or the gas burners, close the lid, and then let the grate get screaming hot for about 10 minutes. The grill temperature should reach at least 500°F.

 CLEAN THE GRATE WHEN IT'S HOT. If you leave "stuff" on the grate from your last barbecue, it can be the glue that holds your new food to the grate a lot longer than you want. As soon as you have preheated the grill for about 10 minutes, brush off that stuff entirely, leaving behind a clean, smooth surface on which your new food can brown evenly. The best tool for the job is a sturdy, long-handled brush with stiff, stainless-steel bristles.

 GET YOUR ACT TOGETHER. Gather all that you will need and put it near the grill before you begin cooking. If you have to run back into the kitchen while your food is on the fire, you might miss (that's code for overcook or burn) something important. So bring your tools, bring your already oiled and seasoned food, bring your mop or glaze or sauce, bring your garnishes—you get the idea. And don't forget clean platters for the cooked food. French chefs call this *mise en place* (literally, "put in place"). We call it getting your act together.

 GIVE YOURSELF AT LEAST TWO HEAT ZONES. If you set up your grill for one type of heat only, your options are limited. What if something is cooking faster than you want? What if your food is causing flare-ups? What if you are grilling two different foods at the same time? You need at least two zones of heat: one for direct heat (where the fire is directly under the food) and one for indirect heat (where the fire is off to the side). That way, you can move your food from one zone to the other whenever you like.

 OIL THE FOOD, NOT THE GRATE. Oil is important for preventing food from sticking, and a high-quality oil can also add flavor. You will get the best possible results when you lightly brush or spray the food itself, not the cooking grate. That way, you can coat the food surfaces evenly without too much oil dripping between the bars of the grate onto the fire, which can cause flare-ups. Plus, if you try to oil a hot grate, the oil tends to smoke and burn almost immediately, creating undesirable flavors.

LEAVE YOURSELF SOME ROOM TO MOVE. Packing a lot of food into a tight space on the grill is asking for trouble. Always leave some space around each piece of food so you can maneuver your tongs or spatula easily to grasp the pieces when necessary. Great grilling often involves jockeying food around the grill and setting it down on clean spots, so leave about one-third of the cooking grate empty at all times.

 PUT A LID ON IT. A grill's lid is there for a lot more than keeping out the rain. It is how you prevent too much air from getting in and too much heat and smoke from getting out. When the lid is closed, the grate is hotter, the grilling times are faster, the smoky tastes are better, and the flare-ups are fewer. So put a lid on it. That said, don't forget to open the vents on the lid of a charcoal grill at least halfway. Every fire needs a little air to keep on burning.

 LEAVE THE FOOD ALONE. Nearly everyone likes food when it is seared to a deep brown with plenty of beautifully charred bits. The trouble is, many people move their food so often that it doesn't get enough time in one place to reach that desirable level of color and flavor. In almost every case, you should turn food just once or twice. If you are fiddling with it more than that, you are also probably opening the lid too much, which can cause another set of problems.

TAKE CHARGE OF THE FIRE. On its own, a charcoal fire reaches its hottest temperatures first and loses heat either quickly or slowly, depending on the type of charcoal and, more important, on you. You need to take charge of the fire by refueling it, by pushing the coals around to suit your needs, by sweeping away ashes that can clog the bottom vents, and by adjusting the vents on the lid for optimal airflow. You should control the fire, not the other way around.

 KNOW WHEN TO STOP. Knowing when to take your food off the grill is crucial. Learn various doneness clues, such as the gently yielding firmness of juicy grilled chicken when you press the surface with a fingertip. For an even more reliable method of judging doneness, get an instant-read thermometer. Its slim probe will help you pinpoint that critical moment when your food is at its peak of perfection.

GETTING STARTED

We grill for fun. It's a chance to get outside and play with fire and savor the results. The general idea is blatantly straightforward: you put food over the fire and cook it until it is done. It seems we could rely mostly on instinct. After all, humankind has been cooking over fire and honing our instincts since the dawn of civilization. That's all true, but so is the fact that our fuel choices and grills have changed a lot, especially in the past few decades. For the best results today, it helps to have a relatively new understanding of how to use them.

CHARCOAL GRILLS

The process of building a fire of burning coals and sustaining it at the right level(s) of heat for whatever we want to eat is immensely gratifying. Perhaps the only thing better is the unmistakable taste of the food. Both experiences depend largely on the design of your charcoal grill and on the kind of charcoal you choose to use.

FUEL CHOICES Briquettes are the most popular fuel choice in North America. Inexpensive and available nearly everywhere, they are most commonly black bundles of compressed sawdust and coal, along with binders and fillers like clay and sodium nitrate. Some are presoaked in lighter fluid for an easier start, but they can impart a chemical taste to food if you don't burn off the lighter fluid completely before the food hits the grill. Standard briquettes produce a predictable, even heat over a long period. A batch of 80 to 100 briquettes will last for about an hour, which is plenty of time to grill most foods without having to replenish the fire.

Pure hardwood (or "all-natural") briquettes have the same pillow shape as standard briquettes but burn at higher temperatures and have none of the questionable fillers and binders. They are typically made of crushed hardwoods bound

together with nothing but natural starches. You'll probably pay more for these briquettes, but many serious grillers and barbecue competitors consider them the gold standard of charcoal.

Lump charcoal (or "charwood") is made by burning hardwood logs in an oxygen-deprived environment, such as an underground pit or a kiln. Over time, the water and resins are burned out of the logs, leaving behind only combustible carbon. This type of charcoal lights faster than briquettes, burns hotter, and burns out faster. It tends to spark and crackle and creates wonderfully smoky aromas like real wood.

LIGHTING THE CHARCOAL If you're outfitted with the proper equipment, firing up a charcoal grill can take as little as 15 to 20 minutes.

The easiest method involves a chimney starter, which is an upright metal cylinder with a handle on the outside and a wire rack inside. You simply fill the space under the wire rack with a few sheets of wadded-up newspaper or a couple of paraffin cubes and then fill the space above the rack with your choice of briquettes, hardwood briquettes, or lump charcoal.

Once you light the newspaper or paraffin, some impressive thermodynamics channels the heat evenly throughout the briquettes.

When the briquettes are lightly covered with white ash, put on two insulated barbecue mitts and grab hold of the two handles on the chimney starter. The swinging handle is there to help you lift the chimney starter and safely aim the coals just where you want them.

HEAT CONFIGURATIONS The most versatile charcoal configuration is a two-zone fire. That means the coals are spread out on one side of the charcoal grate and the other side has no coals at all. This allows you to cook with both direct and indirect heat.

Occasionally, you will prefer a three-zone split fire, with the coals separated into two equal piles on opposite sides of the charcoal grate. That arrangement gives you two zones for direct heat (high, medium-high, medium, or low) and one zone between them for indirect heat. It works especially well for cooking a roast over indirect heat because you have the same level of heat on either side of the roast.

The temperature of your charcoal fire depends on how much charcoal you use and how long it's been burning. The coals are at their hottest when newly lit. They gradually lose heat over time.

Once you have arranged the coals on the charcoal grate, put the cooking grate in place, place the lid on the grill, and wait for about 10 minutes to allow the temperature to rise to at least 500°F. This will preheat the cooking grate, which will make the grate much easier to clean and will ensure a better sear on your food.

GRILL SAFETY

Never use a grill without first reading the owner's guide that came with it. It is important that you familiarize yourself with and heed all "dangers," "warnings," and "cautions" detailed in its pages to be sure you are using your grill safely. Be sure to follow the grilling procedures and maintenance requirements included in the guide as well.

If you have any questions concerning the "dangers," "warnings," and "cautions" in your Weber charcoal, gas, or electric grill owner's guide, or if you do not have an owner's guide for your specific grill model, please visit www.weber.com to access your guide or to locate the toll-free telephone number for Weber-Stephen Products LLC Customer Service.

GAS GRILLS

There are days when nearly everyone prefers the push-button convenience of a gas grill over the fickleness of a live charcoal fire. A gas grill makes it amazingly easy to control the flames, especially with today's new technologies for minimizing flare-ups and channeling away grease. Built-in or portable smoker boxes provide the option for adding real wood smoke, and an array of other accessories, such as griddles, pizza stones, and woks, can quickly turn a gas grill into a fully loaded outdoor kitchen.

STARTING A GAS GRILL Lighting a gas grill is usually as simple as lifting the lid, turning on the gas, and igniting the burners. After you have opened the valve on your propane tank all the way (or turned on the gas at the source), wait for a minute for the gas to travel through the gas line and then turn each burner to high, making sure one burner has ignited before turning on the next. Close the lid and preheat the grill for 10 to 15 minutes. As with a charcoal grill, this step makes the cooking grate easier to clean and helps you get a good sear on your food.

If you smell gas, you may have a leak around the connection or in the hose. First, turn off all the burners. Next, close the valve on your propane tank (or natural gas line) and disconnect the hose. Now, wait for a few minutes and then reconnect the hose. Try lighting the grill again. If you still smell gas, shut the grill down and contact the manufacturer.

HEAT CONFIGURATIONS For direct cooking, leave all the burners on and adjust them for the heat level you want. For example, if you want to cook with direct medium heat, turn all the burners down to medium and wait until the thermometer indicates the temperature is in the range of 350° to 450°F.

For indirect cooking, you can leave some of the burners on and turn one or two of them off.

FOR BOTH GAS AND CHARCOAL GRILLS

Once the cooking grate is preheated, put on an insulated barbecue mitt, grab a long-handled grill brush, and scrape off any particles or residue stuck to the grate. You want a clean, smooth surface for cooking your food. Do not oil the cooking grate before grilling. Any oil you apply would just drip into the fire and likely cause flare-ups. You can avoid wasting oil and improve the chances of food releasing more easily from the grate by oiling the food, not the grate.

Once your grill is preheated and the grate is brushed clean, bring out the food and other supplies you will need for whatever you are cooking and organize them near the grill. Have everything chopped and measured beforehand and within reach to make cooking go faster, and you won't have to run back into the kitchen. Don't forget clean plates and platters for serving the grilled food.

Keeping the grill lid closed as much as possible is important. The lid limits the amount of air that gets to the fire, thus preventing flare-ups, and it helps to cook food on the top and the bottom simultaneously. Although the bottom of the food is almost always exposed to more intense heat than the top, the lid reflects some heat downward, which speeds up the overall cooking time. Without the lid, the fire would lose heat more quickly and many foods would take much longer to cook, possibly drying out in the process.

TOP FIVE TIPS FOR
GRILLING LIKE AN EXPERT

1 BASTING WITH LOVE POTION NO. 10. One of the surest ways of making food taste like it has been cooked by a five-star chef is to baste it with something outrageously good, like gloriously seasoned fat. Start by browning whole garlic cloves in butter or extra-virgin olive oil and then simmer the mixture for a few minutes with fresh herb sprigs, half a lemon, and your favorite spices. A small pot of this potion next to the grill will be your little secret for adding glistening layers of out-of-this-world flavor.

2 SIDING WITH GBD. The standard way to grill meats like steak and pork tenderloin is to cook them on two sides until GBD (golden brown and delicious). But meats have more than two sides, of course, and the more sides you brown, the better the meat will taste. Using tongs to hold meats over the fire on their skinny sides creates not only wonderful new flavor compounds but also more irresistible charred crusts.

3 GETTING DOWN IN THE EMBERS. If you are inclined to play with the fire, you might already know how fun and fabulous it is to cook steaks right in the coals (not on the grate). But you don't need to stop there. You can take full advantage of woodsy charcoal by setting a cast-iron pan directly on the smoldering embers. That's how the pros get a smoky sear on scallops or other small pieces of food that benefit from the fragrance of the fire.

4 REVERSING THE SEAR. Traditionally, grillers sear thick steaks over direct heat and then finish them over indirect heat. But the reverse-sear method is gaining popularity among some top-notch grill chefs. The steaks are roasted slowly over low indirect heat for 20 minutes or so and then finished over a ripping-hot fire. The advantage is that the steak achieves a wider swath of rosy red meat from top to bottom and less of an outer ring of overcooked meat.

5 TRUSTING THE SNAKE. Managing a charcoal fire to maintain a continuous low temperature is crucial for some recipes. But knowing how much charcoal you need to light to begin the cooking and when you should add more to keep the temperature steady is not always easy. One "surefire" way around any confusion is to rely on the so-called snake method: create a C-shaped arc of charcoal briquettes along one side of a grill and light the arc at one end. The briquettes will burn gradually, like a fuse, so you won't need to add more fuel for hours.

SMOKING ON THE GRILL

Barbecue masters and "sultans of smoke" tend to talk a big game and lead you to believe their smoking techniques are far beyond the understanding of backyard grillers. Don't be intimidated by the bravado and secrecy. Smoking is much simpler than it looks—and it doesn't require a humongous barbecue rig, either. It is really a form of seasoning, like rubbing meat with spices or letting meat sit in a marinade. Think of it as cooking your food in an aromatic cloud of seasonings. The key to success is in knowing which seasonings (wood) to use and how much to use.

WHICH WOODS TO USE Like herbs and spices, each type of wood has its own set of characteristics and overall strength. Most of the fruitwoods, such as apple and cherry, are mild, so they pair nicely with mild foods like fish and chicken. The intensity of cedar is comparable to that of the fruitwoods, as the long and delicious history of pairing cedar and salmon illustrates. If you are looking for woodsy aromas that are more pronounced and assertive, consider hickory, oak, and maple. Any one of these is a good choice for pork and beef. And if you like a highly pungent wood smoke, try mesquite. It has the boldest aroma of all. That's why it is the popular choice in Texas and the Southwest for spice-crusted meats like leg of lamb and beef steak.

We're talking about personal preferences here, so there is almost no wrong choice of wood. We do advise you to stay away from some woods, however, such as pine and aspen, which are so soft and resinous that their smoke is bitter and potentially toxic. Stick with the hardwoods. Get started with the popular combinations in the chart above and revise them to suit your taste.

HOW MUCH WOOD TO USE Wood aromas are meant to create an underlying taste that enhances food without overwhelming it. One way to do that is by choosing the correct

FOR SEAFOOD: ALDER OR CEDAR

FOR CHICKEN: CHERRY OR APPLE

FOR PORK: HICKORY OR PECAN

FOR BEEF & LAMB: OAK OR MESQUITE

smoking time. The most common mistake is to smoke food too long. This is particularly easy to do with seafood and light meats, which can soak up smoke in a matter of minutes. At some point, the smoke creeps over a line and changes from being pleasantly fragrant and woodsy to being aggressively bitter and sooty. To steer clear of this, add a few handfuls of water-soaked chips every hour, but *stop smoking your food once the first half of its cooking time is over.*

WHAT YOU'LL NEED If you use a charcoal grill, simply soak your wood chips in water for at least 30 minutes. Then remove the chips from the water, shake off the excess, and use tongs to scatter them over the burning charcoal. Many smoking recipes are true barbecue, with the food remaining over low indirect heat for a few hours or more. For these recipes, you will need to add more soaked wood chips (and charcoal) along the way to keep the smoke flowing.

If you use a gas grill, you will need some sort of box for smoking soaked wood chips, whether it's a built-in smoker box on your grill, a steel smoker box that sits on the cooking grate, or a disposable tin of prepackaged wood chips that you soak in a bowl of water for 30 minutes or so before you set it on the hot cooking grate. If you need to add more chips to a smoker box, do it while some of the previous chips are still burning. The old chips will help to ignite the new ones.

If you use a smoker, wood chunks are a good choice. They last much longer than chips, so you won't have to replenish them as often. You also don't need to soak them, which makes them doubly convenient. As dry as they are, wood chunks don't flame up the way wood chips do.

AMERICA'S TOP FIVE FAVORITES AND
HOW TO GRILL THEM BETTER

1. BURGERS

MEAT MATTERS. Prepackaged "hamburger" often means ground scraps of questionable quality. Once that meat has been compressed in a tray for sale, it will never have the loose, tender texture of a great burger. You are much better off buying a package labeled "ground beef" (by law, it can't include fat scraps), or if a gourmet burger is your goal, buy freshly ground chuck from a butcher you trust.

DIMPLING. Most burgers tend to puff up in the middle as they cook and stay that way once they are off the grill, making it difficult to pile on toppings. To avoid this trouble, use your thumb or the back of a spoon to press a shallow indentation in the center of each raw patty. As each patty cooks, that well will fill in and flatten out, giving you a nice level surface, not a big fat meatball.

MANAGING THE HEAT. The grill must be hot (preheated to medium-high heat, 400° to 500°F; or occasionally medium heat, 350° to 450°F for lamb burgers) and the grate must be clean. You have to be cool and patient. Close the lid as soon as the patties hit the grate. Give ¾-inch burgers 8 to 10 minutes total to reach medium doneness over a medium-hot fire, turning them only once or twice. Don't flip them more often than that or you run the risk of ripping the surface before it can develop a tasty crust. Oh, and don't ever smash burgers with a spatula! That forces out the juices.

2. STEAKS

MARVELOUS MARBLING. Steaks should have a generous amount of milky white fat running through them, not just on the perimeter. If steaks have minimal marbling or if their fat has a brownish or yellowish tint (a sign of old, dry meat), pass them up. What you want are thin, white wisps of luscious fat that will melt during grilling, providing the steaks with succulence.

PLENTY OF SALT. Season steaks with plenty of coarse salt 15 to 30 minutes before grilling. That simple step will improve their flavor dramatically because the salt will mingle with the meat juices, which helps to develop a delicious crust on the meat as it cooks. Kosher salt, with its large crystals and pure flavor, is our top choice, as it is less likely to dissolve completely and lose its character.

MATCHING THE HEAT TO THE MEAT. If your steaks are less than 1½ inches thick, sear and finish cooking them over direct (radiant) high heat. If they are thicker than that, sear them over direct heat and then slide them over to indirect (convection) heat so the inside of each steak has a chance to cook before the outside burns.

4. SAUSAGES

EASY DOES IT. The char of grilled sausages can be tasty, but fresh sausages cooked over high heat can burst apart, losing a lot of juice. If you notice flare-ups, it means you are squandering precious juices. Fresh sausages do much better grilled over direct medium or even medium-low heat.

ANOTHER BEER, PLEASE. Another good option is to poach fresh sausages first. Simmer them in beer until fully cooked and then take them to the hot grate for final browning. Or brown them first over direct medium heat and then finish them in a warm pan of beer.

HURRAY FOR HOT DOGS. Emulsified and fully cooked sausages, like hot dogs and kielbasa, do well over direct medium or medium-high heat. At this temperature, you can give them a little char while they reheat. Try butterflying them open, then lay the exposed surface area on the grate over direct heat.

3. CHICKEN

PAYING FOR FLAVOR. If you are willing to spend more for organic, free-range chicken, you will appreciate some obvious differences. Birds that are able to run around and forage in the great outdoors have a more pronounced chicken flavor and meat that is firmer without being tough.

EVENING OUT. One of the challenges of grilling boneless, skinless chicken breasts is that their thickness varies from end to end. If you find a thin strip of meat (known as the tender) under a breast, remove it and grill it separately. Also, for more even cooking, place each breast between two sheets of plastic wrap and pound it with a mallet or heavy pan to a uniform thickness of about ½ inch.

THE BONE ISSUE. Boneless chicken pieces are thin enough to grill entirely over direct heat. When the bones are involved, however, the parts take longer to cook, so it's important to use both direct and indirect heat.

5. RIBS

NOT TOO CLOSE. Choose the meatiest ribs you can find. It's a bad sign if you see bones peeking through the meat. Those "shiners" mean a butcher cut too close to the bone. Also, ideally, your ribs will have thin streaks of white fat woven within thick cuts of meat.

PEEL AWAY THE MEMBRANE. The tough membrane that covers the bone side of each rack has to go. Slide a dull knife along a bone far enough that you can pry the edge of the membrane loose. Then grab the slippery edge with a paper towel and peel it off. Otherwise you will feel like you are eating tape.

STAYING LOW. Barbecued ribs usually cook for at least 3 hours at temperatures as low as 225° to 250°F, which makes fire management crucial. Once the meat has darkened to a rich mahogany crust, spray or brush it with something moist and delicious (or at least water) and finish cooking each rack individually wrapped in foil. The meat will braise in the juices trapped in the wrapper until it is as tender as you like.

01

STARTERS

SMOKED AND
SPICED NUTS

PREP TIME
5 MINUTES

GRILLING TIME
20 TO 30 MINUTES

1 teaspoon packed light brown sugar

1 teaspoon dried thyme or rosemary, or ½ teaspoon each

¼ teaspoon cayenne pepper

¼ teaspoon mustard powder

2 cups mixed salted nuts (almonds, pecans, cashews, and the like)

2 teaspoons extra-virgin olive oil

A bowl of nuts might seem a lazy and unimpressive way to begin a meal. But with the addition of a little brown sugar, some aromatic seasonings, and especially the heady fragrance of smoldering hickory woods, these nuts take on a special quality. Your guests will be going back to the bowl again and again.

SERVES 8 (MAKES 2 CUPS)

1. Soak 2 handfuls hickory wood chips in water for at least 30 minutes.

2. Prepare the grill for indirect cooking over low heat (250° to 350°F).

3. In a small bowl, using your fingertips, mix together the sugar, thyme, cayenne, and mustard.

4. Pour the nuts into a large disposable foil pan, add the oil and seasoning mixture, and toss to coat the nuts evenly. Spread the nuts in a single layer in the pan.

5. Brush the cooking grates clean. Drain the wood chips, add to the charcoal or to the smoker box of a gas grill, following the manufacturer's instructions, and close the lid. When smoke appears, place the pan of nuts over **indirect low heat** and cook, with the lid closed, until they are toasted, 20 to 30 minutes, shaking the pan a couple of times to prevent burning. Remove the pan from the grill and let the nuts cool completely in the pan. The nuts will become crispier as they cool.

6. Serve at room temperature. Store any leftover nuts in an airtight container at room temperature.

ROASTED EGGPLANT DIP

PREP TIME
10 MINUTES

GRILLING TIME
42 TO 52 MINUTES

1 head garlic

Extra-virgin olive oil

2 globe eggplants, each about 8 ounces

1 tablespoon fresh lemon juice

1 teaspoon fresh oregano leaves

¾ teaspoon kosher salt, divided

½ teaspoon freshly ground black pepper

2 plain bagels

You have our permission to burn the eggplant in this recipe. That's because burning (and then discarding) the skin cooks the flesh to a soft, luscious consistency that is perfect for pureeing with roasted garlic, lemon, and oregano. For a richer flavor, drizzle olive oil over the top.

SERVES 8 TO 10

1. Prepare the grill for direct and indirect cooking over high heat (450° to 550°F).

2. Remove the loose, papery outer skin from the garlic head and cut off the top to expose the cloves. Place the garlic, stem end down, on a large square of aluminum foil and drizzle 1 teaspoon oil over the cut surface. Fold up the sides of the foil to make a sealed packet, leaving a little room for the expansion of steam.

3. Brush the cooking grates clean. Grill the garlic packet over **indirect high heat**, with the lid closed, until the cloves are soft, 40 to 50 minutes. Remove from the grill and let cool until it can be handled.

4. While the garlic cooks, prick the eggplants several times with a fork. Grill over **direct high heat**, with the lid closed, until the skins are charred and the eggplants begin to collapse, 15 to 20 minutes, turning occasionally. A knife should slide in and out of the flesh without resistance. Remove from the grill and let cool until they can be handled. Decrease the temperature of the grill to medium heat (350° to 450°F).

5. Squeeze the garlic cloves from their paper sheaths into a food processor. Cut the still-warm eggplants in half lengthwise and, using a large spoon, scrape the flesh away from the skin. Discard the skin and any large seed pockets. Add the eggplant flesh to the processor bowl and pulse to create a thick paste. Add the lemon juice and oregano and process until the mixture is smooth. Season with ½ teaspoon of the salt and the pepper, then taste and adjust the seasoning.

6. Cut the bagels in half vertically so you have two half-moons. Cut each half-moon horizontally into ¼-inch-thick slices. Lightly brush the bagel slices with oil, season with the remaining ¼ teaspoon salt, and then grill over **direct medium heat** until they begin to brown and crisp, about 2 minutes, turning once. Remove from the grill.

7. Serve the dip warm with the bagel slices.

GRILLED OYSTERS
WITH FOUR SAUCES

PREP TIME
30 MINUTES

GRILLING TIME
2 TO 4 MINUTES

2 dozen large oysters in the shell, each 3 to 4 inches long

Garlic-Thyme Butter (page 302), Grapefruit-Basil Aioli (page 302), Asian Butter Sauce (page 302), or Gorgonzola-Tomato Sauce (page 301)

Lemon wedges

Hot-pepper sauce

Cocktail sauce

In New Orleans, shucked oysters are traditionally grilled until their briny "liquor" bubbles and their soft flesh absorbs a bit of smokiness. To achieve that, you need big oysters, so look for shells that are three to four inches long (but no bigger). The good times get even better when you can pick your favorite sauce, and we provide four great—and very different—choices.

SERVES 4 TO 6

1. Shuck the oysters: With your nondominant hand, grip an oyster, flat side up, with a folded kitchen towel. Find the small opening between the shells near the hinge and pry the shells open with an oyster knife. Try not to spill the delicious juices—the oyster liquor—in the bottom shell. Cut the oyster meat loose from the top shell and then loosen the oyster from the bottom shell by running the knife carefully under the body. Discard the top, flatter shell, keeping the oyster and juices in the bottom, deeper shell. Set aside on a tray sheet pan. Repeat with the remaining oysters.

2. Prepare the grill for direct cooking over high heat (450° to 550°F).

3. Make the dipping sauce of your choice. Spoon some of the sauce on top of each oyster.

4. Brush the cooking grates clean. Grill the oysters, shell sides down, over **direct high heat**, with the lid closed as much as possible, until the oyster juices start to bubble and the edges curl, 2 to 4 minutes. Using tongs, carefully remove the oysters from the grill. Serve with lemon wedges, hot-pepper sauce, cocktail sauce, and more of the dipping sauce.

FIESTA SHRIMP SALSA
WITH CHIPS

★

PREP TIME
20 MINUTES

MARINATING TIME
1 TO 4 HOURS

GRILLING TIME
12 TO 16 MINUTES

★

This boldly flavored appetizer tastes best if allowed to sit for a couple of hours before serving. That way, the grilled shrimp have time to absorb the electric flavors of the roasted chiles, garlic, and lime. Although the shrimp are fully cooked, the result is reminiscent of ceviche. Now, where is that pitcher of margaritas?

SERVES 4

1 poblano chile pepper, about 6 ounces

24 large shrimp (21/30 count), peeled and deveined, tails removed

Extra-virgin olive oil

2 medium tomatoes, seeded and finely diced (about 1 cup)

1 small Fresno chile pepper, seeded and minced

1 jalapeño chile pepper, seeded and minced

¼ cup finely diced red onion

1 large garlic clove, minced

3 tablespoons fresh lime juice

½ teaspoon kosher salt

½ teaspoon freshly ground black pepper

½ cup chopped fresh cilantro leaves

Tortilla chips

1. Prepare the grill for direct cooking over medium heat (350° to 450°F).

2. Brush the cooking grates clean. Grill the poblano over **direct medium heat**, with the lid closed, until blackened and blistered all over, 10 to 12 minutes, turning occasionally. Place the poblano in a medium bowl and cover with plastic wrap to trap the steam. Let stand for about 10 minutes. Remove and discard the charred skin, stem, and seeds and cut into ¼-inch dice. Put the diced poblano back in the bowl.

3. Increase the temperature of the grill to high heat (450° to 550°F). Pat the shrimp dry with paper towels and lightly brush them all over with oil. Grill the shrimp over **direct high heat**, with the lid closed, until firm to the touch and just turning opaque in the center, 2 to 4 minutes, turning once. Remove from the grill and cut into ¼-inch pieces.

4. Add the shrimp, 1 tablespoon oil, the tomatoes, the Fresno and jalapeño chiles, the onion, garlic, lime juice, salt, and pepper to the bowl with the poblano. Toss to mix well. Cover and refrigerate for at least 1 hour or up to 4 hours.

5. Just before serving, stir in the cilantro. Serve the salsa immediately with tortilla chips.

SHRIMP
WITH "OOO-WEE" RÉMOULADE

PREP TIME
15 MINUTES

GRILLING TIME
2 TO 4 MINUTES

SAUCE

½ cup mayonnaise

1 tablespoon drained capers, minced

1 tablespoon sweet pickle relish

1 tablespoon finely chopped fresh tarragon leaves

2 teaspoons minced shallot

1 teaspoon tarragon vinegar or white wine vinegar

1 teaspoon minced garlic

½ teaspoon Dijon mustard

¼ teaspoon paprika

⅛ teaspoon kosher salt

2 pounds extra-large shrimp (16/20 count), peeled and deveined, tails left on

Extra-virgin olive oil

Kosher salt and freshly ground black pepper

In no more than five minutes on the grill, shrimp can reward you with a remarkable appetizer. That's how quickly they pick up the flavors of the fire, especially a lump charcoal fire of aromatic embers. We like to give the shrimp a dip in rémoulade, which is a fancy French name for a mayo-based sauce so good that it might make you shout out a silly expression like "ooo-wee."

SERVES 4 TO 6

1. In a small bowl whisk together the sauce ingredients. If not using right away, cover and refrigerate for up to 24 hours.

2. Have ready 12 metal or bamboo skewers. If using bamboo, soak in water for at least 30 minutes.

3. Prepare the grill for direct cooking over high heat (450° to 550°F).

4. Thread 4 shrimp onto each skewer, bending each shrimp almost in half so the skewer passes through it twice, near the head and near the tail. Lightly brush the shrimp all over with oil and season with salt and pepper.

5. Brush the cooking grates clean. Grill the shrimp over **direct high heat**, with the lid closed, until they are firm to the touch and just turning opaque in the center, 2 to 4 minutes, turning once. Remove from the grill and serve warm with the sauce.

ZESTY GARLIC SHRIMP

**PREP TIME
30 MINUTES**

**MARINATING TIME
30 MINUTES
TO 1 HOUR**

**GRILLING TIME
4 TO 6 MINUTES**

MARINADE

¼ cup extra-virgin olive oil

2 tablespoons fresh
lemon juice

2 tablespoons finely
chopped fresh Italian
parsley leaves and stems

2 teaspoons dried oregano

1½ teaspoons minced garlic

1 teaspoon finely grated
lemon zest

½ teaspoon kosher salt

¼ teaspoon freshly ground
black pepper

¼ teaspoon crushed red
pepper flakes

20 jumbo shrimp
(11/15 count), peeled and
deveined, tails left on

1 tablespoon fine dried
bread crumbs

The coating of crisp bread crumbs and golden garlic makes these shrimp special. But so does the no-fuss marinade of olive oil, herbs, and lemon. For ease, grate the lemon zest when the lemon is whole, then cut the lemon in half and juice it.

SERVES 4 AS AN APPETIZER, 10 AS AN HORS D'OEUVRE

1. In a small bowl whisk together the marinade ingredients. Place the shrimp in a large, resealable plastic bag and pour in the marinade. Press the air out of the bag and seal tightly. Turn the bag to distribute the marinade, place in a bowl, and refrigerate for 30 minutes to 1 hour, turning occasionally.

2. Have ready 4 medium (about 10 inches long) or 20 small (about 4 inches long) metal or bamboo skewers. If using bamboo, soak in water for at least 30 minutes.

3. Prepare the grill for direct cooking over medium heat (350° to 450°F).

4. Remove the shrimp from the bag and discard the marinade. Thread the shrimp onto the skewers, either 2 shrimp per skewer as hors d'oeuvres or 5 shrimp per skewer as appetizers, bending each shrimp almost in half so the skewer passes through it twice, near the head and near the tail. Sprinkle the shrimp evenly on both sides with the bread crumbs.

5. Brush the cooking grates clean. Grill the shrimp over **direct medium heat**, with the lid closed, until they are firm to the touch and just turning opaque in the center, 4 to 6 minutes, turning once. Remove from the grill and serve warm.

CAPONATA
BRUSCHETTA

PREP TIME
15 MINUTES

GRILLING TIME
11 TO 13 MINUTES

CAPONATA

1 globe eggplant, about 12 ounces

Kosher salt

1 small yellow onion, cut crosswise into ½-inch-thick slices

⅓ cup extra-virgin olive oil

1 medium tomato, seeded and roughly chopped

15 Kalamata olives, pitted and finely chopped

2 tablespoons finely chopped fresh basil leaves

1 tablespoon drained capers

2 teaspoons balsamic vinegar

1 teaspoon finely chopped garlic

Freshly ground black pepper

8 slices Italian or other coarse country bread, each about ½ inch thick and 4 inches wide

4 ounces fresh goat cheese, crumbled

Caponata, a Sicilian mixture of cooked eggplant and onion with tomato, olives, and capers, makes an appealing side dish or relish. Mounded on toasted Italian bread with a smear of goat cheese, this tangy-sweet combination makes a terrific appetizer, particularly when you have grilled the eggplant and onions for extra flavor.

SERVES 4 (MAKES 8 PIECES)

1. Remove about ½ inch from both ends of the eggplant. Cut the eggplant crosswise into ½-inch-thick slices. Rub both sides of the eggplant slices thoroughly with salt. Let the slices sit in a colander in the sink or over a plate for about 30 minutes to draw out their bitter juices. Rinse the slices well and pat dry. Lightly brush both sides of the eggplant and onion slices with the oil.

2. Prepare the grill for direct cooking over medium heat (350° to 450°F).

3. Brush the cooking grates clean. Grill the eggplant and onion slices over **direct medium heat**, with the lid closed, until well marked and tender, 10 to 12 minutes, turning once. Remove from the grill.

4. When the eggplant and onion slices are cool enough to handle, coarsely chop them and transfer to a medium bowl. Add the tomato, olives, basil, capers, vinegar, and garlic and mix well. Season with salt and pepper.

5. Grill the bread slices over **direct medium heat**, with the lid closed, until toasted, about 1 minute, turning once. Remove from the grill.

6. Divide the goat cheese evenly among the bread slices, spreading it with a knife. Spoon the caponata over the goat cheese, again dividing evenly. Serve at room temperature.

PEACH AND BLUE CHEESE
BRUSCHETTA
DRIZZLED WITH HONEY

**PREP TIME
10 MINUTES**

**GRILLING TIME
ABOUT 8 MINUTES**

**4 ounces cream
cheese, softened**

**2 tablespoons
granulated sugar**

**1 tablespoon fresh
thyme leaves**

4 firm but ripe peaches

**8 slices Italian or
French bread, each
about ½ inch thick**

Extra-virgin olive oil

**4 ounces blue cheese,
crumbled (scant 1 cup)**

3 tablespoons honey

When it comes to the signs of summer, ripe peaches are up there with baseball games, flip-flops, backyard barbecues, and days at the beach. Warming peaches over a gentle fire turns them sweeter and heightens their flavor, making them glorious companions to the salty pungency of blue cheese and fragrant honey. Apricots or nectarines also work well here.

SERVES 4

1. Prepare the grill for direct cooking over medium-low heat (about 350°F).

2. Stir together the cream cheese, sugar, and thyme until blended. Set aside. Cut each peach in half through the stem end and discard the pit. Lightly brush the peach halves and bread slices on both sides with oil.

3. Brush the cooking grates clean. Grill the peach halves over **direct medium-low heat**, with the lid closed, until lightly charred and beginning to soften, about 8 minutes, turning once. During the last 1 minute of grilling time, toast the bread slices over direct heat, turning once. Remove the peaches and bread from the grill.

4. Spread each bread slice with an equal amount of the cream cheese mixture. Cut the peach halves into ¼-inch-thick slices. Divide the peach slices evenly among the bread slices, overlapping them slightly. Top with the blue cheese and drizzle with the honey. Serve right away.

FILET MIGNON CROSTINI
WITH BALSAMIC ONION JAM

PREP TIME
20 MINUTES,
PLUS **45 MINUTES**
FOR THE JAM

GRILLING TIME
13 TO 16 MINUTES

**3 filet mignon steaks,
each about 8 ounces and
1½ inches thick**

**1 tablespoon extra-virgin
olive oil**

1½ teaspoons kosher salt

**¾ teaspoon freshly ground
black pepper**

CROSTINI

**1 baguette, cut into
25 slices, each about
½ inch thick**

Extra-virgin olive oil

2 garlic cloves

CREAM

⅓ cup sour cream

**3 tablespoons prepared
horseradish**

¼ teaspoon kosher salt

**½ teaspoon freshly ground
black pepper**

**Balsamic Onion Jam
(page 303)**

**1 bunch fresh chives,
chopped (optional)**

If an appetizer is gone in just a few bites, each bite needs to make a fabulous impression. That's why we decided to splurge on filet mignon here. The buttery tenderness of the beef tastes luxurious with the tangle of slow-cooked onions and the dollop of heady horseradish cream.

SERVES 10 TO 12

1. Prepare the grill for direct cooking over medium heat (350° to 450°F).

2. Brush the steaks on both sides with the oil, then season on both sides with the salt and pepper. Let stand at room temperature for 15 to 30 minutes before grilling.

3. Brush the cooking grates clean. Lightly brush one side of each baguette slice with oil. Grill the slices, oiled side down, over **direct medium heat**, until toasted on the underside, 1 to 2 minutes (grill one side only). Remove from the grill, let cool, and rub the grilled side lightly with the garlic.

4. Combine the cream ingredients in a small bowl. Cover and refrigerate until ready to use.

5. Grill the steaks over **direct medium heat**, with the lid closed, until cooked to your desired doneness, 12 to 14 minutes for medium rare, turning once. (If flare-ups occur, move the steaks temporarily over indirect heat.) Remove from the grill and let rest for 3 to 5 minutes. Cut the steaks across the grain into ¼-inch-thick slices.

6. Spread a layer of jam on each toasted baguette slice. Place a slice of meat on the jam and top with a small dollop of the cream. Sprinkle with the chives, if desired.

DO CODFISH REALLY HAVE TONGUES?

BY MIKE KEMPSTER

I grew up in Kansas City, and it's pretty hard to get farther away from an ocean. But Kansas City is famous for barbecue, so I knew plenty about beef brisket and pork ribs when I started working for Weber in 1971.

Back then, Weber grills were an unusual sight, so we relied on in-store demonstrations to build awareness on how they could grill or roast any cut of meat to perfection. I learned

> I FIGURED THIS GUY WAS PULLING MY LEG, SO I ASKED, "DO CODFISH REALLY HAVE TONGUES?" HE LAUGHED AND SAID, "SON, THAT'S ONE OF THE BEST PARTS OF THE COD!"

how to demonstrate a Weber grill from the master, George Stephen, its inventor, and then off I went around the country doing live appearances.

I showed folks how to grill the perfect steak without burning it and how to roast a whole turkey or prime rib for their holiday dinner. I quickly discovered that Americans' taste for barbecue and what they like to grill varied widely depending on their location. In the South and the lower Midwest, folks liked their barbecue hickory smoked. In Texas and Oklahoma, mesquite was the smoky flavor of choice. In the upper Midwest, people wanted a whole lot less smoky flavor. On the East Coast and West Coast, grilling enthusiasts were impressed with roasted turkeys, prime rib, and steak, but they also wanted to know about alder-smoked salmon and how to grill a whole lobster.

Feeling a bit overwhelmed by the seafood requests, I decided to take a crash course in how to grill salmon, swordfish, and halibut. A veteran Weber salesman living in Boston taught me a lot about grilling shellfish, including how to cook a whole lobster over a bed of seaweed. I came away from all my new knowledge amazed by the flavor of grilled seafood.

After a couple of years of learning and demonstrating, I was no longer a rookie, but I was far from an expert. Unfortunately, when you're wearing an apron and grilling in public— and the turkey does not go up in flames— people immediately regard you as an expert. Thinking back on those days brings to mind a story of how folks came to believe I would know how to grill just about anything.

In the late 1970s, Weber was trying to duplicate its U.S. success in Canada. Very few Canadians had ever seen a Weber grill, however, so the task wasn't easy. On a cold, gray day in May, I was trying to sell Weber grills at a hardware store in St. John's, Newfoundland, and I wasn't having much luck. I was beginning to think that my efforts were a complete bust, when a fellow came along and said, "I'll buy one of those grills if you can cook cod tongues with it." I'm sure I looked dumbfounded—and

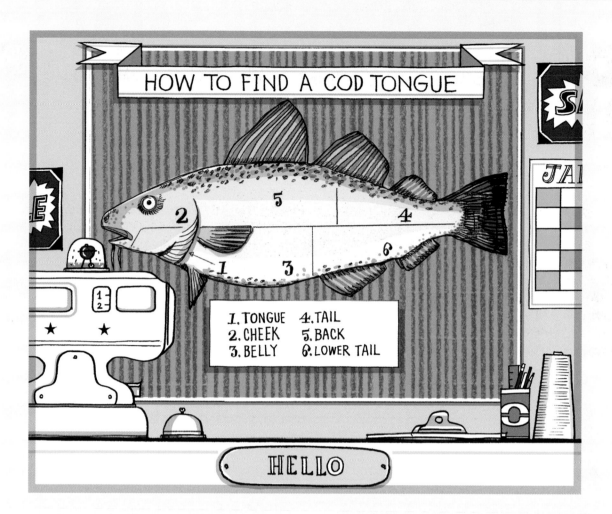

I was!—so I asked him to repeat the question. I figured this guy was pulling my leg, so I asked, "Do codfish really have tongues?" He laughed and said, "Son, that's one of the best parts of the cod!"

When my stint at the hardware store was finished, he took me to a fishmonger who showed me that cod tongues were actually the very tender chunks of meat below the mouth of the fish. I asked how people generally prepared them, and he told me they were usually breaded and fried. I immediately told the fellow that I thought I could cook cod tongues on a Weber grill, and if I proved successful, he would have to buy the grill and one very important accessory. He agreed, and the challenge was on!

The next day I arrived at the gentleman's house with a Weber grill and an accessory that I sometimes used to demonstrate fried rice: a big steel wok. He had bought a pound of cod tongues, and his wife, bless her, had prepared a mixture of flour and cornmeal for the crazy grill salesman on her patio. We dipped the tongues in milk, rolled them in the flour mixture, and then came the test. I was quite nervous at this point.

The coals were red hot and stacked in a pyramid. I set the wok on the rim of the grill and poured in a liberal amount of oil. As the oil began to bubble and smoke, I carefully added the cod tongues, hoping for the best but not really knowing what to expect. I tossed the tongues with wok tools for a few minutes, put the grill lid over the wok to let them cook a while longer, and to everyone's astonishment, they turned out great. Luckily I had cooked chunks of chicken the same way or I would have been clueless.

True to my host's word, he bought the grill and the wok.

GRILLED ROMAINE SALAD
WITH CAESAR DRESSING

PREP TIME
15 MINUTES

GRILLING TIME
2 TO 3 MINUTES

If you have never thought of grilling lettuce, this is a good time to give it a try. The lightly charred leaves taste as if a bit of smoked meat has been tucked into this meatless dish. Romaine hearts work especially well here, as their firm, sturdy structure makes them easy to turn.

DRESSING

1 anchovy fillet packed in olive oil, drained, or ½ teaspoon anchovy paste

2 tablespoons extra-virgin olive oil

1½ tablespoons mayonnaise

1½ teaspoons fresh lemon juice

1 teaspoon Dijon mustard

½ teaspoon Worcestershire sauce

½ small garlic clove, minced

¼ teaspoon freshly ground black pepper

1 French roll, about 6 inches long, cut lengthwise into quarters

1 garlic clove, cut in half

3 hearts of romaine, about 1 pound total, each cut lengthwise into quarters with the stem end intact

2 tablespoons extra-virgin olive oil

2 tablespoons freshly grated Parmigiano-Reggiano® cheese

SERVES 4

1. Prepare the grill for direct cooking over medium heat (350° to 450°F).

2. Put the anchovy fillet in a small bowl and mash to a paste with the back of a fork. Add the remaining dressing ingredients and whisk to combine.

3. Brush the cooking grates clean. Grill the bread quarters over **direct medium heat**, with the lid closed, until lightly toasted, 1 to 2 minutes, turning three times. Remove from the grill and rub the cut sides of the bread with the cut sides of the garlic clove. Set aside.

4. Brush the romaine all over with the oil. Grill the romaine over **direct medium heat**, with the lid open, until slightly wilted, about 1 minute (you may not need to turn the heads). Remove from the grill. Arrange the romaine on a platter and top with the dressing and cheese. Serve immediately with the toasted bread quarters.

CHOPPED CHICKEN SALAD
WITH HONEY-MUSTARD DRESSING

PREP TIME
35 MINUTES

MARINATING TIME
1 HOUR

GRILLING TIME
8 TO 10 MINUTES

You can make the honey-mustard dressing and combine the salad ingredients in the morning—or even the night before—and then lightly coat the salad with the dressing just before serving, leaving you free to handle other menu details. If you like, trade out the romaine hearts for spinach or another salad green.

SERVES 6

MARINADE

2 tablespoons extra-virgin olive oil

2 tablespoons minced fresh rosemary leaves

1 tablespoon fresh lemon juice

1 tablespoon minced garlic

1½ teaspoons kosher salt

¼ teaspoon freshly ground black pepper

6 boneless, skinless chicken thighs, each about 4 ounces

3 hearts of romaine, chopped

2 cups (12 ounces) cherry tomatoes, cut lengthwise into quarters

2 large Hass avocados, diced

½ small red onion, finely diced

8 slices bacon, cooked and crumbled

3 hard-boiled eggs, peeled and cut into wedges

Honey-Mustard Dressing (page 298)

1. In a small bowl whisk together the marinade ingredients. Place the chicken thighs in a large, resealable plastic bag and pour in the marinade. Press the air out of the bag and seal tightly. Turn the bag to distribute the marinade, place in a bowl, and refrigerate for about 1 hour.

2. Prepare the grill for direct cooking over medium heat (350° to 450°F).

3. Brush the cooking grates clean. Remove the thighs from the bag and discard the marinade. Grill the thighs, smooth (skinned) side down first, over **direct medium heat**, with the lid closed as much as possible, until the meat is firm and the juices run clear, 8 to 10 minutes, turning once. Remove from the grill and let rest for 3 to 5 minutes. Cut into bite-sized pieces.

4. Divide the chicken, romaine, tomatoes, avocados, onion, bacon, and eggs evenly among six serving plates. Drizzle the salads with the dressing and serve immediately.

HOT, SWEET, AND STICKY
CHICKEN WINGS

PREP TIME
10 MINUTES

MARINATING TIME
4 TO 6 HOURS

GRILLING TIME
14 TO 26 MINUTES

MARINADE

½ cup ketchup

¼ cup balsamic vinegar

2 tablespoons packed dark brown sugar

4 teaspoons garlic powder

4 teaspoons Worcestershire sauce

1 tablespoon hot-pepper sauce

2 teaspoons Dijon mustard

2 teaspoons paprika

2 teaspoons pure chile powder

20 chicken wings, about 3 pounds total

Extra-virgin olive oil

Some of the marinade ingredients may seem like odd bedfellows, but the combination works deliciously. To ensure juicy meat beneath golden skin, be sure to follow the two-step process of browning the skin over direct heat and then finishing the wings slowly over indirect heat. The wing tips sometimes burn on the grill; to avoid this, you can cut off the tips before marinating the wings.

SERVES 6 TO 8

1. In a bowl whisk together the marinade ingredients. Put the wings in a large, resealable plastic bag and pour in the marinade. Press the air out of the bag and seal tightly. Turn the bag to distribute the marinade, place in a bowl, and refrigerate for 4 to 6 hours, turning the bag occasionally.

2. Prepare the grill for direct and indirect cooking over medium heat (350° to 450°F).

3. Brush the cooking grates clean. Remove the wings from the bag and discard the marinade. Lightly brush the wings with oil. Sear the wings over **direct medium heat**, with the lid closed, until well marked, 4 to 6 minutes, turning once. Move the wings over **indirect medium heat** and continue cooking, with the lid closed, until the skin is dark brown and the meat is no longer pink at the bone, 10 to 20 minutes more, turning once or twice. If desired, during the final few minutes, move the wings over direct heat to crisp the skin a bit more, turning once or twice. Remove from the grill and serve warm.

FOR PARTY MENUS, SEE PAGE 320

JERK CHICKEN SKEWERS
WITH HONEY-LIME CREAM

PREP TIME
30 MINUTES

MARINATING TIME
2 TO 3 HOURS

GRILLING TIME
6 TO 8 MINUTES

This recipe treats naturally mild chicken breasts to a spicy hot paste on the grill followed by a cooling lime-infused sour cream at the table. To ensure the meat turns out as juicy as possible, cut it into uniform pieces and grill them evenly over high heat. The smaller the pieces, the higher the heat should be.

SERVES 4 TO 6

PASTE

1 habanero or Scotch bonnet chile pepper

1 cup loosely packed fresh cilantro leaves and tender stems

½ cup extra-virgin olive oil

4 scallions (white and light green parts only), roughly chopped

2 tablespoons finely chopped, peeled fresh ginger

2 tablespoons granulated sugar

1 tablespoon fresh lime juice

1 tablespoon ground allspice

6 medium garlic cloves, peeled

2 teaspoons kosher salt

1 teaspoon freshly ground black pepper

6 boneless, skinless chicken breast halves, each 6 to 8 ounces, trimmed of excess fat

Honey-Lime Cream (page 298)

1. Both habanero and Scotch bonnet chiles are very hot, so to avoid burning your skin, wear rubber or plastic gloves when you handle the chile. After handling the chile, do not touch your face or any other part of your body, as it might cause a burning sensation. Remove and discard the stem of the chile, then cut away and discard the hot whitish veins and seeds. Put the rest of the chile in the bowl of a food processor. Add the remaining paste ingredients and process until smooth.

2. Remove the tenders from the chicken breasts. Cut the chicken breasts lengthwise into even strips ½ to ¾ inch wide. Put the chicken strips and tenders in a large, resealable plastic bag and spoon in the paste. Work the paste into the chicken, then press the air out of the bag and seal tightly. Place in the refrigerator and marinate for 2 to 3 hours.

3. Have ready 8 to 12 metal or bamboo skewers. If using bamboo, soak in water for at least 30 minutes.

4. Prepare the grill for direct cooking over high heat (450° to 550°F).

5. Put on gloves again, then thread the chicken strips lengthwise onto the skewers, passing the skewer through the meat at least twice and keeping the skewer in the center of the strip. (If you don't wear gloves, be sure to wash your hands thoroughly after this step.)

6. Brush the cooking grates clean. Grill the skewers over **direct high heat**, with the lid closed, until the meat is firm to the touch and opaque all the way to the center, 6 to 8 minutes, turning once. Remove from the grill and serve warm with the honey-lime cream.

TURKEY MEATBALLS
WITH CHILE-GINGER SAUCE

PREP TIME
30 MINUTES
CHILLING TIME
1 HOUR
GRILLING TIME
8 TO 10 MINUTES

The best meatballs are moist and flavorful on the inside and nicely browned on the outside. That's why we start with the dark thigh meat of turkey and then punch up the flavor even more with soy sauce, ginger, and hot sauce. Cook these meatballs gently over medium heat so you don't drive out the juiciness.

SERVES 8 TO 12 (MAKES ABOUT 28 MEATBALLS)

1. In a medium bowl combine all of the meatball ingredients except oil and mix gently until evenly distributed. With wet hands, form into uniform balls, each about 1½ inches in diameter. Cover with plastic wrap and refrigerate for at least 1 hour.

2. In a small saucepan over medium-high heat, combine the vinegar, lime juice, and sugar. Bring to a boil and cook until the sugar dissolves and the liquid is reduced by one-third, about 5 minutes, stirring occasionally. Transfer the mixture to a bowl and stir in the remaining sauce ingredients. Let cool completely.

3. Prepare the grill for direct cooking over medium heat (350° to 450°F).

4. Brush the cooking grates clean. Lightly brush the meatballs with oil. Grill over **direct medium heat**, with the lid closed, until browned and cooked through, 8 to 10 minutes, turning two or three times. Remove from the grill and serve warm with the sauce.

MEATBALLS

1½ pounds ground turkey, preferably thigh meat

¼ cup finely chopped fresh cilantro leaves

2 scallions, minced

1 tablespoon soy sauce

1 tablespoon peeled, grated fresh ginger

2 teaspoons hot chile-garlic sauce, such as Sriracha

2 garlic cloves, minced

1 teaspoon ground coriander

1 teaspoon kosher salt

Vegetable oil

SAUCE

½ cup rice vinegar

¼ cup fresh lime juice

¼ cup granulated sugar

1 tablespoon finely chopped fresh cilantro leaves

2 teaspoons minced red jalapeño chile pepper

2 teaspoons peeled, grated fresh ginger

1 teaspoon kosher salt

1 garlic clove, minced

CHICKEN AND POBLANO
QUESADILLAS

PREP TIME
15 MINUTES

MARINATING TIME
3 TO 4 HOURS

GRILLING TIME
14 TO 18 MINUTES

PASTE

1 jalapeño chile pepper, stem removed

2 large garlic cloves

1 cup tightly packed fresh basil leaves

3 tablespoons extra-virgin olive oil

2 tablespoons tequila

1 teaspoon kosher salt

½ teaspoon freshly ground black pepper

2 boneless, skinless chicken breast halves, each about 8 ounces

2 medium poblano chile peppers, stems removed

4 flour tortillas (10 inches)

2 cups shredded Monterey Jack cheese (8 ounces)

Guacamole (page 300)

People often ask us how to make chicken breasts taste better than, well, chicken breasts. Here, we make that happen by smearing them with a paste of tequila, chile, and basil. Once they are off the grill but still moist, we thinly slice them and mix them with roasted poblanos and shredded Jack to make some sensational quesadillas.

SERVES 4 TO 6

1. Mince the jalapeño and garlic in a food processor. Add the remaining paste ingredients and process until smooth. Smear the paste on all sides of the chicken breasts. Cover and refrigerate for 3 to 4 hours.

2. Prepare the grill for direct cooking over medium heat (350° to 450°F).

3. Brush the cooking grates clean. Grill the chicken, smooth (skinned) side down first, over **direct medium heat**, with the lid closed as much as possible, until the meat is firm to the touch and opaque all the way to the center, 8 to 12 minutes, turning once or twice. Remove from the grill and cut across the grain into thin slices.

4. At the same time, grill the poblano chiles over **direct medium heat** until blackened and blistered all over, 10 to 12 minutes, turning as needed. Place the poblanos in a bowl and cover with plastic wrap to trap the steam. Let stand for about 10 minutes. Remove and discard the charred skin, stems, and seeds and roughly chop the chiles.

5. Lay the tortillas in a single layer on a work surface. Divide the chicken, chiles, and cheese evenly among the tortillas, arranging them over half of each tortilla. Fold the empty half of each tortilla over the filling, creating a half circle, and press down firmly.

6. Grill the quesadillas over **direct medium heat**, with the lid closed, until well marked and the cheese is melted, 4 to 6 minutes, turning once. Let the quesadillas cool for a minute or two before cutting into wedges. Serve warm with the guacamole.

CHEESY NACHOS
WITH STEAK AND BLACK BEANS

PREP TIME
30 MINUTES

GRILLING TIME
9 TO 11 MINUTES

PASTE

1 tablespoon extra-virgin olive oil

1 tablespoon minced garlic

1 teaspoon pure chile powder

1 teaspoon packed light brown sugar

½ teaspoon kosher salt

½ teaspoon chipotle chile powder

¼ teaspoon ground cumin

1½ pounds skirt steak, ½ to ¾ inch thick, trimmed of excess surface fat, cut with the grain into 12-inch-long pieces

1 bag (12 ounces) tortilla chips

1 can (15 ounces) black beans, rinsed and drained

2 cups shredded sharp cheddar cheese (8 ounces)

2 cups shredded Monterey Jack cheese (8 ounces)

Tomato-Avocado Salsa (page 299)

Black beans and skirt steak get our vote for the best pairing for nachos, but feel free to match up your favorite beans and meat. Maybe that's red beans and barbecued chicken? Or perhaps it's pintos and grilled pork? To speed cleanup, line the two sheet pans with aluminum foil.

SERVES 12 TO 15

1. In a small bowl mix together the paste ingredients. Brush the paste on both sides of the steak pieces. Let the steak stand at room temperature for 15 to 30 minutes before grilling.

2. Prepare the grill for direct cooking over high heat (450° to 550°F).

3. Brush the cooking grates clean. Grill the steak pieces over **direct high heat**, with the lid closed, until cooked to your desired doneness, 4 to 6 minutes for medium rare, turning once. Remove from the grill and let rest for 3 to 5 minutes. Cut the steak across the grain into bite-sized pieces.

4. Layer half of the tortilla chips, steak, black beans, and cheddar and Monterey Jack cheeses on a large sheet pan. Place the pan over **direct high heat**, close the lid, and cook until the cheese is melted, about 5 minutes. Remove from the grill and serve immediately with the salsa. Repeat with the remaining ingredients on a second large sheet pan.

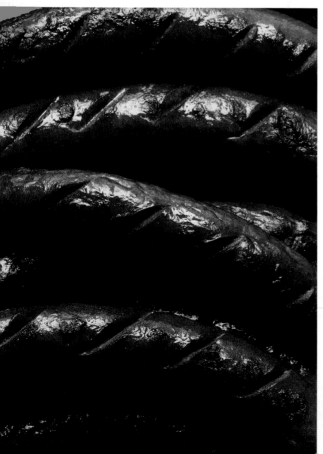

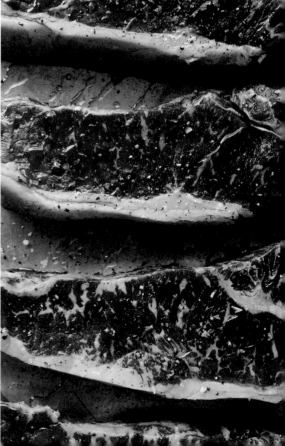

02

BEEF & LAMB

CHICAGO-STYLE
HOT DOGS

**PREP TIME
10 MINUTES**

**GRILLING TIME
4 TO 5 MINUTES**

8 slices tomato, each about ¼ inch thick

8 best-quality all-beef hot dogs with natural casings (slightly longer than the buns)

8 poppy seed hot dog buns, split

16 pickled sport peppers

2 dill pickles, each cut lengthwise into 4 spears

½ cup finely chopped white onion, rinsed in a fine-mesh strainer under cold water

½ cup super green sweet pickle relish

Yellow mustard

Celery salt

Aficionados of the Chicago-style hot dog insist on an all-beef frankfurter on a poppy seed bun topped with sport peppers, a dill pickle spear, diced onion, tomato slices, fluorescent green sweet pickle relish, yellow mustard, and a dusting of celery salt. No substitutions and no additions allowed. We heard about a guy who once tried adding ketchup. Let's just say he didn't suggest it again.

SERVES 8

1. Prepare the grill for direct cooking over medium heat (350° to 450°F).

2. Cut each tomato slice in half to make half-moons. Cut a few well-spaced diagonal shallow slashes crosswise along one side of each hot dog.

3. Brush the cooking grates clean. Grill the hot dogs over **direct medium heat**, with the lid closed, until lightly marked on the outside and hot all the way to the center, 4 to 5 minutes, turning occasionally. Remove from the grill.

4. Place a hot dog in each bun and add 2 tomato half-moons, 2 peppers, 1 pickle spear, some onion, and a spoonful of relish. Add mustard to taste and finish with a pinch of celery salt. Serve warm.

PATAGONIA HOT DOGS
WITH AVOCADO MAYO

PREP TIME
20 MINUTES

GRILLING TIME
4 TO 5 MINUTES

MAYO

1 Hass avocado, roughly chopped

⅓ cup mayonnaise

½ jalapeño chile pepper, seeded and chopped

1 tablespoon chopped shallot

1 tablespoon fresh lemon juice

1 garlic clove, minced

¼ teaspoon kosher salt

¼ teaspoon freshly ground black pepper

8 best-quality all-beef hot dogs with natural casings (slightly longer than the buns)

8 hot dog buns, split

1 jar or bag (1 pound) sauerkraut, drained

1 pound tomatoes, cored, seeded, and chopped

¼ cup roughly chopped fresh cilantro leaves

¼ cup finely chopped red onion

At the southern end of South America, hot dog fanatics in Patagonia, Argentina, revel in a colorful variation that involves sauerkraut, chopped tomatoes, and a creamy avocado mayo. Although it's a combination we probably never would have imagined on our own, it has made it into this collection for a good reason: it tastes great!

SERVES 8

1. In a food processor combine all the mayo ingredients and puree until smooth. Cover and refrigerate until needed.

2. Prepare the grill for direct cooking over medium heat (350° to 450°F). Cut a few well-spaced diagonal shallow slashes crosswise along one side of each hot dog.

3. Brush the cooking grates clean. Grill over **direct medium heat**, with the lid closed, until lightly marked on the outside and hot all the way to the center, 4 to 5 minutes, turning occasionally. During the last 30 seconds to 1 minute of grilling time, toast the buns, cut side down, over direct heat. Remove from the grill.

4. Generously spread the avocado mayo inside each bun. (You will not need all of it, but the unused amount will keep in a covered bowl in the refrigerator for up to 2 days.) Place a hot dog in each bun and add some sauerkraut, tomatoes, cilantro, and onion. Serve warm.

TUBE STEAKS
WITH PICKLED ONIONS

PREP TIME
15 MINUTES

MARINATING TIME
ABOUT 3 HOURS

GRILLING TIME
4 TO 5 MINUTES

PICKLED ONIONS

½ cup cider vinegar

½ cup distilled white vinegar

½ cup granulated sugar

1 tablespoon kosher salt

2 teaspoons celery seed

1 teaspoon crushed red pepper flakes

1 small white or yellow onion, ends trimmed

1 small red onion, ends trimmed

8 best-quality all-beef hot dogs with natural casings (slightly longer than the buns)

8 hot dog buns, split

Mustard

Ketchup

In the 1960s and 1970s, some folks called hot dogs "tube steaks." Instead of going to a restaurant for a sit-down meal with real steaks, people in a hurry or on a tight budget headed to a hot dog stand or cooked these at home. Grilled just right, with a little char and smoke, and topped with tangy onions, these wanna-be steaks still hit the spot.

SERVES 4 TO 8

1. In a large glass bowl whisk together all the pickling ingredients except the onions, until the sugar and salt dissolve.

2. Cut each onion in half lengthwise. Place each half cut side down and cut vertically into paper-thin slices. Add the onions to the pickling liquid and stir to coat them evenly. Set aside at room temperature for about 3 hours, stirring the onions occasionally. Drain the pickled onions and set aside.

3. Prepare the grill for direct cooking over medium heat (350° to 450°F).

4. Brush the cooking grates clean. Cut a few well-spaced diagonal shallow slashes crosswise along one side of each hot dog. Grill over **direct medium heat**, with the lid closed, until lightly marked on the outside and hot all the way to the center, 4 to 5 minutes, turning occasionally. During the last 30 seconds to 1 minute of grilling time, toast the buns, cut side down, over direct heat. Remove from the grill.

5. Place a hot dog in each bun. Invite diners to squeeze the condiment of their choice alongside their hot dog and then top with the pickled onions. Serve warm.

TEXAS BURGERS
WITH BARBECUE SAUCE

**PREP TIME
15 MINUTES,
PLUS 35 MINUTES
FOR THE SAUCE**

**GRILLING TIME
8 TO 10 MINUTES**

Practitioners of Texas barbecue usually serve their slow-smoked briskets without sauce. But burgers offer a lot more leeway, especially when the sauce brings a lot of swagger to the party. To pull off that deep flavor, cook the onions until they are supersoft and as dark as possible before adding the wet ingredients.

SERVES 4

SAUCE

1 tablespoon vegetable oil

½ medium yellow onion, finely chopped

1 cup ketchup

¼ cup water

2 tablespoons Worcestershire sauce

1 tablespoon packed dark brown sugar

1 tablespoon chili powder

1 tablespoon cider vinegar

½ teaspoon garlic powder

PATTIES

1½ pounds ground chuck (80% lean)

1 tablespoon chili powder

½ teaspoon garlic powder

½ teaspoon kosher salt

4 slices cheddar cheese, each about 1 ounce

4 hamburger buns, split

4 leaves romaine lettuce, shredded

16 sweet pickle chips (optional)

1. In a heavy, medium saucepan over medium heat, warm the oil. Add the onion and cook until very soft and as dark as possible without burning, 12 to 15 minutes, stirring occasionally. Add the remaining sauce ingredients, stir well, and bring to a boil over medium-high heat. Adjust the heat so the sauce simmers gently. Cook until thickened, 15 to 20 minutes, stirring frequently. Let cool to room temperature.

2. In a medium bowl mix together all the patty ingredients with your hands. Gently shape the mixture into four patties of equal size and about ¾ inch thick. With your thumb or the back of a spoon, make a shallow indentation about 1 inch wide in the center of each patty to prevent it from doming as it cooks. Refrigerate the patties until ready to grill.

3. Prepare the grill for direct cooking over medium-high heat (400° to 500°F).

4. Brush the cooking grates clean. Grill the patties over **direct medium-high heat**, with the lid closed, until cooked to medium doneness (160°F), 8 to 10 minutes, turning once. During the last 30 seconds to 1 minute of grilling time, place a slice of cheese on each patty to melt, and toast the buns, cut side down, over direct heat. Remove from the grill.

5. Build a burger on each bun with some sauce, lettuce, a patty, a bit more sauce, and 4 pickle chips, if desired. Serve warm. The remaining sauce will keep in a covered container in the refrigerator for up to 1 week.

CRUNCH BURGERS

Credit for this stroke of culinary genius has to go to little kids everywhere who instinctively know that it is fun to make towers of potato chips on top of cheeseburgers and then crush the chips into smithereens. It just so happens that the crunchy bits of salty, oily potato make an irresistible topping.

SERVES 4 (MAKES 8 SLIDERS)

PATTIES

1½ pounds ground chuck (80% lean)

1 tablespoon ketchup

½ teaspoon Worcestershire sauce

½ teaspoon onion powder

½ teaspoon kosher salt

¼ teaspoon freshly ground black pepper

2 slices cheddar cheese, each about 1 ounce, cut into quarters

8 slider buns, split

Ketchup (optional)

16 dill pickle chips

8 handfuls thin potato chips, such as Lay's Classic®

1. In a medium bowl mix together all the patty ingredients with your hands. Gently shape the mixture into eight patties of equal size and about ½ inch thick. With your thumb or the back of a spoon, make a shallow indentation about ½ inch wide in the center of each patty to prevent it from forming a dome as it cooks. Refrigerate the patties until ready to grill.

2. Prepare the grill for direct cooking over medium-high heat (400° to 500°F).

3. Brush the cooking grates clean. Grill the patties over **direct medium-high heat**, with the lid closed, until cooked to medium doneness (160°F), about 6 minutes, turning once. During the last 30 seconds to 1 minute of grilling time, place a quarter of a cheese slice on each patty to melt, and toast the buns, cut side down, over direct heat. Remove from the grill.

4. Build a burger on each bun with ketchup (if using), pickles, a patty, and a handful of chips. Close the burgers with the bun tops and then press down to crunch the chips. Serve right away.

WEBER'S IDEAL
CHEESEBURGERS

PREP TIME
15 MINUTES

GRILLING TIME
9 TO 11 MINUTES

For a cheeseburger to merit the word *ideal* in its title, the meat must ooze with beefy, seasoned juices, the cheese must melt into a smooth, rich blanket, the toppings must be fresh and crisp, and the whole ensemble must travel to your mouth on a toasted bun. Open wide. Here comes that ideal cheeseburger.

PATTIES

1½ pounds ground chuck (80% lean), preferably ground to order by your butcher

2 tablespoons minced white or yellow onion

1 tablespoon ketchup

1½ teaspoons Dijon mustard

½ teaspoon Worcestershire sauce

½ teaspoon dried oregano

½ teaspoon kosher salt

¼ teaspoon freshly ground black pepper

Kosher salt and freshly ground black pepper

4 hamburger buns, split

2 tablespoons unsalted butter, softened

4 slices sharp cheddar cheese, each about 2 ounces

4 leaves butter lettuce

Ketchup (optional)

16 dill pickle chips

SERVES 4

1. In a medium bowl mix together all the patty ingredients with your hands. Gently shape the mixture into four patties of equal size and about 1 inch thick. With your thumb or the back of a spoon, make a shallow indentation about 1 inch wide in the center of each patty to prevent it from doming as it cooks. Refrigerate the patties until ready to grill.

2. Prepare the grill for direct cooking over medium-high heat (400° to 500°F).

3. Brush the cooking grates clean. Lightly season the patties on both sides with salt and pepper. Spread the cut side of the buns with the butter. Grill the patties over **direct medium-high heat**, with the lid closed, until cooked to medium doneness (160°F), 9 to 11 minutes, turning once. During the last 30 seconds to 1 minute of grilling time, place a cheese slice on each patty to melt and toast the buns, cut side down, over direct heat. Remove from the grill.

4. Build a burger on each bun with a lettuce leaf, a patty, ketchup (if using), and 4 pickle chips. Serve warm.

OPEN-FACED
TEX-MEX BURGERS

PREP TIME
25 MINUTES

GRILLING TIME
9 TO 11 MINUTES

PATTIES

1½ pounds ground chuck (80% lean)

1 teaspoon onion powder

½ teaspoon ground cumin

½ teaspoon garlic powder

½ teaspoon chili powder

½ teaspoon kosher salt

¼ teaspoon freshly ground black pepper

Kosher salt and freshly ground black pepper

4 slices thick Texas toast

Extra-virgin olive oil

4 canned whole green chile peppers, chopped

4 slices sharp cheddar cheese, each about 1 ounce

Pico de Gallo 1 (page 300)

½ cup sour cream

The term *Tex-Mex* entered the American lexicon way back in the 1880s, when it was used not for food but for trains, as in the Texas Mexican Railway. Nowadays, the term is most often used to refer to Mexican influences on Texan food, such as these well-seasoned burgers topped with salsa and sour cream and served on thick slices of Texas toast.

SERVES 4

1. In a medium bowl mix together all the patty ingredients with your hands. Gently shape the mixture into four square-shaped patties that are roughly the size of the bread and about 1 inch thick. With your thumb or the back of a spoon, make a shallow indentation about 1 inch wide in the center of each patty to prevent it from doming as it cooks. Refrigerate the patties until ready to grill.

2. Prepare the grill for direct cooking over medium-high heat (400° to 500°F).

3. Brush the cooking grates clean. Lightly season the patties on both sides with salt and pepper. Brush each bread slice lightly with oil. Grill the patties over **direct medium-high heat**, with the lid closed, for 5 minutes. Turn the patties over and top with an equal amount of the green chiles and a cheese slice. Continue grilling until the patties are cooked to medium doneness (160°F), 4 to 6 minutes more. During the last 30 seconds to 1 minute of grilling time, toast the bread slices over direct heat, turning once. Remove from the grill.

4. Stir the pico de gallo to make sure it is well combined. Build a burger on each bread slice with 1 tablespoon of the sour cream, a patty, and 1 tablespoon of the pico de gallo. Serve warm with the remaining pico de gallo and sour cream on the side.

BACON AND EGG BURGERS
WITH CHEDDAR

PREP TIME
25 MINUTES

GRILLING TIME
9 TO 11 MINUTES

This one is for breakfast lovers everywhere. Who says you can't have bacon and eggs for dinner? After you fry the bacon, heat a little of the fat in the pan just until it barely sizzles and then add your eggs. If they are very fresh, the yolks will mound nicely in the center and the whites will not spread too much.

PATTIES

1½ pounds ground chuck
(80% lean)

¼ cup finely chopped
yellow onion

2 tablespoons ketchup

2 teaspoons
Worcestershire sauce

1 teaspoon kosher salt

¼ teaspoon freshly ground
black pepper

8 slices bacon

4 slices cheddar cheese,
each about 1 ounce

4 kaiser rolls, split

4 large eggs

Kosher salt and freshly
ground black pepper

8 slices tomato

SERVES 4

1. In a medium bowl mix together all the patty ingredients with your hands. Gently shape the mixture into four patties of equal size and about 1 inch thick. With your thumb or the back of a spoon, make a shallow indentation about 1 inch wide in the center of each patty to prevent it from doming as it cooks. Refrigerate the patties until ready to grill.

2. In a skillet over medium heat, fry the bacon until crisp, 10 to 12 minutes, turning occasionally. Transfer the bacon to paper towels to drain. Pour off all but 2 tablespoons of the bacon fat from the skillet and reserve for another use or discard.

3. Prepare the grill for direct cooking over medium-high heat (400° to 500°F).

4. Brush the cooking grates clean. Grill the patties over **direct medium-high heat**, with the lid closed, until cooked to medium doneness (160°F), 9 to 11 minutes, turning once. During the last 30 seconds to 1 minute of grilling time, place a slice of cheese on each patty to melt, and toast the rolls, cut side down, over direct heat. Remove from the grill.

5. Return the skillet to the stove over medium heat and warm the bacon fat. Crack the eggs into the skillet, turn down the heat to medium-low, and cook until the whites are just firm and opaque and the yolks have begun to thicken, about 2 minutes. Carefully flip the eggs over and continue to cook until the yolks are cooked but still slightly runny, 30 seconds to 1 minute more. Season with salt and pepper.

6. Build a burger on each bun with 2 tomato slices, 2 bacon slices, a patty, and an egg. Serve warm.

CAPTAIN D'S
LAMB BURGERS

PREP TIME
15 MINUTES

CHILLING TIME
2 TO 4 HOURS

GRILLING TIME
10 TO 13 MINUTES

PATTIES

2 pounds ground lamb

⅓ cup minced red onion

2 tablespoons extra-virgin olive oil

2 tablespoons fresh lemon juice

2 tablespoons finely chopped fresh Italian parsley leaves

2 tablespoons finely chopped fresh oregano leaves

2 teaspoons minced garlic

1½ teaspoons kosher salt

1 teaspoon dried rosemary (optional)

1 teaspoon dried basil (optional)

½ teaspoon freshly ground black pepper

½ teaspoon ground cumin

8 slices sourdough bread, each about ½ inch thick

Extra-virgin olive oil

1½ cups loosely packed baby spinach leaves

8 slices tomato

¾ cup crumbled blue or feta cheese

Years ago we met a United States Marine on a cooking show called *Throwdown! with Bobby Flay*. Captain Eric Dominijanni won the competition against the celebrity chef so handily that we asked to see more of his work at the grill. He contributed this winning recipe to *Weber's Charcoal Grilling*. We salute Captain D, now a major in the Marine Corps, for his service and his grilling.

SERVES 4

1. In a large bowl mix together all the patty ingredients with your hands. Gently shape the mixture into four patties of equal size and about 1 inch thick. With your thumb or the back of a spoon, make a shallow indentation about 1 inch wide in the center of each patty to prevent it from doming as it cooks. Cover and refrigerate the patties for 2 to 4 hours.

2. Prepare the grill for direct cooking over medium heat (350° to 450°F).

3. Brush the cooking grates clean. Lightly brush the bread slices on both sides with oil. Grill the patties over **direct medium heat**, with the lid closed, until cooked to medium doneness (160°F), 10 to 13 minutes, turning once. During the last 30 seconds to 1 minute of grilling time, toast the bread slices over direct heat, turning once.

4. Build a burger on each toasted bread slice with some spinach, 2 tomato slices, a patty, and some cheese. Serve warm.

KOFTA IN PITA POCKETS
WITH CUCUMBER-TOMATO SALAD

PREP TIME
25 MINUTES

GRILLING TIME
7 TO 9 MINUTES

Kofta is a Turkish dish of ground meat mixed with grains, vegetables, and spices. The little patties taste particularly good because they are seasoned not only with parsley and garlic but also with a complex mix of aromatic spices, including some that you may not use regularly, like allspice, cardamom, and turmeric.

SALAD

1 cup chopped English cucumber

1 cup quartered cherry tomatoes

¼ cup finely chopped red onion

Kosher salt

KOFTA

1½ pounds ground chuck (80% lean)

½ cup minced fresh Italian parsley leaves

1 tablespoon minced garlic

2 teaspoons ground coriander

1½ teaspoons ground cumin

1½ teaspoons kosher salt

½ teaspoon freshly ground black pepper

½ teaspoon ground allspice

¼ teaspoon ground cardamom

¼ teaspoon ground turmeric

3 whole-wheat pita breads

Extra-virgin olive oil

Tahini-Yogurt Dressing (page 298)

SERVES 6

1. In a medium bowl combine the cucumber, tomatoes, and onion, stir to mix, and season with salt. Set aside.

2. In a medium bowl mix together all the kofta ingredients with your hands. Gently shape the mixture into six patties of equal size and about ¾ inch thick. With your thumb or the back of a spoon, make a shallow indentation about 1 inch wide in the center of each patty to prevent it from doming as it cooks. Refrigerate the patties until ready to grill.

3. Prepare the grill for direct and indirect cooking over medium-high heat (400° to 500°F).

4. Lightly sprinkle the pita breads with water and wrap them in aluminum foil, sealing the packet closed.

5. Brush the cooking grates clean. Brush the patties on both sides with oil. Grill over **direct medium-high heat**, with the lid closed, until cooked to medium doneness (160°F), 7 to 9 minutes, turning once. At the same time, warm the pita packet over **indirect medium-high heat** for 4 to 5 minutes, turning once. Remove from the grill.

6. Cut each pita in half. Scoop about 3 tablespoons of the salad into each pita half. Spoon some of the dressing over the salad. Place a patty into each pita half and spoon in more dressing, if desired. Serve warm.

BARBECUED
MEAT LOAF

PREP TIME
20 MINUTES

GRILLING TIME
**50 MINUTES
TO 1 HOUR**

Sometimes just one ingredient can set a recipe apart. Here, a teaspoon of dried tarragon elevates what might otherwise be a ho-hum meat loaf. The flaky, crispy panko ensures a light texture, so don't be tempted to trade it out for conventional powdery dried bread crumbs. The ground pork helps to round out the beef flavor and brings some juicy pork fat to the party.

MEAT LOAF

**1¼ pounds ground beef
(80% lean)**

1¼ pounds ground pork

2 cups panko (Japanese-style bread crumbs)

**1 cup finely chopped
yellow onion**

1 large egg

**1 teaspoon
Worcestershire sauce**

1 teaspoon garlic powder

1 teaspoon dried tarragon

1 teaspoon kosher salt

**1 teaspoon freshly ground
black pepper**

SAUCE

**½ cup bottled
barbecue sauce**

¼ cup ketchup

SERVES 8 TO 10

1. In a bowl mix together all the meat loaf ingredients with your hands. Divide the mixture in half and gently shape each half into a loaf about 4 inches wide and 6 to 7 inches long. Place the loaves on a sheet pan.

2. Prepare the grill for indirect cooking over low heat (about 300°F).

3. In a small bowl combine the sauce ingredients and mix well. Set aside half of the sauce to serve with the meat loaf. Use 3 tablespoons of the remaining sauce to coat the top of each meat loaf evenly.

4. Brush the cooking grates clean. Using a metal spatula, gently pick up each loaf from the sheet pan and place directly on the cooking grates over **indirect low heat**. Close the lid and cook until a thermometer inserted through the top of each loaf to the center registers 155°F, 50 minutes to 1 hour. Remove the loaves from the grill and let rest for 10 to 15 minutes (the internal temperature will rise 5 to 10 degrees during this time).

5. Cut the loaves into ½-inch-thick slices and serve warm with the reserved sauce.

TAGLIATA OF FLANK STEAK
WITH ARUGULA AND SHAVED PARMESAN

PREP TIME
15 MINUTES

GRILLING TIME
6 TO 8 MINUTES

1 flank steak, 1½ to 2 pounds and about ¾ inch thick

Extra-virgin olive oil

Kosher salt and freshly ground black pepper

⅓ cup balsamic vinegar

½ teaspoon granulated sugar

6 cups loosely packed baby arugula

1 cup loosely packed shaved Parmigiano-Reggiano® cheese (about 3 ounces)

The Italian word *tagliata* comes from the verb *tagliare*, "to cut." Here, it is used to describe flank steak that is thinly sliced and then dressed with a trio of very Italian ingredients: arugula, balsamic vinegar, and shavings of Parmigiano-Reggiano cheese.

SERVES 4 TO 6

1. Lightly brush the steak on both sides with oil and then season on both sides with salt and pepper. Let the steak stand at room temperature for 15 to 30 minutes before grilling.

2. Prepare the grill for direct cooking over high heat (450° to 550°F).

3. In a small saucepan over medium-high heat on the stove, combine the vinegar and sugar, bring to a boil, and cook until reduced by half, about 6 minutes, stirring occasionally. Remove from the heat and let cool.

4. Brush the cooking grates clean. Grill the steak over **direct high heat**, with the lid closed, until cooked to your desired doneness, 6 to 8 minutes for medium rare, turning once or twice. Transfer to a cutting board and let rest for 3 to 5 minutes.

5. Cut the steak in half lengthwise and then cut each half across the grain into thin slices. Divide the slices evenly among individual plates or arrange on a warm serving platter. Pour any juices captured during cutting over the steak and pile the arugula on top. Drizzle the balsamic reduction over the arugula, then season with salt and pepper and top with the cheese. Serve right away.

CHILE-RUBBED
FLANK STEAK
WITH BLACK BEAN SALAD

★

PREP TIME
25 MINUTES

GRILLING TIME
8 TO 10 MINUTES

★

Make this recipe with whatever kind of charcoal you like, or even with gas, but we have to say, mesquite charcoal and beef are a prized combination in the American southwest. Mesquite burns with a strong (almost bitter) but still pleasant smoke that tastes just right in recipes like this one.

RUB

1 teaspoon chile powder

1 teaspoon ground cumin

1 teaspoon dried oregano

1 teaspoon kosher salt

½ teaspoon freshly ground black pepper

⅛ teaspoon cinnamon

SALAD

1 can (15 ounces) black beans, rinsed and drained

1 cup seeded, finely diced tomatoes

½ cup diced yellow bell pepper

⅓ cup diced red onion

⅓ cup thinly sliced scallions

2 tablespoons extra-virgin olive oil

1 tablespoon fresh lime juice

1 teaspoon minced garlic

1 flank steak, 1½ to 2 pounds and ¾ inch thick

Kosher salt and freshly ground black pepper

SERVES 6

1. In a small bowl combine all the rub ingredients and mix well.

2. In a medium bowl combine all the salad ingredients, including ¾ teaspoon of the rub, and mix gently but thoroughly. Set aside at room temperature. If desired, let stand for at least 1 hour or up to 8 hours to meld the flavors.

3. Lightly coat the steak on both sides with oil and season on both sides with the remaining rub. Let the steak stand at room temperature for 15 to 30 minutes before grilling.

4. Prepare the grill for direct cooking over high heat (450° to 550°F).

5. Brush the cooking grates clean. Grill the steak over **direct high heat**, with the lid closed, until cooked to your desired doneness, 8 to 10 minutes for medium rare, turning once. Remove the steak from the grill and let rest for 3 to 5 minutes.

6. Season the salad with salt and pepper. Cut the steak across the grain into ¼-inch-thick slices. (The thinner the slices, the more tender the meat will be.) Serve the meat warm with the salad. If desired, season the meat with a little more salt.

GINGER FLANK STEAK
WITH ASPARAGUS

PREP TIME
25 MINUTES

MARINATING TIME
3 TO 4 HOURS

GRILLING TIME
14 TO 18 MINUTES

MARINADE

¼ cup plus 1 tablespoon soy sauce

3 tablespoons rice vinegar

2 tablespoons sugar

2 tablespoons toasted sesame oil

1½ tablespoons peeled, grated fresh ginger

1½ tablespoons sambal oelek

1 tablespoon minced garlic

1 cup finely chopped scallions

¼ cup chopped cilantro

1 flank steak, about 1½ pounds and ¾ inch thick

¼ cup sesame seeds

1 teaspoon sea salt

1 pound asparagus, tough ends removed

1 tablespoon extra-virgin olive oil

½ teaspoon kosher salt

2 tablespoons chopped cilantro leaves

The large surface area on a flank steak makes it great for marinating and grilling. Think of all the delicious crust you can develop on the top and bottom. Flank is a fairly lean steak, so be careful not to overcook it. A staple of the Indonesian pantry, *sambal oelek*, a paste of hot red chile peppers, vinegar, and salt, is fiery hot on its own but adds just the right touch of spiciness to this marinade.

SERVES 4

1. In a small bowl whisk together the soy sauce, vinegar, sugar, sesame oil, ginger, sambal oelek, and garlic until the sugar dissolves. Stir in the scallions and cilantro. Place the steak in a glass baking dish, pour in the marinade, and turn the steak to coat evenly. Cover and refrigerate for 3 to 4 hours, turning the steak once or twice. Let the steak stand at room temperature for 15 to 30 minutes before grilling.

2. Prepare the grill for direct cooking over medium heat (350° to 450°F).

3. In a nonstick skillet over low heat on the stove, toast the sesame seeds until they are golden brown but have not begun to pop, 2 to 3 minutes, shaking the pan constantly. Pour the seeds onto a plate and let cool for 10 minutes. Transfer the seeds to a mortar, add the sea salt, and, using a pestle, coarsely grind the seeds (do not grind to a fine powder).

4. Coat the asparagus with the oil and season with the kosher salt.

5. Brush the cooking grates clean. Grill the steak over **direct medium heat**, with the lid closed, until cooked to your desired doneness, 8 to 10 minutes for medium rare, turning once. Remove the steak from the grill and let rest for 3 to 5 minutes. While the steak rests, grill the asparagus over **direct medium heat**, with the lid closed, until lightly charred and crisp-tender, 6 to 8 minutes, turning the spears a quarter turn every 1 to 2 minutes. Remove from the grill.

6. Cut the steak across the grain into thin slices. Serve the steak and asparagus warm, topped with the cilantro and some of the sesame seed mixture. The unused mixture will keep in a tightly capped jar in the refrigerator for up to 2 months.

KOREAN BEEF BARBECUE

PREP TIME
10 MINUTES

MARINATING TIME
2 TO 4 HOURS

GRILLING TIME
3 TO 5 MINUTES

MARINADE

1 Asian pear (baseball size), peeled, cored, and roughly chopped

3 scallions (white and green parts), roughly chopped

6 large garlic cloves

2 cups water

¾ cup soy sauce

⅓ cup granulated sugar

¼ cup rice vinegar

12 flanken-style beef short ribs, about 4 pounds total and ½ inch thick

2 tablespoons sesame seeds, toasted

2 scallions (white and green parts), thinly sliced

One of the distinguishing features of Korean barbecue is its use of flanken-style beef ribs, which look almost nothing like your typical long-bone beef rib. They are cut across (not along) the bones to create three or four thin disks of bone that hold the meat together. To get good char on the ribs, let the excess marinade drip back into the bowl before you set the ribs on the hot grate.

SERVES 4 TO 6

1. In a food processor combine the pear, chopped scallions, and garlic and pulse until finely chopped. Add the water, soy sauce, sugar, and vinegar and process until well combined.

2. Put the ribs in a large bowl and pour in the marinade. Mix well to coat the ribs evenly. Cover and refrigerate for 2 to 4 hours.

3. Prepare the grill for direct cooking over high heat (450° to 550°F).

4. Brush the cooking grates clean. One at a time, lift the ribs from the bowl and let the liquid and solid bits fall back into the bowl. Discard the marinade. Grill the ribs over **direct high heat**, with the lid open, until nicely charred on both sides and cooked to medium or medium-rare doneness, 3 to 5 minutes, turning occasionally. Remove from the grill and sprinkle with the sesame seeds and sliced scallions. Serve warm.

TRI-TIP WITH CORN SALSA

PREP TIME
30 MINUTES

GRILLING TIME
33 TO 45 MINUTES

SALSA

2 ears corn, husked

1 cup cherry tomatoes, cut lengthwise into quarters

⅓ cup finely chopped red onion

2 tablespoons extra-virgin olive oil

2 tablespoons finely chopped fresh basil or cilantro leaves

2 to 3 teaspoons minced serrano chile pepper

2 teaspoons lime juice

½ teaspoon kosher salt

¼ teaspoon freshly ground black pepper

3 tablespoons extra-virgin olive oil, divided

1 teaspoon ancho chile powder

1 teaspoon ground cumin

Kosher salt and freshly ground black pepper

1½ to 2 pounds tri-tip roast, excess fat and silver skin removed

1 can (15 ounces) black beans, rinsed and drained

1½ cups thinly sliced hearts of romaine

½ cup crumbled or coarsely grated Cotija or queso fresco cheese (2 ounces)

Corn salsas taste best when made with freshly harvested summer corn. The kernels lose much of their flavor and sweetness over the course of even a few days, with their natural sugars quickly turning to starch. At the market, look for ears with tight green husks and store them unhusked in the refrigerator until ready to grill.

SERVES 4 TO 6

1. Prepare the grill for direct and indirect cooking over medium heat (350° to 450°F).

2. Brush the cooking grates clean. Grill the corn over **direct medium heat**, with the lid closed, until browned in spots and tender, 10 to 15 minutes, turning occasionally. Remove from the grill and, when the corn is cool enough to handle, cut the kernels off the cobs and put the kernels in a medium bowl. Add all the remaining salsa ingredients and mix well. (The salsa can be made up to 6 hours ahead. Cover and refrigerate. Let stand at room temperature for 1 hour before serving.)

3. In a small bowl mix together 2 tablespoons of the oil, the chile powder, the cumin, 1 teaspoon salt, and ½ teaspoon pepper. Spread the mixture all over the tri-tip. Let the tri-tip stand at room temperature for 15 to 30 minutes before grilling.

4. Grill the tri-tip over **direct medium heat**, with the lid closed, until well marked on both sides, 8 to 10 minutes, turning once. Move the tri-tip over **indirect medium heat**, close the lid, and cook to your desired doneness, 15 to 20 minutes for medium rare. Remove from the grill and let rest for about 5 minutes.

5. Meanwhile, in a heavy, medium saucepan over low heat on the stove, combine the beans and the remaining 1 tablespoon oil and cook until heated through, about 5 minutes, stirring once or twice. Remove from the heat and season with salt and pepper.

6. Cut the meat across the grain into very thin slices. Serve right away with the black beans, lettuce, corn salsa, and cheese.

SANTA MARIA
TRI-TIP SANDWICHES

PREP TIME
20 MINUTES,
PLUS **15 MINUTES**
FOR THE SAUCE

MARINATING TIME
3 TO 24 HOURS

GRILLING TIME
25 TO 35 MINUTES

RUB

1 tablespoon freshly ground black pepper

2 teaspoons garlic salt

1 teaspoon mustard powder

1 teaspoon paprika

¼ teaspoon cayenne pepper

2 to 2½ pounds tri-tip roast, about 1½ inches thick

12 slices French bread

Tri-Tip Barbecue Sauce (page 300)

An epic steak sandwich requires some key elements. First, the steak itself must be tender and thinly sliced for easy chewing. Second, it needs a sauce of remarkable character. Third, the bread should be toasted with a little butter or olive oil to create a crispy texture for soaking up all the flavorful steak juices. This sandwich has it all.

SERVES 6

1. In a small bowl combine all the rub ingredients and mix well. Rub the mixture all over the roast, pressing it into the meat. Cover with plastic wrap and refrigerate for at least 3 hours or up to 24 hours.

2. Soak a handful of oak, mesquite, or hickory wood chips in water for at least 30 minutes.

3. Prepare the grill for direct and indirect cooking over medium heat (350° to 450°F).

4. Brush the cooking grates clean. Drain the wood chips and add to the charcoal or to the smoker box of a gas grill, and close the lid. When smoke appears, place the tri-tip directly over the fire, close the lid, and sear over **direct medium heat** on both sides, about 5 minutes total, turning once. Move to indirect heat, close the lid, and grill over **indirect medium heat** until the internal temperature reaches about 140°F for medium rare, 20 to 30 minutes more. Remove from the grill and let rest for 5 minutes. During the last 30 seconds to 1 minute of grilling time, toast the bread over direct heat. Remove from the grill.

5. Cut the meat on the diagonal across the grain into thin slices. Build each sandwich with 2 slices of French bread, meat, and a dollop of sauce. Serve warm or at room temperature.

STEAK AND TOMATO KABOBS
WITH AVOCADO SAUCE

PREP TIME
15 MINUTES

GRILLING TIME
8 MINUTES

This recipe dates back to a 1999 book called *Weber's Art of the Grill*. We think the flavors—tender sirloin treated to an aromatic rub, ripe tomatoes, and a sauce of avocado, cucumber, and lime—work as well today as they did back then. Don't skimp on the size of the steak cubes, as they must be big enough to char on the outside without overcooking on the inside.

SAUCE

1 Hass avocado

2-inch piece English cucumber, peeled and roughly chopped

¼ cup sour cream

¼ cup sliced scallions

¼ cup chopped fresh dill

Juice of 1 lime

About ⅛ teaspoon hot-pepper sauce

Kosher salt

RUB

1 teaspoon minced garlic

1 teaspoon mustard powder

1 teaspoon pure chile powder

½ teaspoon paprika

½ teaspoon ground coriander

½ teaspoon ground cumin

½ teaspoon kosher salt

2 pounds top sirloin, about 1¼ inches thick, trimmed of excess fat, cut into 1¼-inch cubes

24 cherry tomatoes

Vegetable oil

SERVES 4

1. In a food processor or blender combine the avocado, cucumber, sour cream, scallions, dill, and lime juice and process until smooth. Stir in the hot-pepper sauce, adjusting the amount to your taste, and then season with salt. Pour the sauce into a bowl, cover, and refrigerate. Bring to room temperature before serving.

2. Have ready metal or bamboo skewers. If using bamboo, soak in water for at least 30 minutes.

3. Prepare the grill for direct cooking over medium heat (350° to 450°F).

4. In a small bowl combine all the rub ingredients and mix well. Season the meat cubes with the rub, coating them evenly. Thread the meat onto the skewers, alternating them with the tomatoes. Lightly brush the skewers with oil.

5. Brush the cooking grates clean. Grill the kabobs over **direct medium heat**, with the lid closed, until the meat is cooked to your desired doneness, about 8 minutes for medium rare, turning occasionally. Remove from the grill.

6. Serve the kabobs warm with the sauce.

T-BONES
WITH AVOCADO SALSA

PREP TIME
20 MINUTES

GRILLING TIME
10 TO 12 MINUTES

SALSA

2 Hass avocados, finely
diced or mashed

1 cup finely diced tomato

4 scallions (white and light
green parts only), finely
chopped

2 tablespoons fresh
lime juice

1 tablespoon extra-virgin
olive oil

2 tablespoons finely
chopped fresh basil leaves

1 teaspoon minced garlic

1 teaspoon minced jalapeño
chile pepper

¾ teaspoon kosher salt

¼ teaspoon freshly
ground pepper

¼ teaspoon
Worcestershire sauce

2 tablespoons roughly
chopped garlic

2 teaspoons kosher salt,
divided

2 T-bone steaks, each
1 to 1¼ pounds and about
1¼ inches thick, trimmed
of excess fat

Extra-virgin olive oil

1 teaspoon freshly ground
black pepper

You can grill whatever cut of steak you like for this recipe, but the T-bone has at least one great advantage: while most of the meat will develop some nice char, which we definitely want, the meat alongside the bone will be a little less cooked and a little juicier. The salsa here is similar to guacamole but with two offbeat additions, basil and Worcestershire sauce.

SERVES 4

1. In a medium bowl combine all the salsa ingredients and mix well. Set aside at room temperature for up to 2 hours before serving.

2. Make a little pile of the garlic on a cutting board. Sprinkle 1 teaspoon of the salt over the garlic. Use a chef's knife to finely chop the garlic with the salt and then use the side of the knife to crush the garlic with the salt to a smooth paste.

3. Prepare the grill for direct and indirect cooking over high heat (450° to 550°).

4. Lightly brush the steaks on both sides with oil and then spread the garlic paste evenly on both sides. Season both sides of the steaks with the remaining 1 teaspoon salt and the pepper. Let the steaks stand at room temperature for 15 to 30 minutes before grilling.

5. Brush the cooking grates clean. Sear the steaks over **direct high heat**, with the lid closed, for 6 minutes, turning once. Move the steaks over **indirect high heat** and continue cooking to your desired doneness, 4 to 6 minutes more for medium rare. Remove the steaks from the grill and let rest for 3 to 5 minutes.

6. Serve the steaks warm with the salsa.

GINGER
PORTERHOUSE STEAKS
WITH ROASTED SESAME SALT

PREP TIME
20 MINUTES

GRILLING TIME
6 TO 8 MINUTES

3 tablespoons vegetable oil

2 tablespoons peeled, grated fresh ginger

3 teaspoons kosher salt, divided

2 teaspoons freshly ground black pepper, divided

2 porterhouse steaks, each about 1¼ pounds and 1 inch thick, trimmed of excess fat

3 tablespoons sesame seeds

What makes these steaks both unusual and fun to eat is that guests dip as many edges of each slice as they like into a crunchy, nutty mix of sesame seeds, salt, and pepper. This Japanese style of eating allows everyone to customize the amount of seasoning to suit his or her palate.

SERVES 4

1. In a small bowl mix together the oil, ginger, 2 teaspoons of the salt, and 1½ teaspoons of the pepper. Smear the mixture on both sides of each steak. Let the steaks stand at room temperature for 15 to 30 minutes before grilling.

2. Prepare the grill for direct cooking over high heat (450° to 550°F).

3. Meanwhile, heat a 10-inch skillet over medium heat on the stove. Add the sesame seeds, the remaining 1 teaspoon salt, and the remaining ½ teaspoon pepper to the hot pan and toast until the sesame seeds are deep golden brown, 5 to 10 minutes, stirring occasionally with a wooden spoon to prevent burning. Pour the roasted sesame salt into four small dipping bowls, dividing it evenly.

4. Brush the cooking grates clean. Grill the steaks over **direct high heat**, with the lid closed, until cooked to your desired doneness, 6 to 8 minutes for medium rare, turning once. Remove the steaks from the grill and let rest for 3 to 5 minutes.

5. Cut off the strip from one side of the bone and the filet from the other, then cut each steak across the grain into slices. Serve warm with the sesame salt. Invite diners to dip an edge of each slice of steak in the salt.

BLACK PEPPER
NEW YORK STRIP STEAKS
WITH HORSERADISH SAUCE

PREP TIME
10 MINUTES

GRILLING TIME
6 TO 8 MINUTES

A classic steakhouse cut, the strip steak is cut from the center of the top loin. If you can find these steaks with some bone attached along one edge, that's a bonus. There are many regional names for this cut: New York strip, Kansas City strip, shell, Delmonico, Ambassador, hotel cut, and top loin. They are all very gratifying, no matter what you call them.

SERVES 4

SAUCE

¾ cup sour cream

2 tablespoons prepared horseradish

2 tablespoons finely chopped fresh Italian parsley leaves

2 teaspoons Dijon mustard

2 teaspoons Worcestershire sauce

½ teaspoon kosher salt

¼ teaspoon freshly ground black pepper

4 New York strip steaks, each 10 to 12 ounces and about 1 inch thick, trimmed of excess fat

2 tablespoons extra-virgin olive oil

2 tablespoons Dijon mustard

¾ teaspoon kosher salt

¾ teaspoon freshly ground black pepper

1. In a small bowl whisk together all the sauce ingredients. Cover and refrigerate until serving.

2. Brush the steaks on both sides with the oil. Spread the mustard evenly on both sides and then season both sides with the salt and pepper. Let the steaks stand at room temperature for 15 to 30 minutes before grilling.

3. Prepare the grill for direct cooking over high heat (450° to 550°F).

4. Brush the cooking grates clean. Grill the steaks over **direct high heat**, with the lid closed, until cooked to your desired doneness, 6 to 8 minutes for medium rare, turning once. Remove the steaks from the grill and let rest for 3 to 5 minutes.

5. Serve the steaks warm with the sauce on the side.

NEW YORK STRIP STEAKS
WITH RED-EYE BARBECUE SAUCE

PREP TIME
20 MINUTES,
PLUS **15 MINUTES**
FOR THE SAUCE

GRILLING TIME
6 TO 8 MINUTES

SAUCE

1 tablespoon unsalted butter

2 teaspoons minced shallot

1 teaspoon minced garlic

½ cup ketchup

¼ cup brewed dark-roast coffee or espresso

1 tablespoon balsamic vinegar

1 tablespoon packed light brown sugar

2 teaspoons ancho chile powder

4 New York strip steaks, each 10 to 12 ounces and about 1 inch thick, trimmed of excess fat

2 tablespoons extra-virgin olive oil

¾ teaspoon kosher salt

¾ teaspoon freshly ground black pepper

People often ask how to create handsome diamond-shaped grill marks on steaks. It's pretty easy. Lay the steaks on the cooking grate over direct heat so they are pointing to ten o'clock, then close the lid. After a couple of minutes, lift the steaks, rotate them so they are at two o'clock, close the lid, and let them sear for another minute or two. Flip each steak over and repeat.

SERVES 4

1. In a saucepan over medium heat, melt the butter. Add the shallot and cook until it begins to brown, about 3 minutes, stirring often. Add the garlic and cook until fragrant, about 1 minute. Stir in the remaining sauce ingredients, bring to a simmer, and reduce the heat to low. Simmer until slightly reduced, about 10 minutes, stirring often. Transfer to a bowl to cool.

2. Brush the steaks on both sides with the oil and then season on both sides with the salt and pepper. Let the steaks stand at room temperature for 15 to 30 minutes before grilling.

3. Prepare the grill for direct cooking over high heat (450° to 550°F).

4. Brush the cooking grates clean. Grill the steaks over **direct high heat**, with the lid closed, until cooked to your desired doneness, 6 to 8 minutes for medium rare, turning once. Remove the steaks from the grill and let rest for 3 to 5 minutes.

5. Serve the steaks warm with the sauce on the side.

NEW YORK STRIP STEAKS
WITH BASIL-ARUGULA PESTO

PREP TIME
15 MINUTES

GRILLING TIME
6 TO 8 MINUTES

PESTO

1½ cups loosely packed baby arugula

½ cup loosely packed fresh basil leaves

2 tablespoons roughly chopped toasted walnuts

½ teaspoon finely grated lemon zest

1 garlic clove

¼ cup extra-virgin olive oil

Kosher salt and freshly ground black pepper

6 New York strip steaks, each 8 to 10 ounces and about 1 inch thick, trimmed of excess fat

Extra-virgin olive oil

Kosher salt and freshly ground black pepper

This bright green pesto wanders a little from tradition by swapping out some of the basil for peppery arugula and substituting walnuts for pine nuts. The result is a sauce with more savory oomph than usual. For the best flavor and color, make the pesto the day you serve it.

SERVES 6

1. In a food processor combine the arugula, basil, walnuts, lemon zest, and garlic and pulse until coarsely chopped. With the machine running, gradually add the oil and process until well blended. Season the pesto with salt and pepper and set aside.

2. Lightly brush the steaks on both sides with oil and then season on both sides with salt and pepper. Let the steaks stand at room temperature for 15 to 30 minutes before grilling.

3. Prepare the grill for direct cooking over high heat (450° to 550°F).

4. Brush the cooking grates clean. Grill the steaks over **direct high heat**, with the lid closed, until cooked to your desired doneness, 6 to 8 minutes for medium rare, turning once. Remove the steaks from the grill and let rest for 3 to 5 minutes.

5. Top each steak with a generous dollop of the pesto and serve warm.

DIJON AND GARLIC
RIB EYES
SMOKED WITH A LITTLE THYME

PREP TIME
15 MINUTES

MARINATING TIME
2 TO 4 HOURS

GRILLING TIME
6 TO 8 MINUTES

We usually use hardwood chips for smoking, but here we turn to wood of another sort: the thin branch-like stems of thyme sprigs. The thyme leaves go into the mustard-garlic paste that is smeared onto the steaks, and then the steaks are grilled in aromatic smoke created by tossing both wood chips and the thyme stems onto the hot charcoal.

SERVES 4 TO 6

PASTE

1 small handful fresh thyme sprigs

3 tablespoons extra-virgin olive oil

1 tablespoon Dijon mustard

1 tablespoon balsamic vinegar

1 tablespoon minced garlic

1 teaspoon kosher salt

½ teaspoon celery seed

¼ teaspoon freshly ground black pepper

4 boneless rib-eye steaks, each 12 to 16 ounces and about 1 inch thick

½ teaspoon kosher salt

¼ teaspoon freshly ground black pepper

1. Strip the leaves from the thyme sprigs. Reserve the stems for tossing onto the charcoal later. Finely chop enough leaves to yield 2 tablespoons. In a small bowl combine the chopped thyme with all the remaining paste ingredients and mix to make a paste. Brush the paste evenly on both sides of the steaks. Cover and refrigerate for 2 to 4 hours.

2. Soak 2 small handfuls hickory or mesquite wood chips in water for at least 30 minutes.

3. Prepare a charcoal grill for direct cooking over high heat (450° to 550°F).

4. Remove the steaks from the refrigerator and season on both sides with the salt and pepper. Let the steaks stand at room temperature for 15 to 30 minutes before grilling.

5. Brush the cooking grates clean. Drain the wood chips, add the chips and thyme stems to the charcoal, and put the lid on the grill. When smoke appears, grill the steaks over **direct high heat**, with the lid closed, until cooked to your desired doneness, 6 to 8 minutes for medium rare, turning once. Remove the steaks from the grill and let rest for 3 to 5 minutes. Serve warm.

COMBAT STEAKS

★

PREP TIME
15 MINUTES

GRILLING TIME
6 TO 8 MINUTES

★

In 2006, Weber produced a cookbook of steak recipes to raise funds for U.S. Marines wounded or killed in action. Grilling contests were held at ten Marine Corps installations, and many awesome recipes were created. But in the end, only one recipe could be declared the big winner. Here it is, courtesy of Colonel Stewart Navarre, Marine Corps Base Camp Pendleton, California.

RUB

1 tablespoon garlic powder

1 teaspoon kosher salt

½ teaspoon freshly ground black pepper

4 bone-in rib-eye steaks, each about 10 ounces and 1 inch thick

3 portabello mushrooms, each about 4 ounces

½ cup (1 stick) unsalted butter, divided

2 teaspoons minced garlic

¼ teaspoon kosher salt

⅛ teaspoon freshly ground black pepper

¼ cup red wine

½ cup crumbled blue or feta cheese (2½ ounces), optional

SERVES 4

1. In a small bowl combine all the rub ingredients and mix well. Season the steaks on both sides with the rub. Let the steaks stand at room temperature for 15 to 30 minutes before grilling.

2. Prepare the grill for direct cooking over high heat (450° to 500°F).

3. Remove the stems from the mushrooms and discard. Wipe the mushroom caps with a damp paper towel. With a teaspoon, scrape out the dark gills and discard. Cut each mushroom cap in half and then cut each half crosswise into ½-inch-thick slices.

4. In a large skillet over medium-high heat on the stove, melt half of the butter. Add the mushrooms and garlic, spreading the mushrooms in a single layer, and season with the salt and pepper. Cook until the mushrooms are barely tender, 4 to 5 minutes, stirring two or three times. Add the wine and cook until it nearly evaporates, about 3 minutes, stirring once. Set aside.

5. Brush the cooking grates clean. Grill the steaks over **direct high heat**, with the lid closed, until cooked to your desired doneness, 6 to 8 minutes for medium rare, turning once. Remove the steaks from the grill and let rest for 3 to 5 minutes. Meanwhile, reheat the mushrooms over medium heat on the stove, adding the remaining butter and heating until the butter is melted.

6. Serve the steaks warm with the mushrooms spooned on top. Finish with the cheese, if desired.

BEEF TENDERLOIN STEAKS
WITH SEARED MUSHROOMS AND RED WINE VINAIGRETTE

PREP TIME
15 MINUTES

GRILLING TIME
14 TO 18 MINUTES

4 beef tenderloin steaks, each about 6 ounces and 1¼ inches thick

Extra-virgin olive oil

Kosher salt and freshly ground black pepper

3 thick-cut slices bacon, cut into ¼-inch dice (2 ounces)

⅓ cup finely diced red onion

VINAIGRETTE

3 tablespoons red wine vinegar

2 teaspoons Dijon mustard

2 garlic cloves, minced

¼ cup extra-virgin olive oil

½ teaspoon kosher salt

¼ teaspoon freshly ground black pepper

8 ounces cremini mushrooms, stems removed and caps cut into quarters

2 tablespoons finely chopped fresh chives

Nearly everyone likes filet mignon hot off the grill, making this your go-to recipe for that special dinner party. When cooking the mushrooms, spread them so they are not touching one another. That way, they will roast rather than steam, developing a rich flavor.

SERVES 4

1. Brush the steaks on both sides with oil and season generously on both sides with salt and pepper. Let the steaks stand at room temperature for 15 to 30 minutes before grilling.

2. Prepare the grill for direct cooking over high heat (450° to 550°F) and medium heat (350° to 450°F).

3. In a skillet over medium-low heat on the stove, cook the bacon and onion until the bacon is crisp and the onion is tender, 6 to 8 minutes, stirring occasionally. Remove from the heat.

4. In a small bowl whisk together the vinegar, mustard, and garlic. Gradually whisk in the oil until emulsified and then whisk in the salt and pepper. Put the mushrooms in a medium bowl, add ¼ cup of the vinaigrette, and mix well. Set aside the remaining vinaigrette.

5. Brush the cooking grates clean. Preheat a perforated grill pan over medium heat. Remove the mushrooms from the marinade and spread in a single layer on the pan. Cook over **direct medium heat**, with the lid closed, until golden brown and tender, 6 to 8 minutes, turning once or twice. Don't move the mushrooms until the undersides are nicely browned.

6. Meanwhile, grill the steaks over **direct high heat**, with the lid closed, until cooked to your desired doneness, 8 to 10 minutes for medium rare, turning once. Remove from the grill and let rest for 3 to 5 minutes.

7. Transfer the mushrooms to the skillet with the bacon and onions and warm over medium heat on the grill for about 1 minute, stirring often. Add the chives and mix well. Serve the steaks warm with the mushroom mixture spooned on top. If desired, whisk the reserved vinaigrette to recombine and drizzle some over each steak.

BEEF TENDERLOIN ROAST
WITH WHITE WINE–CREAM SAUCE

FAN
★★★★★
FAVORITE

PREP TIME
40 MINUTES,
PLUS **15 MINUTES**
FOR THE SAUCE

GRILLING TIME
35 TO 45 MINUTES

RUB

1½ tablespoons dried tarragon

2½ teaspoons kosher salt

2 teaspoons freshly ground black pepper

1½ teaspoons dried thyme

1 teaspoon packed rubbed dried sage

1 whole beef tenderloin, 6 to 7 pounds, untrimmed

Extra-virgin olive oil

SAUCE

½ cup minced shallot

½ cup rice vinegar

1½ teaspoons dried tarragon

¼ teaspoon dried thyme

½ cup dry white wine

½ cup low-sodium chicken broth

1½ cups heavy whipping cream

Kosher salt

½ cup packed minced fresh Italian parsley leaves

Here is a beef recipe that makes most other beef recipes jealous. It has it all: a high-end cut seasoned with earthy herbs, fire roasted, and then finished with a classic French cream sauce. To nail the doneness of the meat, use direct and indirect heat and a meat thermometer.

SERVES 10 TO 12

1. In a small bowl combine all the rub ingredients and mix well.

2. Trim off and discard the excess fat and silver skin from the tenderloin. Part of the thin "tail" end may separate, but leave it connected to the main muscle as much as possible. Lay the tenderloin out straight, with the smoother side up. Align the narrow pieces at the tail end, then fold the tail end under itself to form an even thickness (one end of the tenderloin may be larger). Tie the roast snugly with butcher's twine at 2-inch intervals. Secure the folded end with two strings. Lightly coat the roast with oil and season all over with the rub. Let the roast stand at room temperature for 30 minutes to 1 hour before grilling.

3. Prepare the grill for direct and indirect cooking over medium heat (350° to 450°F).

4. In a skillet over high heat on the stove, combine the shallot, vinegar, tarragon, and thyme and cook until the vinegar evaporates, 3 to 4 minutes, stirring often. Add the wine and broth and boil until reduced to ½ cup, 3 to 4 minutes. Add the cream and boil until the surface is covered with large, shiny bubbles and the sauce is reduced to 1½ cups, stirring, 5 to 7 minutes. Adjust the seasoning with salt, and set aside.

5. Brush the cooking grates clean. Sear the roast over **direct medium heat**, with the lid closed, for about 15 minutes, rotating it a quarter turn every 3 to 4 minutes, to sear evenly on all sides. Then slide the roast over **indirect medium heat**, close the lid, and continue cooking until the internal temperature reaches 120° to 125°F for medium rare, 20 to 30 minutes, turning once. Remove the roast from the grill, tent loosely with aluminum foil, and let rest for 10 to 15 minutes (the internal temperature will rise 5 to 10 degrees during this time).

6. Reheat the sauce over medium heat, adding the parsley before serving. Remove the twine from the roast and cut the meat across the grain into slices ½ to 1 inch thick. Season with salt. Serve warm with the sauce.

EXTREME GRILLING

BY MIKE KEMPSTER

In the mid-1970s, Weber set out to achieve national distribution. We had a strong foothold in the Midwest, thanks in part to our relationship with Sears. But we had yet to convince Sears that our grills would sell just as well in the South, East, and West.

One day I learned that all of Sears's regional vice presidents were coming to Chicago, Weber's hometown, for a January meeting. I volunteered to grill a special dinner of aged prime rib roast beef for them. When it comes to

> ONCE THE RUSH OF MY INITIAL SUCCESS WORE OFF, I BEGAN TO WORRY. CHICAGO IS COLD IN JANUARY! WE DECIDED TO SET UP THE GRILLS ON THE ROOFTOP OF THE TOWERS JUST OUTSIDE THE DINING ROOM. . .

beef, there's nothing like prime rib grilled over a smoky hickory fire. If you've never tried it, it's really quite easy. But when the stakes are great and expectations are high, grilling prime rib can be daunting. A lowly grill peddler cooking

for the top brass of Sears was a brash proposal, but I knew if I could wow them with a grilled dinner, I could convince them to carry our grills in their stores across the nation. It took a little persistence, but they agreed to let us entertain them at the Lake Point Towers on the shores of Lake Michigan in mid-January.

Once the rush of my initial success wore off, I began to worry. Chicago is cold in January! We decided to set up the grills on the rooftop of the towers just outside the dining room, where floor-to-ceiling windows provided a panoramic view of the Chicago skyline—a view that included the newly erected Sears Tower. In addition to enjoying that beautiful view, our guests would be able to watch us grilling their dinner on Weber charcoal kettles.

The executive chef, an enthusiastic griller and proud Weber grill owner, helped me with the menu: a hickory-smoked shrimp appetizer followed by a grilled lobster salad, then the prime rib, stuffed with garlic and walnuts and crowned with a garlicky horseradish aioli. It was ambitious, but I was confident that Mother Nature would provide a crisp, clear, windless night.

She sent a major storm instead, starting with freezing rain, followed by ten inches of blowing snow.

The next morning, when the temperature dropped below zero and powerful winds were blowing off Lake Michigan, I took my grilling team to a local ski shop to stock up on expedition-grade parkas rated to -50°F. We loaded up our vans and made the slippery drive in horrible conditions. Once out on the roof, we were nearly blown over by the wind gusts. Bundled like mountaineers, we shoveled, de-iced, and then set our grills as close as we could to the restaurant's windows. The temperature continued to drop.

In good conditions, a whole prime rib roast will take two to four hours to cook, so I added another hour to the cooking time. The wind actually helped start the charcoal and keep it blazing. When we placed two beautiful prime rib roasts on our largest kettle grills at 3:00 p.m., the chef told us the temperature had dropped to -10ºF, with a windchill of -30ºF.

Promptly at 6:00 p.m., the Sears vice presidents and their staff arrived in pristine dark suits, starched white shirts, and red ties and, despite the weather, without a lock of hair out of place. They were greeted by the sight of six masked men in parkas and chef aprons grilling shrimp and lobsters in a cloud of steam and smoke driven by a fierce wind against the lights of Chicago's frigid skyline. Although our guests were clearly stunned, they did not lack for a conversation starter.

The smoked shrimp was a hit, and the group marveled at the grilled lobster salad. I checked the prime rib at 7:00 p.m. My meat thermometer registered 135˚F. After resting,

the roasts would be at a perfect medium-rare temperature. The air temperature was now -15ºF and the windchill at ground level was -40ºF.

Our guests left their tables and gathered at the window as we lifted the roasts off the grills and carried them into the room on cutting boards. I'm sure they will never forget the image of our grill team in expedition clothing and grilling aprons as we triumphantly placed the steaming prime rib roasts on silver carving carts.

Dinner was a success and Sears started offering our grills in all their sales territories the next spring. I still have my expedition parka rated to -50ºF. Years later, one brisk winter, I dusted it off and cooked a dinner of grill-roasted duck for some friends during an outrageous storm. Like the Sears brass, they gathered at my patio door and watched me add charcoal to the fire as the wind blew sparks sideways. I couldn't help but remember that night so many years ago and the fact that a Weber grill has never let me down, no matter what the weather.

PEPPER-CRUSTED
RIB ROAST
WITH HAZELNUT PESTO

PREP TIME
30 MINUTES

GRILLING TIME
ABOUT 2¼ HOURS

2 tablespoons coarsely
crushed black peppercorns

1 tablespoon kosher salt

1 three-bone prime rib
roast, about 7¼ pounds

1 tablespoon canola oil

PESTO

½ cup loosely packed fresh
cilantro leaves

½ cup loosely packed fresh
Italian parsley leaves

¼ cup loosely packed fresh
oregano leaves

¼ cup hazelnuts, toasted
and skins removed

¼ cup sherry vinegar

3 to 5 medium garlic cloves,
roughly chopped

½ teaspoon crushed red
pepper flakes

½ cup extra-virgin olive oil

Kosher salt and freshly
ground black pepper

Ta-da! Behold the magnificent roast that family and friends will cheer. The hardest part of this recipe will be shelling out big money for the meat. The hazelnuts give the pesto sauce a distinctive flavor that is in line with the extravagance of this meal. To toast and skin the nuts, bake them on a sheet pan at 350°F for 10 minutes. Transfer to a kitchen towel and rub to remove the skins.

SERVES 6 TO 8

1. In a small bowl mix together the peppercorns and salt. Coat the roast on all sides with the canola oil and season with the peppercorn mixture. Let the roast stand at room temperature for 1 hour before grilling.

2. Soak 2 large handfuls apple or oak wood chips in water for at least 30 minutes.

3. In a food processor or blender combine the cilantro, parsley, oregano, hazelnuts, vinegar, garlic, and pepper flakes and process until finely chopped. Then, with the motor running, slowly add the oil and process until a thin paste forms. Season with salt and pepper, pour into a serving bowl, cover, and let stand at room temperature while the roast cooks.

4. Prepare the grill for indirect cooking over medium-low heat (about 350°F).

5. Brush the cooking grates clean. Drain 1 handful of the wood chips and add to the charcoal or to the smoker box of a gas grill, then close the lid. When smoke appears, place the roast, bone side down, over **indirect medium-low heat** and cook, with the lid closed, until the internal temperature reaches 120° to 125°F for medium rare, about 2¼ hours. After the first hour of cooking, drain the remaining wood chips and add to the charcoal or smoker box. Remove the roast from the grill and let rest for about 20 minutes (the internal temperature will rise 5 to 10 degrees during this time). Cut the roast across the grain into thick slices. Serve warm with the pesto.

LAMB LOIN CHOPS
WITH LEMON-MINT SALSA VERDE

PREP TIME
20 MINUTES

GRILLING TIME
8 TO 10 MINUTES

SALSA

1 cup loosely packed fresh mint leaves

1 cup loosely packed fresh Italian parsley leaves and tender stems

1 teaspoon finely grated lemon zest

2 tablespoons fresh lemon juice

1 tablespoon roughly chopped shallot

1 tablespoon drained capers, rinsed

1 garlic clove, roughly chopped

½ teaspoon kosher salt

¼ teaspoon crushed red pepper flakes

¼ cup extra-virgin olive oil

8 lamb loin chops, each about 1¼ inches thick, trimmed of excess fat

Extra-virgin olive oil

Kosher salt and freshly ground black pepper

We are crazy about the flavor of lamb and have made it our mission to come up with recipes that encourage others to like it as much as we do. For a less gamy, more subtle flavor, choose young lamb chops. To make the flavors of lamb shine here, we've paired the chops with an herb-heavy salsa that also contains plenty of lemon, capers, and excellent-quality olive oil.

SERVES 4

1. In a food processor or blender combine the mint, parsley, lemon zest and juice, shallot, capers, garlic, salt, and pepper flakes and pulse to chop roughly. Then, with the motor running, slowly add the oil and process until a chunky salsa forms. Transfer to a small bowl, cover with plastic wrap, pressing it directly onto the surface to prevent discoloration, and set aside at room temperature. (The salsa can be made up to 4 hours in advance. Cover and refrigerate. Bring to room temperature and stir to combine before serving.)

2. Lightly brush the lamb chops on both sides with oil and season on both sides with salt and pepper. Let the chops stand at room temperature for 15 to 30 minutes before grilling.

3. Prepare the grill for direct cooking over medium heat (350˚ to 450˚F).

4. Brush the cooking grates clean. Grill the chops over **direct medium heat**, with the lid closed, until cooked to your desired doneness, 8 to 10 minutes for medium rare, turning once. Remove from the grill and let rest for 3 to 5 minutes.

5. Serve the chops warm, two to a plate, with the salsa spooned on top.

FOR PARTY MENUS, SEE PAGE 320

CURRIED LAMB CHOPS
WITH YOGURT SAUCE

★

PREP TIME
20 MINUTES

MARINATING TIME
2 TO 4 HOURS

GRILLING TIME
8 TO 10 MINUTES

★

SAUCE

½ cup plain whole-milk Greek yogurt

1 tablespoon finely chopped cilantro leaves

2 teaspoons lime juice

1 teaspoon chile-garlic paste

½ garlic clove, minced

¼ teaspoon kosher salt

⅛ teaspoon garam masala

MARINADE

3 tablespoons lime juice

2 tablespoons peeled, finely grated fresh ginger

2 tablespoons extra-virgin olive oil

2 teaspoons Madras curry powder

1 teaspoon smoked paprika

1 teaspoon ground turmeric

1 teaspoon cayenne pepper

1 teaspoon kosher salt

1 teaspoon freshly ground black pepper

8 lamb loin chops, each 1½ inches thick, trimmed

Lamb has a stronger flavor than beef or pork, which makes it a good partner for bold marinades and sauces. Here, we take the meat in an Indian direction, using spices that pack a lot of pizzazz. It's easy to modify the sauce to your liking and convenience. For example, if you don't have garam masala, a blend of roasted and ground spices, use a little curry powder instead.

SERVES 4

1. In a small bowl whisk together all the sauce ingredients. Cover and refrigerate until 30 minutes before serving. (The sauce can be made up to 8 hours in advance.)

2. In a separate small bowl whisk together all the marinade ingredients. Place the lamb chops in a large glass baking dish, pour the marinade over them, and turn the chops to coat evenly. Cover and refrigerate for at least 2 hours or up to 4 hours. Let the chops stand at room temperature for 15 to 30 minutes before grilling.

3. Prepare the grill for direct cooking over medium heat (350° to 450°F).

4. Brush the cooking grates clean. Remove the chops from the dish and discard the marinade. Grill over **direct medium heat**, with the lid closed, until cooked to your desired doneness, 8 to 10 minutes for medium rare, turning once. Remove from the grill and let rest for 3 to 5 minutes.

5. Serve the chops warm, with the yogurt sauce alongside.

BUTTERFLIED LEG OF LAMB

PREP TIME
35 MINUTES
MARINATING TIME
2 TO 12 HOURS
GRILLING TIME
25 TO 37 MINUTES

MARINADE

¼ cup extra-virgin olive oil

1 tablespoon finely chopped fresh rosemary leaves

1 tablespoon minced garlic

1 teaspoon kosher salt

½ teaspoon coarse-ground black pepper

1 boneless leg of lamb, 3 to 4 pounds, butterflied, trimmed of fat, and cut into 3 or 4 equal sections

SALAD

12 ounces small zucchini, trimmed and halved lengthwise

1 small red onion, cut into ½-inch-thick slices

Extra-virgin olive oil

8 ounces cherry tomatoes, cut into halves

2 tablespoons pitted, chopped Kalamata olives

2 tablespoons drained, finely chopped oil-packed sun-dried tomatoes

2 tablespoons finely chopped fresh mint leaves

Lemon-Parsley Dressing (page 298)

After a butcher has deboned a leg of lamb, you are left with a slab of meat of varying thicknesses. To ensure all the meat cooks to the same doneness, cut the slab into sections that separate the thicker areas from the thinner ones. Then, grill the sections in succession, starting with the thicker ones.

SERVES 6 TO 8

1. In a small bowl whisk together all the marinade ingredients. Place the lamb in a large, resealable plastic bag and pour in the marinade. Press the air out of the bag and seal tightly. Turn the bag to distribute the marinade evenly, place the bag in a bowl, and refrigerate for 2 to 12 hours, turning the bag occasionally.

2. Prepare the grill for direct cooking over medium heat (350° to 450°F).

3. Brush the cooking grates clean. Brush the zucchini and onion evenly with oil. Grill over **direct medium heat**, with the lid closed, until barely tender, 5 to 7 minutes, turning once. Remove from the grill. Let cool slightly, then cut the zucchini on the diagonal into ½-inch-thick slices and chop the onion. In a serving bowl combine the zucchini, onion, cherry tomatoes, olives, sun-dried tomatoes, and mint.

4. Spoon 3 tablespoons of the dressing over the salad. Toss to coat evenly. Reserve the remaining dressing.

5. Grill the lamb pieces over **direct medium heat**, with the lid closed, until cooked to your desired doneness, turning once. Pieces more than 2 inches thick will take 20 to 30 minutes to reach medium rare (145°F); pieces 1 to 2 inches thick will take 15 to 20 minutes. Remove the lamb from the grill and let rest for 5 minutes.

6. Cut the lamb across the grain into thin slices. Spoon the reserved dressing over the meat. Serve warm with the salad.

03

PORK

SPICY PORK
MEATBALL SLIDERS

PREP TIME
30 MINUTES,
PLUS **35 MINUTES**
FOR THE SAUCE

CHILLING TIME
2 HOURS

GRILLING TIME
8 TO 10 MINUTES

MEATBALLS

2 tablespoons whole-milk ricotta cheese

1 large egg

1½ pounds ground pork

½ cup drained and minced jarred hot cherry peppers or Calabrian chiles

½ cup panko bread crumbs

¼ cup freshly grated Parmigiano-Reggiano® cheese (scant 1 ounce)

¼ cup finely chopped fresh Italian parsley leaves

3 garlic cloves, minced

1 teaspoon dried oregano

1 teaspoon paprika

1 teaspoon kosher salt

1 teaspoon freshly ground black pepper

½ teaspoon crushed red pepper flakes

Spicy Tomato Sauce (page 302)

12 slider buns or small, soft dinner rolls, split

Extra-virgin olive oil

12 large fresh basil leaves

Meatballs are usually browned in a skillet and then simmered with sauce. That technique is fine, though it doesn't deliver a smoky char. By grilling the meatballs first, you turn the volume of flavors way up. Here, we mix a little ricotta with the pork to keep the meatballs moist, grill them, and then coat them in a spicy tomato sauce before tucking them into soft buns.

SERVES 6 (MAKES 12 MEATBALLS)

1. Have ready a platter or small sheet pan. In a small bowl whisk together the ricotta and egg. In a large bowl combine all the remaining meatball ingredients. Pour the ricotta-egg mixture into the meat mixture and, using a fork, gently mix together. With wet hands, form the mixture into twelve 2-inch balls and then flatten each ball slightly. Place on the platter or pan, cover with plastic wrap, and refrigerate for 2 hours.

2. Prepare the grill for direct cooking over medium heat (350° to 450°F).

3. Prepare the sauce as directed and cover to keep warm.

4. Brush the cooking grates clean. Lightly brush the meatballs on all sides and the cut sides of the buns with oil. Grill the meatballs over **direct medium heat**, with the lid closed, until cooked through, 8 to 10 minutes, turning them two or three times. During the last 30 seconds to 1 minute of grilling time, toast the buns, cut side down, over direct heat. Transfer the buns to a work surface. Transfer the meatballs to the sauce. Simmer on the stove over medium-low heat to heat through.

5. To assemble each slider, place a bun bottom cut side up. Using a spoon, scoop up a meatball with some sauce and place it on the bun bottom. Top the meatball with a basil leaf, close the slider with a bun top, and, if you want to keep the slider in place, secure with a toothpick. Repeat with the remaining meatballs and buns. Serve right away.

GINGER PORK BURGERS
WITH SESAME SPINACH

PREP TIME
30 MINUTES

GRILLING TIME
8 TO 10 MINUTES

Bulking up burgers with more than beef can sometimes yield great rewards. Pairing equal amounts of beef and pork and adding an array of Korean-inspired ingredients will give your burgers fantastic layers of flavor. As long as you are being creative, trade out the usual lettuce and tomato for spicy spinach with sesame.

PATTIES

12 ounces lean ground pork

12 ounces ground chuck (80% lean)

½ cup thinly sliced scallions (white and light green parts only)

2-inch piece fresh ginger, peeled and grated

1 tablespoon soy sauce

2 teaspoons toasted sesame oil

2 garlic cloves, minced

½ teaspoon kosher salt

½ teaspoon freshly ground black pepper

2 teaspoons vegetable oil

2 teaspoons toasted sesame oil

2 tablespoons plus 1 teaspoon hot chile-garlic sauce, such as Sriracha, divided

8 ounces baby spinach

1 tablespoon sesame seeds, toasted

½ cup ketchup

4 sesame seed buns, split

SERVES 4

1. In a large bowl mix together all the patty ingredients with your hands. Gently shape the mixture into four patties of equal size and about ¾ inch thick. With your thumb or the back of a spoon, make a shallow indentation about 1 inch wide in the center of each patty to prevent it from doming as it cooks. Refrigerate the patties until ready to grill.

2. Prepare the grill for direct cooking over medium-high heat (450° to 500°F).

3. In a large skillet over medium heat on the stove, warm the vegetable oil, sesame oil, and 1 teaspoon of the chile-garlic sauce. Add the spinach by the handful and stir just until it begins to wilt, 2 to 3 minutes. Remove from the heat and add the sesame seeds.

4. In a small bowl combine the ketchup with the remaining 2 tablespoons chile-garlic sauce and mix well.

5. Brush the cooking grates clean. Grill the patties over **direct medium-high heat**, with the lid closed, until cooked to medium doneness (160°F), 8 to 10 minutes, turning once. During the last 30 seconds to 1 minute of grilling time, toast the buns, cut side down, over direct heat. Remove from the grill.

6. Build a burger on each bun with some chile-garlic ketchup, a patty, and some sesame spinach. Serve warm.

PULLED PORK SANDWICHES

★

PREP TIME
30 MINUTES

COOKING TIME
8 TO 10 HOURS

RESTING TIME
1 HOUR

★

1 bone-in pork shoulder roast (Boston butt), 7 to 8 pounds

½ cup unsweetened apple juice

¼ cup water

1 tablespoon Worcestershire sauce

2 tablespoons kosher salt

1 tablespoon packed light brown sugar

RUB

2 tablespoons kosher salt

1 tablespoon packed light brown sugar

2 teaspoons paprika

1 teaspoon chili powder

1 teaspoon garlic powder

1 teaspoon mustard powder

1 teaspoon freshly ground black pepper

Tangy Barbecue Sauce (page 301)

12 hamburger buns

4 cups purchased coleslaw

Quintessential pulled pork requires the patience to cook the shoulder meat long enough at very low temperatures that it shreds apart into juicy morsels.

SERVES 12

1. Using a sharp knife, trim the exterior fat layer of the roast so it is no more than ¼ inch thick. In a small bowl whisk together the apple juice, water, Worcestershire sauce, salt, and sugar until the salt and sugar dissolve. Load a food syringe with the apple juice mixture and inject the roast with the liquid: with the fat side facing down, imagine the roast in 1-inch squares and, using the syringe, inject each square with some of the liquid, slowly pulling the needle out as you inject the liquid. Some liquid will seep out, but try to keep as much as possible inside the roast.

2. In a small bowl combine all the rub ingredients and mix well. Coat the surface of the roast evenly with the rub, pressing it into the meat. Allow the roast to stand at room temperature for 30 minutes before cooking.

3. Prepare the smoker for indirect cooking with very low heat (200° to 250°F). When the temperature reaches 225°F, add 2 large handfuls hickory wood chunks to the charcoal.

4. Smoke the roast, fat side up, over **indirect very low heat**, with the lid closed, for 5 hours, adjusting the vents so the temperature stays close to 225°F. At the start of every hour, add 2 more handfuls hickory wood chunks to the charcoal. If the temperature falls below 200°F and can't be raised by adjusting the vents, add more lit briquettes as needed.

5. After 5 hours, check the internal temperature of the meat using an instant-read thermometer; it should read 160°F. If not, continue cooking. Remove the meat from the smoker. Close the lid to maintain the heat.

6. On a work surface, lay out two sheets of heavy-duty aluminum foil, each about 3 feet long, overlapping the sheets slightly along their longer sides. Place the roast, fat side up, in the center of the foil. Wrap the roast securely, sealing the edges. Return the roast to the smoker and cook over **indirect very low heat**, with the lid closed, until the internal temperature reaches 190°F, at least 3 hours and as long as 5 hours. Remove from the smoker and let rest, still in the foil, for 1 hour.

7. Unwrap the roast and, when cool enough to handle, shred the meat, discarding excess fat and sinew. In a saucepan over low heat, moisten the pork with some of the sauce, cooking until warmed through. Pile the pork on buns and top with the coleslaw and additional sauce.

BRATS
WITH SPICY STEWED PEPPERS

PREP TIME
10 MINUTES

GRILLING TIME
35 TO 45 MINUTES

¼ cup (½ stick) unsalted butter

1 large red bell pepper, cut lengthwise into ⅓-inch-wide strips

1 large yellow bell pepper, cut lengthwise into ⅓-inch-wide strips

1 medium jalapeño chile pepper, finely chopped

1 medium red onion, cut in half and thinly sliced

1 teaspoon fennel seed

½ teaspoon kosher salt

¼ teaspoon freshly ground black pepper

1 cup beer, preferably lager or ale, plus more if needed

2 tablespoons spicy brown mustard

6 bratwursts

6 large hot dog buns, split

It's hard to beat the simple satisfaction of charred bratwurst simmered in a bath of peppers and onions with beer and mustard. A disposable foil pan does double duty here, first used for browning the vegetables and then for stewing them with the brats. Crack open a cold one and you are all set to watch the game in style.

SERVES 6

1. Prepare the grill for direct and indirect cooking over medium heat (350° to 450°F).

2. Brush the cooking grates clean. In a large disposable foil pan over **direct medium heat**, melt the butter. Add the peppers, onion, fennel seed, salt, and pepper and mix well. Close the lid and cook the vegetables until tender and golden brown in spots, 10 to 15 minutes, stirring occasionally. If any of the vegetables are browning too quickly, slide the pan over indirect heat and finish cooking the vegetables there.

3. Add the beer and mustard to the vegetables and mix well with tongs. Slide the pan over indirect heat to keep warm.

4. Grill the bratwursts over **direct medium heat**, with the lid closed, until lightly charred on all sides, about 15 minutes, turning occasionally. Transfer the bratwursts to the pan, smother them with the peppers and onion, and cook over **indirect medium heat**, with the lid closed, until fully cooked (160°F), 10 to 15 minutes. If the pan is getting too dry, add a little more beer. During the last 30 seconds of grilling time, toast the buns, cut side down, over direct heat. Remove from the grill.

5. Serve the bratwursts warm in the buns with the spicy peppers on top.

ITALIAN SAUSAGES
WITH PEPPERS, ONION, AND PROVOLONE

★

PREP TIME
20 MINUTES

GRILLING TIME
8 TO 10 MINUTES

★

4 tablespoons extra-virgin olive oil, divided, plus more for brushing

¾ teaspoon kosher salt, divided

½ teaspoon freshly ground black pepper, divided

2 medium bell peppers, 1 red and 1 green, cut lengthwise into ⅓-inch-wide strips

1 medium yellow onion, cut crosswise into ⅓-inch-thick slices

4 fresh Italian sausages, sweet and/or hot, each about 5 ounces

1 baguette, about 8 ounces and 2 feet long

2 tablespoons red wine vinegar

1 garlic clove, minced

4 strips provolone cheese, each about ½ ounce and 6 inches long

1 tablespoon roughly chopped fresh Italian parsley leaves

Everyone knows what melted cheese can do for plain burgers. Imagine grilled sausages draped in that same rich creaminess. The "trick" here is to tuck the cheese into a long slit cut along the length of each sausage. A medley of peppers and onions cooked on a grill pan suits the combination nicely, as does plenty of cold beer.

SERVES 4

1. Prepare the grill for direct cooking over medium heat (350° to 450°F).

2. In a medium bowl whisk together 2 tablespoons of the oil, ½ teaspoon of the salt, and ¼ teaspoon of the black pepper. Add the bell peppers and onion and turn to coat.

3. Cut each sausage in half lengthwise about three-fourths of the way through. You want to create a slit to hold the cheese later. Lightly brush the sausages on all sides with oil. Cut the baguette in half lengthwise but not all the way through, so it will lie flat on the grill but remain hinged. Brush the cut sides of the baguette with oil.

4. In a small bowl whisk together the vinegar, garlic, the remaining 2 tablespoons oil, and the remaining ¼ teaspoon each salt and pepper to make a vinaigrette.

5. Brush the cooking grates clean. Preheat a perforated grill pan over medium heat. Spread the bell peppers and onion in a single layer on the preheated grill pan and place the sausages on the cooking grates. Grill over **direct medium heat**, with the lid closed, until the vegetables are tender and the sausages are browned and fully cooked (160°F), 8 to 10 minutes, turning the vegetables and sausages occasionally. During the last 30 seconds to 1 minute of grilling time, place a strip of cheese inside each sausage slit to melt, and toast the baguette, cut side down, over direct heat. Remove everything from the grill.

6. Transfer the vegetables to a bowl, add the parsley, and toss to combine.

7. Cut the baguette crosswise into four 6-inch-long pieces. Tuck a sausage into each baguette piece and top with an equal amount of the vegetables and then the vinaigrette. Serve warm.

WHY WOULD ANYONE EAT A HEDGEHOG?

BY MIKE KEMPSTER

I n the early 1990s, Weber was working hard to build its brand in the South African marketplace. South Africa is a beautiful country with a long and rich history of outdoor cooking. South Africans love barbecue meals, but they don't invite you to a barbecue. Instead, they invite you to a *braai*. And while Americans refer to Weber's classic charcoal grill as a kettle barbecue, South Africans call it a kettle *braai*.

When we arrived in South Africa, we discovered that people typically barbecued only steaks, chops, burgers, and sausages (*wors*). Charcoal briquettes were hard to find, and a hardwood fire on an open grill was the most common way of barbecuing. We didn't have to introduce South Africans to the fun and flavor of a barbecue party, but we had to be careful not to insult outdoor cooking enthusiasts by telling them that they could improve on their barbecues by using an American-made covered kettle grill.

We decided to conduct barbecue demonstrations at retail stores throughout the country, showing people how to cook beef roasts, whole chickens, and fish. We also demonstrated how to bake pizzas and bread. Those demonstrations were a hit, drawing big crowds of interested grillers. On a beautiful day in December—that's summertime in the Southern Hemisphere—I was demonstrating how to roast whole chickens. I was enjoying the interaction with folks living in Cape Town who loved to barbecue, and they were amazed to see how a whole chicken could be roasted without burning it to a crisp.

A gentleman watched me for a while and then asked if a leg of lamb could be cooked the same way. I replied yes and told him how I

BECAUSE OF MY LIMITED ZOOLOGICAL KNOWLEDGE, I IMMEDIATELY THOUGHT HEDGEHOG, NOT WARTHOG. I TRIED TO IMAGINE WHY ANYONE WOULD WANT TO EAT A HEDGEHOG, ESPECIALLY BECAUSE THERE COULDN'T BE MUCH MEAT ON A HEDGEHOG'S LEG.

usually prepared it. He then asked, "Well, what about a leg of warthog? Could you do it the same way?" Because of my limited zoological knowledge, I immediately thought hedgehog, not warthog. I tried to imagine why anyone would want to eat a hedgehog, especially because there couldn't be much meat on a hedgehog's leg. Much to my embarrassment, he got a great laugh out of a Yank who had never seen a warthog. As he walked away, still chuckling, I wasn't sure if I had just been hoodwinked or if there really were animals called warthogs running around South Africa.

This was a long time before we had the Internet everywhere for quick reference, so

I called Shirley Guy, a great chef and grilling enthusiast whom I had met when I was in Johannesburg. She assured me that there were indeed warthogs on this planet and they resembled wild boars.

Our business grew in South Africa, and we teamed up with Shirley to produce our first South African cookbook. We included a recipe for roasted leg of warthog to make sure we satisfied the needs of wild-game hunters. Whenever I mention that recipe in the United States, I get the same "is he pulling my leg?" look. I recognize that look because it was on my face many years ago on that Cape Town day.

SAVORY PORK SOUVLAKI
WITH GREEK SALAD

PREP TIME
25 MINUTES

MARINATING TIME
6 TO 8 HOURS

GRILLING TIME
8 TO 10 MINUTES

MARINADE

¼ cup extra-virgin olive oil

2 tablespoons lemon juice

1 teaspoon ground cumin

1 teaspoon dried oregano

1 teaspoon chile powder

1 teaspoon kosher salt

¾ teaspoon freshly ground
black pepper

1½ pounds boneless pork
loin, trimmed of excess fat
and cut into 1-inch chunks

SALAD

¼ cup extra-virgin olive oil

1 tablespoon red wine
vinegar

2 cups cherry tomatoes,
halved or quartered

1 large cucumber, peeled,
seeded, and diced

4 ounces feta cheese,
cut into ½-inch cubes

1 medium shallot, cut
lengthwise into slivers

Kosher salt

Lemon wedges

A good way to get a mix of flavors into pork is to cut the meat into chunks to expose more surface area to an herb-and-spice-rich marinade, as we have done here. Be sure to mark the meat with the fire on as many sides as possible for the fullest grill flavor. Souvlaki is a Greek dish that usually features skewered lamb and vegetables, but we like it with pork, too.

SERVES 4

1. In a small bowl whisk together all the marinade ingredients. Put the pork chunks in a large, resealable plastic bag and pour in the marinade. Press the air out of the bag and seal tightly. Turn the bag to distribute the marinade evenly, place the bag on a plate, and refrigerate for 6 to 8 hours, turning the bag occasionally.

2. Have ready metal or bamboo skewers. If using bamboo, soak in water for at least 30 minutes.

3. Prepare the grill for direct cooking over medium-high heat (400° to 500°F).

4. Remove the pork chunks from the bag and discard the marinade. Thread the pork snugly onto the skewers.

5. In a medium serving bowl whisk together the oil and vinegar until emulsified. Fold in the tomatoes, cucumbers, cheese, and shallot. Cover and refrigerate until ready to serve.

6. Brush the cooking grates clean. Grill the souvlaki over **direct medium-high heat**, with the lid closed, until the outsides are evenly seared and the pork is just barely pink in the center, 8 to 10 minutes, turning the skewers as needed to ensure all four sides come in contact with the grates. Remove from the grill.

7. Check the salad for seasoning and add salt if needed (if the feta is very salty, the salad may not need salt). Squeeze the lemon wedges over the souvlaki and serve warm with the salad.

GRILLED PIZZAS
WITH SAUSAGE AND PEPPERS

PREP TIME
30 MINUTES

GRILLING TIME
18 TO 22 MINUTES

2 balls prepared pizza dough, each about 1 pound

1 tablespoon extra-virgin olive oil

1 medium red or green bell pepper, cut into ¼-inch-wide strips

½ small yellow onion, thinly sliced

8 ounces sweet or hot fresh Italian sausages, removed from casings

Unbleached all-purpose flour

1 can (8 ounces) tomato sauce

¼ cup thinly sliced black olives

2 tablespoons finely chopped fresh Italian parsley leaves

1 tablespoon finely chopped fresh thyme leaves

2 teaspoons finely chopped fresh rosemary leaves

1½ cups shredded mozzarella cheese (about 5½ ounces)

Serve these pizzas to guests and they may think you've built a brick pizza oven in your backyard. A pizza stone that turns searingly hot on the grill guarantees you will be enjoying a classic firm but chewy crust.

SERVES 6 TO 8

1. Remove the balls of dough from the refrigerator, if necessary, about 1 hour before grilling so the dough will be easier to roll.

2. In a large skillet over medium-high heat, warm the oil. Add the bell pepper and onion and cook until softened but not browned, about 3 minutes, stirring occasionally. Remove the vegetables from the skillet and set aside. Add the sausage to the same skillet, breaking it into medium-sized pieces. Cook over medium-high heat until lightly browned and fully cooked, about 3 minutes, stirring occasionally and breaking the sausage into smaller pieces. Remove the skillet from the heat and let the sausage cool in the skillet.

3. Prepare the grill for direct cooking over medium heat (350° to 450°F). Brush the cooking grates clean. Preheat a pizza stone for at least 15 minutes, following the manufacturer's instructions.

4. Using a rolling pin on a lightly floured work surface, roll out a ball of dough into a round about 12 inches in diameter and ⅓ inch thick. (If the dough shrinks back, cover it with a kitchen towel, let it rest for 5 minutes, and then continue rolling.) Set the first round aside and roll out the second ball the same way.

5. Dust a pizza peel or rimless sheet pan with flour and carefully transfer the first round of dough to the peel or pan. Spread ½ cup of the sauce evenly over the dough, leaving a ½-inch border uncovered. Scatter half each of the sausage, the pepper-and-onion mixture, the olives, and the parsley, thyme, and rosemary over the sauce. Finish by scattering half of the cheese evenly over the top.

6. Slide your first pizza onto the preheated pizza stone and cook over **direct medium heat**, with the lid closed, until the crust is golden brown and the cheese is melted, 9 to 11 minutes. Using the peel or a large spatula, transfer the pizza to a cutting board and let rest for a few minutes. Cut into wedges and serve warm. Repeat steps 5 and 6 with the second dough round and the remaining sauce and toppings.

STUFFED PIZZA
WITH THE WORKS

PREP TIME
45 MINUTES,
PLUS **15 MINUTES**
FOR THE FILLING

GRILLING TIME
40 TO 50 MINUTES

FILLING

1 tablespoon extra-virgin olive oil

3 cups finely chopped yellow onion

1½ cups diced green bell pepper

1 pound button mushrooms, trimmed and sliced

4 large garlic cloves, minced

1 teaspoon kosher salt

½ teaspoon freshly ground black pepper

Extra-virgin olive oil

1½ pounds prepared pizza dough, at room temperature

Unbleached all-purpose flour

2 cups shredded mozzarella cheese (about 7 ounces)

5 ounces pepperoni, sliced

Pizza Sauce (page 301)

With Weber's headquarters in the Chicago area, it was only a matter of time before we figured out how to make a great stuffed deep-dish pizza on the grill.

SERVES 6 TO 8

1. Prepare the grill for direct and indirect cooking over medium heat (350° to 450°F).

2. In a skillet over medium heat on the stove, warm the oil. Add the onion and bell pepper and cook until softened, about 3 minutes, stirring occasionally. Add the mushrooms and cook until lightly browned and any liquid has evaporated, about 12 minutes. During the last minute, add the garlic, salt, and pepper. Remove from the heat and set aside to cool.

3. Lightly coat a 10-inch cast-iron skillet with oil. Divide the dough into two balls, one twice as large as the other. On a lightly floured work surface, stretch the larger ball into a 14-inch round. (If the dough shrinks back, cover it with a kitchen towel, let it rest for 5 minutes, and then continue rolling.) Transfer the dough round to the skillet, letting the excess hang over the sides. Gently stretch the dough to fit the skillet, pressing it into the corners. Spread 1 cup of the mozzarella on top of the dough, then spread half of the cooled filling over the cheese. Top with half of the pepperoni slices in a single layer. Repeat the filling layers, then top with ½ cup of the remaining mozzarella. On a floured surface, stretch the remaining ball of dough into a 10-inch round. Place the round on top of the filling and press down to remove any air pockets. Brush the edges of the top and bottom rounds of dough where they come together with water, then roll and pinch the edges together to seal. Prick the dough in several places to release any air pockets. Spread the sauce over the top crust, leaving the sealed edges uncovered. Top the sauce evenly with the remaining ½ cup mozzarella.

4. Brush the cooking grates clean. Place the skillet over **direct medium heat**, close the lid, and cook until the edges of the dough look set and somewhat dry, about 5 minutes. Move the skillet over **indirect medium heat**, close the lid, and continue cooking until the crust is golden brown, 35 to 45 minutes. Remove the skillet from the grill and let the pizza rest for 10 minutes. Using a wide spatula, slide the pizza onto a serving platter. Cut into wedges and serve warm.

BONELESS PORK CHOPS
WITH TOMATILLO SAUCE

PREP TIME
30 MINUTES

BRINING TIME
1 HOUR

GRILLING TIME
18 TO 22 MINUTES

BRINE

2 cups water

2 tablespoons kosher salt

2 teaspoons ground cumin

½ teaspoon cayenne pepper

4 boneless pork chops, each 6 to 8 ounces and about 1 inch thick

SAUCE

8 medium tomatillos, husks removed and rinsed

1 poblano chile pepper, 3 to 4 ounces

2 slices bacon

1 white onion, about 8 ounces, cut into ¼-inch dice

2 teaspoons minced garlic

1 cup loosely packed fresh cilantro leaves

½ teaspoon packed light brown sugar

½ teaspoon kosher salt

¼ teaspoon freshly ground black pepper

Extra-virgin olive oil

Tomatillos, a staple of the Mexican pantry, look like green tomatoes with a papery husk. Grilling enhances their tangy taste and softens their skin, making them easy to puree for a sauce that benefits from the addition of roasted poblanos and bacon. Brining the pork chops helps to ensure a moist, evenly cooked result.

SERVES 4

1. In a large bowl combine the brine ingredients and stir until the salt dissolves. Submerge the pork chops in the brine, topping them with a plate to keep them submerged. Cover and refrigerate for 1 hour.

2. Prepare the grill for direct cooking over medium heat (350° to 450°F).

3. Brush the cooking grates clean. Grill the tomatillos and poblano over **direct medium heat**, with the lid closed, until the tomatillos are blistered and soft and the poblano is blackened and blistered but still holds its shape, 10 to 12 minutes, turning occasionally. Remove from the grill. Place the poblano in a bowl and cover with plastic wrap to trap the steam. Let stand for about 10 minutes. Remove and discard the charred skin, stem, and seeds.

4. In a medium skillet over medium heat on the stove, fry the bacon until crisp, about 10 minutes, turning occasionally. Transfer the bacon to paper towels to drain. Add the onion and garlic to the bacon drippings remaining in the pan and cook over medium heat until the onion is soft, about 4 minutes, stirring occasionally. Remove from the heat.

5. In a food processor or blender combine the tomatillos and poblano and puree until smooth. Add all the remaining sauce ingredients, including the bacon, and process until smooth. Transfer to a medium sauté pan, place on the stove over medium heat, and bring to a simmer, stirring occasionally. If the sauce seems too thick, add 2 to 3 tablespoons water. Keep warm over low heat.

6. Lift the chops from the brine and pat dry with paper towels. Discard the brine. Lightly brush the chops on both sides with oil. Grill the chops over **direct medium heat**, with the lid closed, until still barely pink in the center, 8 to 10 minutes, turning once. Remove from the grill and let rest for 3 to 5 minutes. Serve the chops warm with the sauce.

BRINED PORK CHOPS
WITH APPLE-TARRAGON RELISH

★

PREP TIME
30 MINUTES

BRINING TIME
**30 MINUTES
TO 2 HOURS**

GRILLING TIME
5 TO 7 MINUTES

★

BRINE

4 cups cold water

⅓ cup kosher salt

**⅓ cup packed light
brown sugar**

3 bay leaves

**2 teaspoons freshly ground
black pepper**

1 quart ice cubes

**6 bone-in pork loin chops,
each about 6 ounces and
¾ inch thick, trimmed of
excess fat**

**3 tablespoons extra-virgin
olive oil**

**2 tablespoons Dijon
mustard**

**¼ teaspoon freshly ground
black pepper**

**Apple-Tarragon Relish
(page 303)**

**About 3 tablespoons
pistachios, roughly
chopped**

Brining doesn't have to take a lot of time. A few
handfuls of ice cubes will quickly cool down a hot
brine, and then you need no more than about a half
hour for the brine to impart flavor and juiciness to
the pork. While the brine is working its magic, you
can assemble the relish of sweet apples and onions.

SERVES 6

1. In a large saucepan combine the water, salt, and sugar and whisk over
medium heat until the salt and sugar dissolve. Remove from the heat
and stir in the bay leaves and pepper. Add the ice cubes and stir a few
times to cool down the water. Submerge the pork chops in the brine,
topping them with a plate if needed to keep them submerged. Cover
and let stand at room temperature for about 30 minutes or refrigerate
for up to 2 hours.

2. Prepare the grill for direct cooking over medium heat (350° to 450°F).

3. In a small bowl, whisk together the oil, mustard, and pepper. Lift the
pork chops from the brine and pat them dry with paper towels. Discard
the brine. Brush the chops on both sides with the mustard mixture.

4. Brush the cooking grates clean. Grill the chops over **direct medium
heat**, with the lid closed, until the meat is still slightly pink in the center,
5 to 7 minutes, turning once after 3 minutes. Remove from the grill and
let rest for 3 to 5 minutes.

5. Reheat the relish over medium heat. Top the chops with the relish,
garnish with the pistachios, and serve warm.

PORK RIB CHOPS
WITH SASSY BARBECUE SAUCE

FAN
★★★★★
FAVORITE

★

PREP TIME
20 MINUTES

GRILLING TIME
8 TO 10 MINUTES

When time is short, we all reach for preground pepper for quick spice rubs and for store-bought barbecue sauce for serving. But if you are grilling on a lazy weekend, take the time and effort to grind whole peppercorns and make barbecue sauce from scratch and you will be rewarded with superior flavors at the table.

RUB

1½ teaspoons black peppercorns

1½ teaspoons yellow mustard seed

1½ teaspoons paprika

1½ teaspoons packed light brown sugar

1½ teaspoons kosher salt

1 teaspoon garlic powder

1 teaspoon onion powder

¼ teaspoon cayenne pepper

6 bone-in pork rib chops, each 10 to 12 ounces and about 1 inch thick

Canola oil

Sassy Barbecue Sauce (page 301)

SERVES 6

1. In a spice mill pulse together the peppercorns and mustard seed until coarsely ground. Transfer to a small bowl, add all the remaining rub ingredients, and mix well.

2. Allow the chops to stand at room temperature for 15 to 30 minutes before grilling.

3. Prepare the grill for direct cooking over medium heat (350° to 450°F).

4. Brush the cooking grates clean. Lightly brush the chops on both sides with oil and season evenly with the rub, pressing the spices into the meat. Grill the chops over **direct medium heat**, with the lid closed, until still barely pink in the center, 8 to 10 minutes, turning once. Remove the chops from the grill and let rest for 3 to 5 minutes.

5. Reheat the sauce over medium heat. Serve the chops warm with the sauce on the side.

DISAPPEARING
PORK TENDERLOINS
WITH PICO DE GALLO

PREP TIME
30 MINUTES

MARINATING TIME
1 TO 2 HOURS

GRILLING TIME
15 TO 20 MINUTES

MARINADE

⅓ cup fresh orange juice

2 tablespoons
Worcestershire sauce

2 tablespoons extra-virgin
olive oil

1 tablespoon unsulfured
molasses (not blackstrap)

1 tablespoon minced garlic

2 pork tenderloins, each
about 1 pound, trimmed of
silver skin and excess fat

RUB

2 teaspoons pure chile
powder

1 teaspoon freshly ground
black pepper

1 teaspoon kosher salt

½ teaspoon ground cumin

½ teaspoon dried oregano

¼ teaspoon garlic powder

Extra-virgin olive oil

Pico de Gallo 2 (page 300)

Slices of this spice-rubbed pork tenderloin have been disappearing ever since this recipe was first published in 2001. Marvelous in its own right, the pork becomes even more appealing when served with the fresh tomato salsa known as *pico de gallo*, literally "beak of rooster," so named for how the spiciness of the chile pepper bites your tongue like the beak of a rooster.

SERVES 4 TO 6

1. In a small bowl whisk together all the marinade ingredients. Place the pork tenderloins in a large, resealable plastic bag and pour in the marinade. Press the air out of the bag and seal tightly. Turn the bag to distribute the marinade evenly, place the bag in a bowl, and refrigerate for 1 to 2 hours, turning the bag occasionally.

2. In a bowl combine all the rub ingredients and mix well. Remove the pork from the bag and discard the marinade. Brush the pork all over with oil. Spread the rub evenly over the pork, pressing it into the meat. Let the pork stand at room temperature for 15 to 30 minutes before grilling.

3. Prepare the grill for direct cooking over medium heat (350° to 450°F).

4. Brush the cooking grates clean. Grill the pork over **direct medium heat**, with the lid closed, until the outsides are evenly seared and the centers are barely pink, 15 to 20 minutes, turning three times. Remove from the grill and let rest for 3 to 5 minutes.

5. Cut the pork across the grain into slices. Serve warm with the pico de gallo.

FOR PARTY MENUS, SEE PAGE 320

FIVE-SPICE
PORK MEDALLIONS
WITH RED CURRY SAUCE

PREP TIME
25 MINUTES

BRINING TIME
1 HOUR

GRILLING TIME
15 TO 20 MINUTES

4 cups water

½ cup kosher salt

¼ cup packed dark brown sugar

2 garlic cloves, roughly chopped

2 pork tenderloins, about 1 pound each, trimmed of silver skin and excess fat

RUB

1 tablespoon Chinese five-spice powder

½ teaspoon freshly ground black pepper

¼ teaspoon kosher salt

Vegetable oil

Red Curry Sauce (page 302)

Searing pork tenderloin over direct heat helps to keep the meat succulent and gives the dish a smoky finish. We like to boost those flavors with spices and a brief stint in a brine. Be sure to keep your instant-read thermometer handy to ensure against overcooking the tenderloins.

SERVES 4 TO 6

1. In a large bowl whisk together the water, salt, sugar, and garlic until the salt and sugar dissolve. Submerge the pork in the brine, topping it with a plate if needed to keep it submerged. Cover and refrigerate for 1 hour.

2. In a small bowl combine all the rub ingredients and mix well. Remove the pork from the brine and discard the brine. Pat the pork dry with paper towels, then coat lightly with oil. Spread the rub evenly over the pork, pressing it into the meat. Let the pork sit at room temperature for 20 to 30 minutes before grilling.

3. Prepare the grill for direct cooking over medium heat (350° to 450°F).

4. Brush the cooking grates clean. Grill the tenderloins over **direct medium heat**, with the lid closed as much as possible, until they are barely pink at the center and the internal temperature reaches 150°F, 15 to 20 minutes, turning every 5 minutes or so and swapping their positions as needed for even cooking. Remove the pork from the grill and let rest for 3 to 5 minutes.

5. Reheat the sauce over medium heat. Cut the pork across the grain into thick slices. Serve warm with the sauce.

JERK PORK TENDERLOIN
WITH GLAZED SWEET POTATOES

PREP TIME
20 MINUTES

MARINATING TIME
2 TO 4 HOURS

GRILLING TIME
15 TO 20 MINUTES

PASTE

½ habanero chile pepper

8 scallions, chopped

2 garlic cloves, crushed

¼ cup canola oil

2 tablespoons peeled, chopped fresh ginger

2 tablespoons lime juice

1 tablespoon ground allspice

1 teaspoon kosher salt

½ teaspoon dried thyme

¼ teaspoon cinnamon

¼ teaspoon freshly ground black pepper

2 pork tenderloins, each about 1 pound, trimmed of silver skin and excess fat

Finely grated zest of 2 limes

¼ cup lime juice

¼ cup canola oil

2 tablespoons honey

½ teaspoon kosher salt

¼ teaspoon freshly ground black pepper

2 large sweet potatoes, each about 1 pound

The most exciting taste in this recipe comes from the charred crust of the meat. That's because when the jerk paste cooks into the pork, several bold flavors emerge. To maximize that delicious effect, rotate the tenderloins as needed to brown them on all sides.

SERVES 4 TO 6

1. To avoid burning your skin, wear rubber or plastic gloves when you handle the habanero, and after handling the chile, do not touch your face or any other part of your body. Wearing gloves, remove and discard the stem of the chile, then cut away and discard the hot whitish veins and seeds. Put the rest of the chile in a blender or food processor. Add all the remaining paste ingredients and process until smooth, about 2 minutes.

2. Brush the paste evenly over the tenderloins. Cover and refrigerate for 2 to 4 hours. Let the pork stand at room temperature for 15 to 30 minutes before grilling.

3. Prepare the grill for direct cooking over medium heat (350° to 450°F).

4. In a small bowl whisk together the lime zest and juice, oil, honey, salt, and pepper. Peel the sweet potatoes, trim off the pointed ends, and cut each potato into ½-inch-thick slices. Brush the slices on both sides with the oil mixture.

5. Brush the cooking grates clean. Grill the pork and the potatoes over **direct medium heat**, with the lid closed, until the pork is still barely pink in the center and the potatoes are easily pierced with a knife, 15 to 20 minutes, turning them both and brushing them with the oil mixture about every 5 minutes. Remove the pork and potatoes from the grill, let the pork rest for 3 to 5 minutes, and keep the potatoes warm.

6. Cut the pork across the grain into slices. Serve warm with the potatoes.

A FIRST-CLASS LUAU

BY MIKE KEMPSTER

In the early 1970s, airlines were taking delivery of a new and now legendary plane, the Boeing 747. Its range and comfort allowed travelers to fly from more cities of the U.S. mainland to the beautiful fiftieth state of Hawaii. The airlines promoted the new destination with stunning photographs of breathtaking scenery and of native Hawaiian culture, including luaus.

Hawaiian mania captured my attention, and we decided to conduct in-store luaus featuring roasted suckling pigs on our huge Ranch charcoal grills. We set the scene elaborately, with Hawaiian dress, pineapple desserts, colorful leis, and ukulele music. If I could have rented mini volcanoes, I probably would have done it.

> ...THE AROMA OF ROASTING PORK DREW THEM CLOSER, WHERE THEY COULD SEE THE CRAZY WEBER FOLKS DRESSED LIKE DON HO AND HANDING OUT FREE BITES...

My colleagues and I donned Hawaiian shirts and shorts and generally looked completely out of place roasting suckling pigs in department-store parking lots. For live talent, we tried to recruit professional hula dancers, but they were not easily found in New York, Chicago, and Minneapolis. So we ended up hiring local dance students willing to debut their careers at the nearby Sears or Macy's.

Our colorful promotions proved a big hit. Shoppers were drawn to the camera flashes as proud parents photographed their dancing preteen daughters. The melodic strains of the greatest ukulele hit of all times, "Tiny Bubbles," and the aroma of roasting pork drew them even closer, where they could see the crazy Weber folks dressed like Don Ho and handing out free bites. What a way to make a living! But retailers loved those luaus and racked up sales of Weber grills and island-vacation apparel.

My most memorable luau took place in St. Louis at a Famous-Barr store, and I wasn't even supposed to be there. It all started when a fellow Weberhead called me at home late one Friday night. In a sheepish, somewhat inebriated voice, he explained that he and his coworker were pigless. Not surprisingly, you can't always fly into a town and find a butcher shop that just happens to have a whole pig on hand. So Weber had hired Meeske's Market in Mount Prospect, Illinois, to prepare and box whole pigs for us. Our grill teams would pick them up on their way to the airport and check them with their luggage to their luau destination. It turned out that this time each of the Weber pig roasters thought the other had picked up the pig. The airline was serving free booze all the way to St. Louis, so it wasn't until they happily landed (and I do mean happily) that they discovered neither of them had the pig. Frantic, they had called all over St. Louis and, to their dismay, were unable to find a pig. The big luau was scheduled to start the next day at 11:00 a.m.

We quickly hatched the following plan: I would pick up their pig, head to O'Hare, buy a plane ticket, check the pig, but not get on the flight myself. They would then retrieve the pig from baggage claim in St. Louis and race to the luau. Our mission was all the more critical

because the president of the Famous-Barr stores was to be there. He had said that if he liked what he saw, he would place our products in every store in the chain. The only problem was that after checking with all the airlines, only one seat was left—in first class. It departed Chicago at 9:00 a.m. on Saturday, arriving in St. Louis at 9:50 a.m. That was cutting it close, but if all went smoothly, we could still have the pig on the grill before the first notes of "Tiny Bubbles" were played.

When Saturday dawned, I was already camped out at Meeske's. Unfortunately, the night before had been Grandpa and Grandma Meeske's fiftieth wedding anniversary party, and the family was running fifteen minutes late. I wasn't out of there with my boxed pig until 8:20 a.m., and now I had a twenty-minute ride to O'Hare. Several red lights and a slow-moving freight train later, I realized it was too close to departure time to check my luggage, so I moved on to Plan B. Fortunately, I had a good-size duffle bag in the trunk of my car and was able to find a parking spot close to the terminal. People looked

at me strangely as I removed a plastic-wrapped, semifrozen pig from a box and stuffed it into the duffle bag. But then they just walked on by, probably thinking to themselves that anything can happen at O'Hare.

I raced to the ticket counter, lugging my pig. The agent told me I'd have to run to make the flight. Let me tell you, a pig gets mighty heavy when you're sprinting with it through an airport. I made it to the plane just as the door was closing and then found that the ticket holder in the seat next to mine was a no-show. What a relief. I stuffed my duffled companion under the two seats in front of me. As I caught my breath and the plane gained altitude, I contemplated asking the flight attendant for one of those little wing pins for my pig, then decided not to press my luck.

The good news is that we beat the president to the luau. When he did arrive, he was pleased with the size of the crowd and complimented us on the food. "Well," I told him, as my hungover colleagues choked back laughter, "at Weber we like to do everything first class."

TERIYAKI PORK BELLY
WITH CASHEW JASMINE RICE

PREP TIME
30 MINUTES

BRAISING TIME
ABOUT 3 HOURS

CHILLING TIME
ABOUT 2 HOURS

REDUCING TIME
1 TO 1¼ HOURS

COOKING TIME
ABOUT 1½ HOURS

BRAISING LIQUID

4 cups water

½ cup soy sauce

⅓ cup bourbon

¾ cup roughly chopped scallions (white and light green parts only)

⅓ cup packed light brown sugar

2 ounces fresh ginger, peeled and cut into ½-inch-thick slices

3 tablespoons hoisin sauce

2 whole star anise

2 garlic cloves, crushed

2½ pounds pork belly with rind, in a single piece

Cashew Jasmine Rice (page 303)

2 scallions (green parts only), sliced

Look for pork belly in a well-stocked butcher shop or an Asian market. It will have three layers: rind, fat, and meat. Choose a piece with a good proportion of pink meat to white fat. To create a crisp surface, fry the slices on a grill-top griddle until dark brown and delicious.

SERVES 6

1. In a 5-quart grill-proof Dutch oven over high heat on the stove, combine all the braising liquid ingredients and bring to a simmer, stirring constantly until the sugar dissolves. Place the pork belly, rind side down, in the braising liquid and add more water if needed to cover barely. Raise the heat to high and bring the liquid to a boil. Turn down the heat to low, cover, and simmer until the pork is very tender when pierced with the tip of a sharp knife, about 3 hours, turning occasionally and adding more water if needed to keep the pork covered. Transfer the pork to a platter and let cool. Reserve the liquid to make a sauce. Cover the cooled pork with plastic wrap and refrigerate until chilled, about 2 hours.

2. Set a fine-mesh strainer over a large bowl and strain the braising liquid through it. Discard the solids in the strainer. Let the liquid stand for 10 minutes, then skim the fat from the surface with a large spoon. Rinse the Dutch oven, return the liquid to it, and bring to a boil over high heat. Lower the heat to a simmer and cook until reduced to 1 cup, 1 to 1¼ hours. Remove from the heat, let cool, cover, and refrigerate until ready to use.

3. Prepare a smoker for indirect cooking with very low heat (200° to 250°F). When the temperature reaches 225°F, add 3 handfuls large apple or cherry wood chunks to the charcoal.

4. Brush the cooking grates clean. Smoke the pork belly, rind side up, over **indirect very low heat**, with the lid closed, for 1 hour. Add another large handful wood chunks to the charcoal and continue to smoke the pork until the internal temperature reaches 140°F, about 30 minutes more. Transfer to a cutting board and let rest for about 10 minutes (the internal temperature will rise 5 to 10 degrees during this time).

5. About 25 minutes before the pork is done, make the rice as directed. Reheat the sauce on the stove. To serve, cut the pork across the grain into ½-inch-thick slices. Divide the rice between bowls, top with the pork, and drizzle with plenty of sauce. Garnish with the sliced scallions.

BEST-ON-THE-BLOCK
BABY BACK RIBS

PREP TIME
30 MINUTES

STANDING TIME
**30 MINUTES
TO 1 HOUR**

GRILLING TIME
ABOUT 3 HOURS

RUB

2 tablespoons kosher salt

1 tablespoon smoked paprika

1 tablespoon garlic powder

1 tablespoon pure chile powder

2 teaspoons mustard powder

2 teaspoons dried thyme

1 teaspoon ground cumin

1 teaspoon celery seed

1 teaspoon freshly ground black pepper

4 racks baby back ribs, each 2½ to 3 pounds

(continued on next page)

To qualify as "best on the block," the seasoned "bark" (crust) and natural flavors of the pork ribs must complement the hickory smoke and the sweet-tart sauce. We use some potent spices to accomplish this, but if you prefer milder ribs, add about half the recommended amount of chile powder to the rub and leave the hot-pepper sauce out of the sauce.

SERVES 8 TO 10

1. Have ready a rib rack. In a small bowl combine all the rub ingredients and mix well. Using a dull dinner knife, slide the tip under the membrane covering the back of each rack of ribs. Lift and loosen the membrane until it breaks, then grab a corner of it with a paper towel and pull it off. Season the ribs evenly with the rub, pressing it into the meat. Arrange the racks in the rib rack, standing each rack up and facing them all in the same direction. Let the racks stand at room temperature for 30 minutes to 1 hour before grilling.

2. Soak 4 large handfuls hickory wood chips in water for at least 30 minutes.

3. Prepare the grill for indirect cooking over low heat (300° to 350°F).

4. Brush the cooking grates clean. Drain 2 handfuls wood chips and add them to the charcoal or to the smoker box of a gas grill and close the lid. When smoke appears, place the rib rack with the ribs over **indirect low heat** and cook, with the lid closed, for 1 hour. Maintain the temperature of the grill between 300° and 350°F.

(continued on next page)

BEST-ON-THE-BLOCK
BABY BACK RIBS (CONTINUED)

SAUCE

4 slices bacon

1 cup ketchup

½ cup unsweetened apple juice

¼ cup cider vinegar

1 tablespoon unsulfured molasses (not blackstrap)

2 teaspoons Worcestershire sauce

½ teaspoon smoked paprika

½ teaspoon ground cumin

¼ teaspoon kosher salt

¼ teaspoon freshly ground black pepper

Hot-pepper sauce (optional)

MOP

½ cup unsweetened apple juice

1 tablespoon cider vinegar

5. While the ribs are cooking, make the sauce. In a medium skillet on the stove, fry the bacon over low heat until browned and crisp, 10 to 15 minutes, turning occasionally. Transfer the bacon to paper towels to drain. Let the bacon drippings in the skillet cool to room temperature. Eat the bacon or save for another use. In a medium saucepan combine all the remaining ingredients except the hot sauce, if using. Add 3 tablespoons of the reserved bacon fat and whisk until smooth. Place over low heat and cook for about 5 minutes, stirring occasionally. If you prefer a spicy sauce, season with the hot sauce. Remove the pan from the heat.

6. Combine the mop ingredients in a small spray bottle. After the first hour of cooking, drain the remaining handful of wood chips and add them to the charcoal or smoker box. Lightly spray the racks with the mop, particularly the areas that are looking a little dry. Close the lid and cook for 1 hour longer. Maintain the temperature of the grill between 300° and 350°F.

7. When the second hour of cooking has finished, lightly spray the racks with the mop, particularly the areas that are looking a little dry. If any of the racks are cooking faster than the others or look much darker, swap their positions for even cooking. Close the lid and cook for another 30 minutes.

8. After 2½ hours of cooking, the meat will have shrunk back from most of the bones by ¼ inch or more. If it has not, continue to cook the racks until it does. When the racks are done, remove the rib rack from the grill. Close the lid of the grill to maintain the heat. Remove the racks from the rib rack and lightly brush each rack on both sides with some of the sauce.

9. Return the racks to the grill over **indirect low heat**. At this point you can pile all the racks on top of one another or stack the racks two to a pile. Continue to cook over **indirect low heat**, with the lid closed, until tender and succulent, 15 to 30 minutes. To test if the racks are done, one at a time, lift them, bone side up, at one end with tongs; if a rack bends so much in the middle that the meat tears easily, it is ready. If the meat does not tear easily, continue to cook until it does. When the racks are ready, transfer them to a platter and let rest for 5 to 10 minutes.

10. Just before serving, lightly brush the racks with sauce again. Cut the racks into individual ribs and serve warm.

JERK-SPICED RIBS
WITH PINEAPPLE-RUM SALSA

PREP TIME
20 MINUTES
MARINATING TIME
3 TO 4 HOURS
GRILLING TIME
2½ TO 4 HOURS

PASTE

½ cup roughly chopped white onion

6 garlic cloves, chopped

3 scallions (white and green parts), roughly chopped

1 or 2 serrano chile peppers, seeded

2 tablespoons extra-virgin olive oil

2 tablespoons fresh lime juice

2 tablespoons granulated sugar

1 tablespoon ground allspice

1½ teaspoons kosher salt

1 teaspoon dried thyme

¾ teaspoon freshly ground black pepper

2 racks baby back ribs, each 2 to 2¼ pounds

Pineapple-Rum Salsa (page 299)

Not all racks of baby back ribs are the same, so how you cook them should also not be the same. If one rack is getting too dark, move it farther from the fire. If a rack looks dry, spray or baste it with water. The same idea holds true for when the racks are done. Just because one rack is ready to come off the grill doesn't mean the other is too. Always give each rack the attention it needs.

SERVES 4 TO 6

1. In a food processor, combine all the paste ingredients and process until fairly smooth. Using a dull dinner knife, slide the tip under the membrane covering the back of each rack of ribs. Lift and loosen the membrane until it breaks, then grab a corner of it with a paper towel and pull it off. Spread the paste evenly all over the racks. Cover and refrigerate for 3 to 4 hours, turning occasionally. Let the racks stand at room temperature for 45 minutes before grilling.

2. Prepare the grill for indirect cooking over low heat (250° to 350°F).

3. Brush the cooking grates clean. Grill the racks, bone side down first, over **indirect low heat**, with the lid closed, for 2½ to 3 hours, turning the racks over, rotating them, and switching their positions about every 40 minutes so both sides of each rack spend the same amount of time closest to the heat. Also, baste them occasionally with water to keep the surface moist. The racks are done when the meat has shrunk back from the ends of most of the bones by ¼ inch or more. To test if the racks are done, one at a time, lift them, bone side up, at one end with tongs; if a rack bends so much in the middle that the meat tears easily, it is ready. If the meat does not tear easily, continue to cook until it does, up to 1 hour more. When the racks are ready, transfer them to a platter and let rest for 5 to 10 minutes.

4. Cut each rack in half or into individual ribs and serve warm with the salsa.

CHAMPIONSHIP SPARERIBS
WITH APPLE BARBECUE SAUCE

PREP TIME
45 MINUTES,
PLUS **20 MINUTES**
FOR THE SAUCE

COOKING TIME
4¾ TO 6 HOURS

RUB

3 tablespoons kosher salt

2 tablespoons ancho chile powder

2 tablespoons packed light brown sugar

2 tablespoons garlic powder

1 tablespoon ground cumin

2 teaspoons freshly ground black pepper

4 racks spareribs, each 2½ to 3½ pounds

¾ cup unsweetened apple juice

¼ cup cider vinegar

SAUCE

2 cups ketchup

½ cup unsweetened apple juice

¼ cup cider vinegar

¼ cup yellow mustard

2 tablespoons unsulfured molasses (not blackstrap)

2 tablespoons Worcestershire sauce

1 teaspoon garlic powder

¼ teaspoon chipotle chile powder

To achieve championship-level ribs with a nice dark crust, we use a true smoker, which can maintain low temperatures for hours without additional charcoal.

SERVES 8 TO 10

1. Prepare the smoker for indirect cooking with very low heat (225° to 250°F).

2. In a bowl combine the rub ingredients. Put a rack of the ribs, meaty side up, on a cutting board. Following the line of fat that separates the meaty ribs from the tougher tips at the base of each rack, cut off the tips. Turn the rack over and cut off the flaps of meat attached in the center of the rack and that hang below the shorter end of the ribs. Slide the tip of a dinner knife under the membrane covering the back of the rack. Lift and loosen it, then grab a corner with a paper towel and pull it off. Repeat with the remaining 3 racks. Season the spareribs all over with the rub, putting more of it on the meaty side and pressing it into the meat.

3. In a small spray bottle combine the apple juice and cider vinegar.

4. Add 2 large handfuls hickory wood chunks to the charcoal. Brush the cooking grates clean. Smoke the rib racks, bone side down, over **indirect very low heat**, with the lid closed, until the meat has shrunk back from the bones at least ½ inch, 4 to 5 hours. After each hour, add another handful hickory chunks to the charcoal (until you have added 5 handfuls total), and spray the ribs on both sides with the apple juice mixture.

5. In a medium saucepan over medium heat on the stove, combine all the sauce ingredients and bring to a simmer. Reduce the heat to low and cook for 15 to 20 minutes, stirring occasionally. Remove the pan from the heat.

6. When the spareribs are ready, remove them from the smoker. Close the lid of the smoker to maintain the heat. Brush the racks on both sides with some of the sauce and wrap each rack in heavy-duty aluminum foil. Return the foil-wrapped racks to the smoker, stacking them on the top cooking grate. Continue to cook over **indirect very low heat**, with the lid closed, until the meat is tender enough to tear with your fingers, 45 minutes to 1 hour.

7. Remove the spareribs from the smoker, unwrap, and lightly brush the racks on both sides with sauce again. Cut the racks into individual ribs. Serve warm with the remaining sauce on the side.

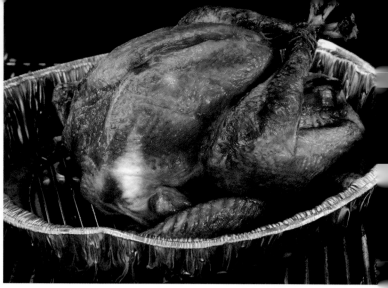

04

POULTRY

CHICKEN POPEYE SLIDERS
WITH MOZZARELLA AND PESTO

PREP TIME
20 MINUTES

GRILLING TIME
18 TO 22 MINUTES

PATTIES

1½ pounds ground chicken thigh meat

1 package (10 ounces) frozen chopped spinach, thawed and squeezed dry

1 cup shredded mozzarella cheese (about 4 ounces)

¼ cup fine dried bread crumbs

¼ cup finely chopped yellow onion

2 tablespoons balsamic vinegar

1 teaspoon kosher salt

2 garlic cloves, minced

½ teaspoon freshly ground black pepper

2 medium red bell peppers

Extra-virgin olive oil

12 slices mozzarella cheese, trimmed roughly to size of sliders

12 slider buns, split

Store-bought pesto

In the 1930s, Popeye, the lovable roughneck cartoon character, was best known for consuming spinach, which gave him superhuman strength and talents. Spinach growers credited the sailor man with increasing American spinach consumption by more than one-third. This good-for-you green remains popular today, here adding flavor to these sliders.

SERVES 6

1. In a medium bowl mix together the patty ingredients with your hands. Gently shape the mixture into 12 patties of equal size and about ½ inch thick (about the size of the buns). Refrigerate the patties until ready to grill.

2. Prepare the grill for direct cooking over medium heat (350° to 450°F).

3. Brush the cooking grates clean. Grill the bell peppers over **direct medium heat**, with the lid closed, until blackened and blistered all over, 10 to 12 minutes, turning occasionally. Place the peppers in a bowl and cover with plastic wrap to trap the steam. Let stand for about 10 minutes. Remove and discard the charred skin, stem, and seeds, then cut each pepper lengthwise into 6 equal strips.

4. Brush the patties on both sides with oil. Grill the patties over **direct medium heat**, with the lid closed, until fully cooked (165°F), 8 to 10 minutes, turning once. During the last 30 seconds to 1 minute of grilling time, place a slice of cheese on each patty to melt, and toast the buns, cut side down, over direct heat.

5. Build a slider on each bun with a patty, a thin layer of pesto, and a bell pepper strip. Serve warm.

TURKEY BURGERS
WITH JALAPEÑO MAYO

PREP TIME
25 MINUTES

GRILLING TIME
11 TO 13 MINUTES

PATTIES

1½ pounds ground turkey, preferably thigh meat

¼ small green bell pepper, finely chopped

¼ small red bell pepper, finely chopped

3 tablespoons finely chopped yellow onion

2 tablespoons minced fresh cilantro leaves

2 garlic cloves, minced

1 teaspoon kosher salt

½ teaspoon freshly ground black pepper

½ teaspoon dried oregano

½ teaspoon pure chile powder

Extra-virgin olive oil

4 thick slices pepper Jack cheese

4 kaiser rolls, split

Jalapeño Mayo (page 303)

4 leaves crisp lettuce

We have all been disappointed by dry, bland turkey burgers. This recipe promises to put an end to that. First, we use thigh meat, which has more flavor and moisture than breast meat. Then we add bell pepper, herbs, and spices to ratchet up the flavor even more. Finally, we finish the burger with melted cheese and spicy mayo to send it over the top.

SERVES 4

1. In a bowl mix together the patty ingredients with your hands. Gently shape the mixture into four patties of equal size and about 1 inch thick. With your thumb or the back of a spoon, make a shallow indentation about 1 inch wide in the center of each patty to prevent it from doming as it cooks. Refrigerate the patties until ready to grill.

2. Prepare the grill for direct cooking over medium heat (350° to 450°F).

3. Brush the cooking grates clean. Brush the patties on both sides with oil. Grill the patties over **direct medium heat**, with the lid closed, until fully cooked (165°F), 11 to 13 minutes, turning once. During the last 30 seconds to 1 minute of grilling time, place a slice of cheese on each patty to melt, and toast the rolls, cut side down, over direct heat.

4. Build a burger on each roll with some mayo, a lettuce leaf, and a patty. Serve warm.

CHICKEN SATAY
WITH BALINESE PEANUT SAUCE

PREP TIME
30 MINUTES

MARINATING TIME
1 TO 4 HOURS

GRILLING TIME
4 TO 6 MINUTES

MARINADE

¼ cup peanut oil

Finely grated zest and juice of 1 lime

1 tablespoon fish sauce

2 teaspoons hot chile-garlic sauce, such as Sriracha

1 teaspoon ground coriander

1 teaspoon ground cumin

4 boneless, skinless chicken breast halves (without tenders), each about 6 ounces

SALAD

8-inch piece English cucumber

1 tablespoon minced fresh mint leaves

2 teaspoons fresh lime juice

1 teaspoon granulated sugar

½ teaspoon kosher salt

Balinese Peanut Sauce (page 299)

We like satay of all types, and this Indonesian version is one of our favorites. Keep the chicken strips about the same size: thick enough to slide a skewer through but not so thick that they look like shish kebabs. If using bamboo skewers, lay a folded piece of foil on the cooking grate and set the bare wooden sections of the skewers over the foil to prevent burning.

SERVES 4

1. In a medium bowl combine all the marinade ingredients. Cut each chicken breast crosswise into ½-inch-wide slices. Add the chicken slices to the marinade and mix to coat thoroughly. Cover and refrigerate for at least 1 hour or up to 4 hours.

2. Quarter the cucumber lengthwise, and then cut the quarters crosswise as thinly as possible. In a medium bowl mix the cucumber slices with all the remaining salad ingredients. Set aside at room temperature for at least 30 minutes before serving.

3. Have ready 16 metal or bamboo skewers. If using bamboo, soak in water for at least 30 minutes.

4. Prepare the grill for direct cooking over high heat (450° to 550°F).

5. Remove the chicken from the bowl and discard the marinade. Thread 2 or 3 chicken slices lengthwise onto each skewer, keeping the skewers inside the meat as much as possible.

6. Brush the cooking grates clean. Grill the chicken skewers over **direct high heat**, with the lid closed, until the meat is firm to the touch and no longer pink in the center, 4 to 6 minutes, turning once. Remove from the grill.

7. Just before the skewers are ready, reheat the sauce over very low heat on the stove. Serve the chicken warm with the salad and the sauce.

CHICKEN AND APPLE SALAD
WITH CHEDDAR AND CASHEWS

PREP TIME
20 MINUTES

MARINATING TIME
15 TO 30 MINUTES

GRILLING TIME
8 TO 12 MINUTES

DRESSING

¼ cup fresh lime juice

3 tablespoons honey

2 tablespoons minced shallot

1 tablespoon Dijon mustard

1 tablespoon minced fresh rosemary leaves

1 teaspoon kosher salt

½ teaspoon freshly ground black pepper

⅓ cup extra-virgin olive oil

3 boneless, skinless chicken breast halves, each about 6 ounces

1 medium red onion, cut crosswise into ⅓-inch-thick slices

1 romaine lettuce heart, torn or cut crosswise into ½-inch-wide strips

2 small red apples, halved, cored, and cut into ¼-inch-thick slices

1 cup green grapes

½ cup roasted cashews

½ cup diced cheddar cheese (scant 2½ ounces)

Here's a recipe for all the kids in your life. They tend to be happy when you serve them cheddar cheese, red apples, cashews, and grapes. Many of them like grilled chicken, too, especially if it is coated in a sweet honey dressing. Of course, some kids will pick around the lettuce, but this will still be a hit with them—and with any grown-ups, too.

SERVES 4 TO 6

1. In a small nonreactive bowl whisk together all the dressing ingredients except the oil. Slowly whisk in the oil to make a smooth dressing. Set aside at room temperature.

2. Prepare the grill for direct cooking over medium heat (350° to 450°F).

3. Place the chicken breasts in a large nonreactive bowl, add ¼ cup of the dressing, and turn the chicken to coat evenly. Marinate at room temperature for 15 to 30 minutes before grilling. Put the onion slices in a small bowl, spoon 2 tablespoons of the dressing over the top, and turn gently to coat evenly.

4. Brush the cooking grates clean. Remove the chicken from the marinade. Grill, smooth (skinned) side down first, over **direct medium heat**, with the lid closed as much as possible, until the meat is firm to the touch and opaque all the way to the center, 8 to 12 minutes, turning once or twice. At the same time, grill the onion slices over **direct medium heat** until charred in spots and tender, about 8 minutes, turning once. Remove the chicken and the onions from the grill and let the chicken rest for 3 to 5 minutes.

5. In a large serving bowl combine the lettuce, apples, grapes, cashews, and cheese. Cut the chicken into thin strips across the grain and roughly chop the onions. Add the chicken and onions to the bowl. Add enough of the remaining dressing to coat the ingredients lightly (you may not need all of it) and stir and toss to mix well. Serve at room temperature.

CHICKEN PANZANELLA
WITH BASIL VINAIGRETTE

PREP TIME
40 MINUTES,

GRILLING TIME
12 TO 18 MINUTES

DRESSING

½ cup fresh basil leaves

¼ cup fresh Italian parsley leaves with tender stems

1 tablespoon lemon juice

1 tablespoon red wine vinegar

1 small garlic clove, minced

⅓ cup extra-virgin olive oil

½ teaspoon kosher salt

¼ teaspoon freshly ground black pepper

3 medium zucchini and/or crookneck squash, trimmed and cut lengthwise into ½-inch-thick slices

1 red bell pepper, cut lengthwise into ½-inch strips

½ loaf (8 ounces) country-style white bread, cut crosswise into 1-inch-thick slices

Extra-virgin olive oil

Kosher salt and freshly ground black pepper

2 boneless, skinless chicken breast halves, each about 6 ounces

1 pound tomatoes, cored and cut into ½-inch cubes

½ cup crumbled feta cheese (about 2½ ounces)

Panzanella is a traditional Tuscan salad made with tomatoes and chunks of stale bread that soak up the tomato juices and dressing. Our grilled version, made by toasting fresh bread over the fire, is equally tasty. Add some grilled chicken and vegetables and you have a bread salad substantial enough for a main course. This recipe doubles nicely, too.

SERVES 4 TO 6

1. In a food processor combine the basil, parsley, lemon juice, vinegar, and garlic and pulse until coarsely chopped. With the machine running, slowly add the oil, processing until emulsified. Transfer to a small nonreactive bowl and season with the salt and pepper.

2. Prepare the grill for direct cooking over medium heat (350° to 450°F).

3. Brush the cooking grates clean. Lightly brush the squash, bell pepper, and bread on both sides with oil and then season with salt and pepper. Grill the vegetables and bread over **direct medium heat**, with the lid closed, until the vegetables are slightly charred and the bread has grill marks, turning once. The vegetables will take 4 to 6 minutes and the bread will take 2 to 4 minutes. Remove them from the grill as they are ready and let cool.

4. Coat the chicken breasts on both sides with 3 tablespoons of the dressing. Grill, smooth (skinned) side down first, over **direct medium heat**, with the lid closed, until the meat is firm to the touch and opaque all the way to the center, 8 to 12 minutes, turning once. Remove the chicken from the grill and let rest for 3 to 5 minutes.

5. Cut the vegetables, bread, and chicken into ½-inch cubes and transfer to a large serving bowl. Add the tomatoes and feta, drizzle with the remaining dressing, and toss to coat evenly. Serve right away.

BEER-MARINATED
CHICKEN TACOS

PREP TIME
20 MINUTES
MARINATING TIME
2 TO 4 HOURS
GRILLING TIME
8 TO 10 MINUTES

We have concocted marinades with twice as many ingredients, and have fussed with spice rubs that are much more complicated, yet none works quite as well for chicken tacos as this magic combination of flavors. Drain the chicken thoroughly before setting it on the hot grate, as it will stick and steam if wet and won't brown like it should.

MARINADE

1 cup dark Mexican beer

2 tablespoons toasted sesame oil

1 tablespoon finely chopped garlic

1 teaspoon dried oregano

1 teaspoon kosher salt

½ teaspoon freshly ground black pepper

¼ teaspoon ground cayenne pepper

6 boneless, skinless chicken thighs, each about 4 ounces

2 Hass avocados

1 tablespoon fresh lime juice

¼ teaspoon kosher salt

6 flour or corn tortillas (6 to 7 inches)

¼ cup crumbled queso fresco or feta (optional)

¼ cup roughly chopped fresh cilantro leaves (optional)

Lime wedges

SERVES 4 TO 6

1. In a small bowl whisk together all the marinade ingredients. Place the thighs in a large, resealable plastic bag and pour in the marinade. Press the air out of the bag and seal tightly. Turn the bag to distribute the marinade, place the bag in a bowl, and refrigerate for 2 to 4 hours, turning the bag occasionally.

2. Scoop the avocado flesh into a bowl. Add the lime juice and salt. Using a fork, mash the ingredients together. Cover with plastic wrap, pressing the wrap directly onto the surface of the guacamole to prevent browning, and refrigerate until about 1 hour before serving.

3. Preheat the grill for direct cooking over high heat (450° to 550°F).

4. Brush the cooking grates clean. Remove the thighs from the bag and discard the marinade. Grill the thighs over **direct high heat**, with the lid closed, until the meat is firm and the juices run clear, 8 to 10 minutes, turning once or twice. During the last 1 minute of grilling time, warm the tortillas over direct heat, turning once. Remove the chicken and tortillas from the grill. Let the chicken rest for 3 to 5 minutes. Wrap the tortillas in foil to keep warm.

5. Cut the chicken across the grain into thin strips. Pile the chicken strips on the tortillas and top the chicken with the guacamole, a sprinkle of queso fresco, and some cilantro. Fold and serve right away with the lime wedges alongside.

MOROCCAN-SPICED
CHICKEN KABOBS

★

PREP TIME
30 MINUTES

MARINATING TIME
4 HOURS

GRILLING TIME
8 TO 10 MINUTES

★

MARINADE

¼ cup extra-virgin olive oil

¼ cup chopped fresh cilantro leaves

¼ cup chopped fresh mint leaves

2 tablespoons fresh lemon juice

2 teaspoons honey

1½ teaspoons kosher salt

1 teaspoon paprika

1 teaspoon ground cumin

2 garlic cloves, minced

½ teaspoon ground coriander

½ teaspoon ground cinnamon

¼ teaspoon cayenne pepper

4 boneless, skinless chicken breast halves, each about 6 ounces

2 large bell peppers, 1 green and 1 red, cut into 1½-inch squares

1 small red onion, cut into 8 wedges and separated into layers

Lemon Yogurt Sauce (page 299)

Greek yogurt is all the rage these days because somehow it manages to be as healthy as it is gratifying. If you add a little lemon, fresh mint, garlic, and salt to it, the yogurt transforms into a tangy and savory sauce for all kinds of grilled meats, including these marinated, spice-rubbed chicken kabobs.

SERVES 4

1. In a small bowl whisk together the marinade ingredients. Pour ¼ cup of the marinade into a medium nonreactive bowl and reserve for the vegetables.

2. Cut each chicken breast in half lengthwise and then cut each half crosswise into 1½-inch pieces. Place the chicken pieces in a large, resealable plastic bag and pour in the remaining marinade. Press the air out of the bag and seal tightly. Turn the bag to distribute the marinade, place in a bowl, and refrigerate for 4 hours, turning the bag occasionally.

3. Have ready metal or bamboo skewers. If using bamboo, soak in water for at least 30 minutes.

4. Prepare the grill for direct cooking over medium heat (350° to 450°F).

5. Add the bell peppers and onion to the reserved marinade in the medium bowl and turn to coat evenly. Remove the chicken from the bag and discard the marinade. Remove the vegetables from the bowl. Thread the chicken pieces onto the skewers, alternating them with the pepper and onion pieces.

6. Brush the cooking grates clean. Grill the kabobs over **direct medium heat**, with the lid closed, until the meat is firm to the touch and opaque all the way to the center, 8 to 10 minutes, turning once or twice. Remove from the grill and let rest for 2 to 3 minutes.

7. Serve the kabobs warm with the sauce.

TURKISH CHICKEN KABOBS
WITH PEPPER-WALNUT SAUCE

**PREP TIME
15 MINUTES**

**MARINATING TIME
UP TO 1 HOUR**

**GRILLING TIME
8 TO 10 MINUTES**

Every once in a while you come across a dish that shows no signs of sacrificing flavor in the interest of good health. This is one of those dishes. Lean pieces of spice-rubbed chicken breast are grilled on skewers and served with a puree of roasted peppers thickened with toasted walnuts and bread crumbs. It's all very Turkish and very delicious.

MARINADE

¼ cup extra-virgin olive oil

1 teaspoon mustard powder

1 teaspoon garlic powder

1 teaspoon kosher salt

½ teaspoon freshly ground black pepper

½ teaspoon ground cumin

6 boneless, skinless chicken breast halves, each about 6 ounces

SAUCE

1½ roasted red bell peppers (from a jar), drained

½ cup extra-virgin olive oil

½ cup walnuts, toasted

¼ cup fine dried bread crumbs

2 tablespoons balsamic vinegar

½ teaspoon ground cumin

¼ teaspoon kosher salt

¼ teaspoon freshly ground black pepper

SERVES 6

1. Have ready metal or bamboo skewers. If using bamboo, soak in water for at least 30 minutes.

2. In a large bowl combine all the marinade ingredients and mix well.

3. Cut each chicken breast in half lengthwise and then cut each half crosswise into 1- to 1½-inch pieces. Add the chicken pieces to the marinade and turn to coat evenly. Thread the chicken pieces onto skewers so they are touching but not crammed together. Cover and refrigerate for up to 1 hour.

4. In a food processor or blender combine all the sauce ingredients and process until you have a pesto-like consistency. If you prefer a thinner sauce, add a little warm water.

5. Prepare the grill for direct cooking over medium heat (350° to 450°F).

6. Brush the cooking grates clean. Grill the kabobs over **direct medium heat**, with the lid closed, until the meat is firm to the touch and opaque all the way to the center, 8 to 10 minutes, turning once. Remove the kabobs from the grill and let rest for 2 to 3 minutes.

7. Serve the kabobs warm with the sauce.

CHILE-RUBBED CHICKEN
WITH JICAMA, AVOCADO, AND ORANGE SALSA

PREP TIME
20 MINUTES

GRILLING TIME
8 TO 12 MINUTES

Who said every salsa needs tomatoes? Sweet, juicy jicama, a root vegetable with a distinctive crunch, is a tasty alternative when mixed with orange segments and creamy avocado. On its own, the chile-rubbed chicken can be intense, but the salsa tamps down the spicy heat just enough.

SALSA

2 oranges, peeled, segmented, and each segment cut in half

1½ cups peeled, finely diced jicama

1 Hass avocado, diced

¾ cup finely diced red onion, rinsed in a fine-mesh strainer under cold water

½ cup finely diced red bell pepper

¼ cup fresh lime juice

1 teaspoon minced jalapeño chile pepper

¼ teaspoon kosher salt

RUB

2 tablespoons pure chile powder

1 teaspoon kosher salt

¼ teaspoon freshly ground black pepper

4 boneless, skinless chicken breast halves, each about 6 ounces

1 tablespoon extra-virgin olive oil

SERVES 4

1. In a medium nonreactive bowl combine all the salsa ingredients and mix gently but thoroughly. Set aside at room temperature.

2. Prepare the grill for direct cooking over medium heat (350° to 450°F).

3. In a small bowl combine all the rub ingredients and mix well. Lightly brush the chicken on both sides with the oil and then season evenly with the rub.

4. Brush the cooking grates clean. Grill the chicken, smooth (skinned) side down first, over **direct medium heat**, with the lid closed as much as possible, until the meat is firm to the touch and opaque all the way to the center, 8 to 12 minutes, turning once or twice. Remove from the grill and let rest for 3 to 5 minutes.

5. Serve the chicken warm with the salsa.

TEQUILA-ORANGE
CHICKEN BREASTS

PREP TIME
15 MINUTES

MARINATING TIME
2 TO 4 HOURS

GRILLING TIME
8 TO 12 MINUTES

MARINADE

½ cup tightly packed fresh mint leaves

½ cup tightly packed fresh Italian parsley leaves with tender stems

½ cup fresh orange juice

2 tablespoons tequila

2 tablespoons extra-virgin olive oil

2 medium garlic cloves, crushed

2 teaspoons minced jalapeño chile pepper, without seeds

1½ teaspoons kosher salt

½ teaspoon ground cumin

½ teaspoon pure chile powder

¼ teaspoon freshly ground black pepper

4 boneless, skin-on chicken breast halves, each about 6 ounces

You don't often see stores offering boneless skin-on chicken breasts. Either you must bone them yourself or ask a butcher to do it. Your reward is the dry heat of the grill creating a burnished bronze color and, more important, a crisp, delectable skin. If skin-on breasts are not an option, use skinless breasts, which will also marry well with the marinade.

SERVES 4

1. In a food processor combine all the marinade ingredients and process until smooth.

2. Place the chicken breasts in a large, resealable plastic bag and pour in the marinade. Press the air out of the bag and seal tightly. Turn the bag several times to distribute the marinade, place in a bowl, and refrigerate for 2 to 4 hours, turning the bag occasionally.

3. Prepare the grill for direct cooking over medium heat (350° to 450°F).

4. Remove the chicken breasts from the bag and reserve the marinade. Pour the marinade into a small saucepan, bring to a boil over high heat on the stove, and boil for 1 full minute.

5. Brush the cooking grates clean. Grill the breasts, skin side down, over **direct medium heat**, with the lid closed as much as possible, until the meat is firm to the touch and opaque all the way to the center, 8 to 12 minutes, turning and basting with the boiled marinade once. Remove from the grill and let rest for 3 to 5 minutes, then serve warm with the warm marinade alongside.

CHICKEN PAILLARDS
WITH TOMATO-OLIVE RELISH

PREP TIME
30 MINUTES

GRILLING TIME
4 TO 5 MINUTES

RUB

1 tablespoon ground fennel seed

1½ teaspoons kosher salt

½ teaspoon garlic powder

½ teaspoon freshly ground black pepper

4 boneless, skinless chicken breast halves (without tenders), each about 6 ounces

Extra-virgin olive oil

RELISH

¾ cup diced tomato (¼-inch dice)

⅔ cup diced celery heart with light green leaves (¼-inch dice)

½ cup pitted Kalamata olives, rinsed and cut into ¼-inch dice

½ cup pitted green olives, rinsed and cut into ¼-inch dice

2 tablespoons extra-virgin olive oil

2 teaspoons minced fresh thyme leaves, or ½ teaspoon dried thyme

Kosher salt

1 lemon, halved

Don't skip the pounding step here. Chicken breasts are never the same thickness from end to end, which means they will grill unevenly. Pounding them between sheets of plastic wrap solves the problem. Grill the chicken breasts quickly over high heat so they retain their moisture, then top them with our Italian-inspired relish.

SERVES 4

1. In a small bowl combine all the rub ingredients and mix well.

2. One at a time, place each breast, smooth (skinned) side down, between two sheets of plastic wrap and pound to an even thickness of ¼ inch. Lightly brush the chicken on both sides with oil and then season on both sides with the rub.

3. Prepare the grill for direct cooking over high heat (450° to 550°F).

4. In a medium bowl combine all the relish ingredients, seasoning to taste with salt.

5. Brush the cooking grates clean. Grill the chicken, smooth (skinned) side down, over **direct high heat**, with the lid closed, until opaque all the way to the center, 3 to 4 minutes. Turn the chicken over and grill just to sear the surface, about 1 minute. Remove from the grill.

6. Arrange the chicken, with the first grilled side facing up, on individual plates. Spoon some relish over each piece, squeeze fresh lemon juice on top, and serve right away.

ANCHO CHILE
CHICKEN THIGHS
WITH TOMATO CHUTNEY

★

PREP TIME
20 MINUTES,
PLUS
25 TO 35 MINUTES
TO COOK THE
CHUTNEY

GRILLING TIME
36 TO 40 MINUTES

★

The ancho chile—aka dried poblano—is on the lower end of the heat spectrum, so ancho chile powder is fairly mild and has a pleasantly sweet, almost raisiny flavor. Here, it marries well with the other flavors in the spice rub for the chicken and complements the sweet-and-sour chutney. Watch the chicken closely while over direct heat, as the fat can cause flare-ups.

SERVES 4 TO 6

CHUTNEY

1 can (14 ounces) diced tomatoes in juice

½ cup minced red onion

⅓ cup packed light brown sugar

⅓ cup cider vinegar

1 tablespoon balsamic vinegar

1 teaspoon kosher salt

¼ teaspoon crushed red pepper flakes

¼ cup dried currants or raisins

RUB

2 teaspoons ancho chile powder

1 teaspoon paprika

1 teaspoon kosher salt

½ teaspoon freshly ground black pepper

8 bone-in, skin-on chicken thighs, each 5 to 6 ounces, trimmed of excess fat and skin

1. In a small saucepan combine the tomatoes, onion, sugar, vinegars, salt, and pepper flakes and bring to a boil over high heat, stirring to dissolve the sugar. Turn down the heat to low and simmer until almost all of the liquid has evaporated and the mixture is thick and syrupy, 20 to 30 minutes, stirring occasionally. Remove from the heat, stir in the currants, and let the chutney cool to room temperature before serving.

2. Prepare the grill for direct and indirect cooking over medium heat (350° to 450°F).

3. In a small bowl combine all the rub ingredients and mix well. Season the thighs evenly with the rub.

4. Brush the cooking grates clean. Grill the thighs, skin side down first, over **direct medium heat**, with the lid closed as much as possible, until golden brown, 6 to 10 minutes, turning occasionally. Move the thighs over **indirect medium heat** and cook, with the lid closed as much as possible, until the juices run clear and the meat is no longer pink at the bone, about 30 minutes. Remove from the grill and let rest for 3 to 5 minutes.

5. Serve the chicken warm with the chutney.

CRISPY CHICKEN THIGHS
WITH BASIL AND PROSCIUTTO BUTTER

PREP TIME
20 MINUTES

GRILLING TIME
20 TO 24 MINUTES

BUTTER

¼ cup (½ stick) unsalted butter, softened

1 ounce prosciutto, very finely chopped

1 medium shallot, minced

1 tablespoon finely chopped fresh basil leaves

1 tablespoon freshly grated Parmigiano-Reggiano® cheese

¼ teaspoon kosher salt

1/4 teaspoon freshly ground black pepper

8 bone-in, skin-on chicken thighs, each 5 to 6 ounces, trimmed of excess fat and skin

½ teaspoon kosher salt

¼ teaspoon freshly ground black pepper

The richly seasoned butter slathered between the skin and the meat of the chicken makes this dish sing. Be careful not to separate the skin from the meat any more than necessary to apply the butter or you risk detaching the skin completely. To avoid flare-ups from dripping butter, grill the chicken over indirect heat, skin side up, for most of the cooking time.

SERVES 4 TO 6

1. In a small bowl combine all the butter ingredients and mix together with a fork. Divide the butter into eight equal portions.

2. Prepare the grill for direct and indirect cooking over medium-high heat (400° to 500°F).

3. Pat the chicken thighs dry with paper towels. Using your fingertips, gently loosen the skin on the thighs, being careful not to separate the skin completely from the meat. Lift the skin up and place a portion of the butter underneath. Smooth the skin over the butter and massage gently to spread the butter evenly over the meat. Season the thighs on both sides with the salt and pepper.

4. Brush the cooking grates clean. Grill the thighs, skin side up first, over **indirect medium-high heat**, with the lid closed, until sizzling, slightly firm, and lightly marked on the underside, 18 to 20 minutes. Turn the thighs over, move to **direct medium-high heat**, and cook, with the lid closed, until the juices run clear, the skin is blistered and crisp, and the meat is no longer pink at the bone, 2 to 4 minutes more (if flare-ups occur, move the thighs temporarily over indirect heat). Remove the thighs from the grill, let rest for 3 to 5 minutes, and then serve warm.

EASY ROSEMARY
ROASTED CHICKEN

PREP TIME
15 MINUTES

MARINATING TIME
UP TO 4 HOURS

GRILLING TIME
45 TO 55 MINUTES

MARINADE

2 tablespoons extra-virgin olive oil

1 tablespoon Dijon mustard

1 tablespoon Worcestershire sauce

1 tablespoon cider vinegar

1 tablespoon finely chopped fresh rosemary leaves

½ teaspoon kosher salt

¼ teaspoon freshly ground black pepper

1 whole chicken, about 4 pounds, neck, giblets, wing tips, and any excess fat removed

Here is an easy recipe for those long, busy days when you don't feel like jumping through hoops to make dinner. It's amazing how well this marinade works in just an hour or two, and the grilling couldn't be simpler. Roast the chicken pieces over indirect heat until fully cooked and then roll them around over direct heat for a few minutes to brown them.

SERVES 4

1. In a small bowl whisk together all the marinade ingredients.

2. Cut the chicken into six pieces: two breast halves, two whole legs (thigh and drumstick), and two wings. Brush each chicken piece on both sides with the marinade. If you have time, marinate the chicken in the refrigerator for up to 4 hours. If not, you can roast the chicken right away.

3. Prepare the grill for direct and indirect cooking over medium heat (350° to 450°F).

4. Brush the cooking grates clean. Grill the chicken pieces, skin side down, over **indirect medium heat**, with the lid closed, until fully cooked, turning once or twice. The breasts and wing pieces will take 30 to 40 minutes and the whole legs will take 40 to 50 minutes. During the last 5 minutes of grilling time, move the chicken over **direct medium heat** and cook until well browned all over, turning once or twice. Remove from the grill and let rest for 3 to 5 minutes, then serve warm.

TRIPLE PLAY
BARBECUED CHICKEN

PREP TIME
30 MINUTES,
PLUS
20 TO 25 MINUTES
FOR THE SAUCE
GRILLING TIME
43 TO 45 MINUTES

SAUCE

2 tablespoons extra-virgin olive oil

½ cup finely chopped yellow onion

2 teaspoons minced garlic

1 cup ketchup

½ cup lemon-lime carbonated beverage (not diet)

¼ cup fresh lemon juice

¼ cup packed light brown sugar

2 tablespoons whole-grain mustard

RUB

2 teaspoons smoked paprika

2 teaspoons kosher salt

Finely grated zest of 1 lemon

½ teaspoon garlic powder

½ teaspoon freshly ground black pepper

4 whole chicken legs, each 10 to 12 ounces, trimmed of excess fat and skin and cut into thighs and drumsticks

The triple-play reference here has nothing to do with baseball but everything to do with how this dish is made. First, you rub chicken pieces with a mixture of smoked paprika, salt, lemon zest, garlic, and pepper. Then, hickory smoke perfumes the slow-cooked meat. And finally, the chicken is brushed with a terrific barbecue sauce sweetened with lemon-lime soda.

SERVES 4

1. In a saucepan over medium heat, warm the oil. Add the onion and garlic and cook until golden, about 10 minutes, stirring often. Stir in all the remaining sauce ingredients and bring to a simmer. Turn down the heat to low and cook until the sauce is slightly thickened, 10 to 15 minutes, stirring often.

2. Soak 2 large handfuls hickory wood chips in water for at least 30 minutes.

3. Prepare the grill for direct and indirect cooking over medium heat (350° to 450°F).

4. In a small bowl combine all the rub ingredients and mix well. Season the chicken pieces all over with the rub.

5. Brush the cooking grates clean. Grill the chicken, skin side down first, over **direct medium heat**, with the lid closed, until golden brown, 8 to 10 minutes, turning occasionally. Move the chicken over **indirect medium heat**. Drain the wood chips, add to the charcoal or to the smoker box of a gas grill, and continue grilling, with the lid closed, for about 20 minutes. Brush the chicken with a thin layer of the sauce and continue to cook, with the lid closed, until the juices run clear and the meat is no longer pink at the bone, about 15 minutes more, turning and brushing occasionally with the sauce. Remove the chicken from the grill and let rest for 3 to 5 minutes.

6. Serve the chicken warm with the remaining sauce on the side.

ROTISSERIE CHICKEN
WITH APRICOT GLAZE

PREP TIME
25 MINUTES

MARINATING TIME
2 TO 4 HOURS

GRILLING TIME
1 TO 1¼ HOURS

MARINADE

2 cups buttermilk

¼ cup roughly chopped fresh rosemary leaves

4 large garlic cloves, finely chopped

2 tablespoons kosher salt

1 teaspoon freshly ground black pepper

1 whole chicken, 4½ to 5 pounds, neck, giblets, wing tips, and excess fat removed

GLAZE

1 cup apricot nectar

3 tablespoons maple syrup

1 tablespoon Dijon mustard

1 tablespoon white wine vinegar

A buttermilk marinade gives this chicken a crazy-good texture and flavor, plus you get the benefit of the chicken basting itself as it turns.

SERVES 4

1. In a medium bowl combine all the marinade ingredients and mix well. Truss the chicken with butcher's twine, securing the legs and wings. Place the chicken in a large, resealable plastic bag and pour in the marinade. Press the air out of the bag and seal it tightly. Turn the bag several times to coat the chicken evenly, place in a large bowl, starting with the breast side facing down, and refrigerate for 2 to 4 hours, turning the bag once or twice. Allow the chicken to stand at room temperature for about 30 minutes before grilling.

2. Place a large, disposable foil pan underneath the cooking grates to catch the drippings. You may have to smash the pan a bit, but that's okay. If you're using a charcoal grill, place the pan on the charcoal grate between two piles of charcoal. Then prepare the grill for rotisserie cooking over **indirect medium heat** (as close to 400°F as possible).

3. In a saucepan whisk together the glaze ingredients, place over medium-high heat on the stove, and bring to a boil, stirring often. Turn down the heat to a gently simmer and cook until reduced to 1 cup, about 5 minutes. Reserve half of the glaze to use as a sauce.

4. Remove the chicken from the bag. Wipe off the marinade and discard. Following the grill's instructions, secure the chicken in the middle of a rotisserie spit, put the spit in place, and turn on the motor. Grill the chicken over **indirect medium heat**, with the lid closed, until the juices run clear when a thigh is pierced in the thickest part, or until an instant-read thermometer inserted into the thickest part of the thigh (not touching the bone) registers 160° to 165°F, 1 to 1¼ hours. During the last 30 minutes, brush the chicken with the glaze a few times.

5. When the chicken is fully cooked, turn off the rotisserie motor and carefully remove the spit from the grill. Tilt the chicken, cavity end down, over the foil pan so the liquid that has accumulated inside the bird empties into the pan. Gently loosen the chicken from the spit and slide it onto a cutting board. Let rest for 10 minutes (the internal temperature will rise 5 to 10 degrees during this time). Cut the chicken into serving pieces. Serve warm with the reserved sauce.

HICKORY-SMOKED
BEER CAN CHICKEN

PREP TIME
15 MINUTES

DRY-BRINING TIME
2 HOURS

GRILLING TIME
1¼ TO 1½ HOURS

2 tablespoons kosher salt

**1 whole chicken, 4 to
5 pounds, neck, giblets,
and any excess fat
removed**

RUB

2 teaspoons onion powder

2 teaspoons paprika

**1 teaspoon packed light
brown sugar**

**½ teaspoon freshly ground
black pepper**

**1 tablespoon extra-virgin
olive oil**

Extra-virgin olive oil

**1 can (12 ounces) beer, at
room temperature**

When it's time to entertain friends, pull out this laughter-inducing classic that involves shoving a beer can up the (ahem) "bottom end" of a chicken. The beer steams while the chicken roasts and absorbs aromatic smoke.

SERVES 4

1. Sprinkle the salt over the meaty parts of the chicken and inside the cavity. Cover with plastic wrap and refrigerate for 2 hours.

2. In a bowl combine all the rub ingredients and mix well. Soak 4 large handfuls hickory or oak wood chips in water for at least 30 minutes.

3. Prepare the grill for indirect cooking over medium heat (350° to 450°F). Keep the temperature around 400°F throughout the cooking time.

4. Rinse the chicken with cold water, then pat dry with paper towels. Brush the chicken all over with oil and season all over, including inside the cavity, with the rub. Fold the wing tips behind the back.

5. Open the beer and pour out about two-thirds of it. Using a church key–style can opener, make two more holes in the top of the can. Place the can on a solid surface and then lower the chicken over the can.

6. Brush the cooking grates clean. Drain 2 handfuls wood chips, add to the charcoal or the smoker box of a gas grill, and close the lid. When smoke appears, transfer the chicken-on-a-can to the grill, placing it over **indirect medium heat**. Close the lid and cook the chicken until the juices run clear when a thigh is pierced in the thickest part, or an instant-read thermometer inserted into the thickest part of the thigh (not touching the bone) registers 160° to 165°F, 1¼ to 1½ hours. After the first 15 minutes, drain the remaining 2 handfuls wood chips and add to the charcoal or the smoker box. If using a charcoal grill, replenish the charcoal as needed to maintain the temperature, adding 6 to 10 unlit briquettes after 45 minutes. Leave the lid off the grill for 5 minutes to ignite the briquettes.

7. Carefully remove the chicken-on-a-can from the grill (do not spill the contents of the beer can, which will be very hot) and stand it on a heatproof surface. Let the chicken rest for 10 to 15 minutes (the internal temperature will rise 5 to 10 degrees during this time) before lifting it from the beer can and carving it into serving pieces. Serve warm.

GARLIC-SAGE
TURKEY CUTLETS
WITH CRANBERRY SAUCE

★

PREP TIME
15 MINUTES,
PLUS
10 MINUTES
TO COOK
THE SAUCE

GRILLING TIME
4 TO 6 MINUTES

★

**3 tablespoons extra-virgin
olive oil**

**1 tablespoon minced
fresh sage leaves**

2 teaspoons minced garlic

1½ teaspoons kosher salt

**½ teaspoon freshly
ground black pepper**

**8 turkey cutlets, each
3 to 4 ounces and about
½ inch thick**

SAUCE

**1 Granny Smith apple,
peeled, cored, and cut into
½-inch pieces**

12 ounces fresh cranberries

**½ cup unsweetened
apple juice**

½ cup granulated sugar

¼ teaspoon ground cloves

¼ teaspoon kosher salt

It's a mystery why we don't cook turkey cutlets more often. They take no time on the grill, and when they are dressed up a bit—here covered with garlic and sage and then served topped with a cranberry sauce—they are delicious.

SERVES 4 TO 6

1. Prepare the grill for direct cooking over medium heat (350° to 450°F).

2. In a shallow baking dish combine the oil, sage, garlic, salt, and pepper and mix well. Put the cutlets in the dish and turn to coat them evenly. Set aside at room temperature for up to 20 minutes while you make the sauce.

3. In a medium saucepan over medium-high heat, combine all the sauce ingredients and bring to a boil on the stove. Turn down the heat to a simmer, cover, and cook until all the cranberries have popped, 6 to 10 minutes. Set aside to cool.

4. Brush the cooking grates clean. Grill the cutlets over **direct medium heat**, with the lid closed, until the meat is firm to the touch and no longer pink in the center, 4 to 6 minutes, turning once. Remove the cutlets from the grill and serve warm with the sauce spooned on top.

FIRING UP THE FIREFIGHTERS

BY MIKE KEMPSTER

Firefighters work long shifts, and they bunk overnight and take their meals in the firehouse. That way, they are always ready to go when an alarm sounds. It's common for one or two firefighters to become the designated cooks, and their job is to keep the troops fed. Many of these cooks are appointed by default, and because they are often without an ounce of culinary training, firehouse food can be less than satisfying. The confluence of these circumstances sparked (pardon the pun) an idea that solved a big challenge.

In my early days at Weber, it was my job to set up grilling demonstrations in retail stores across the nation. Product exhibitions were our signature way to illustrate the versatility of our

THE ONLY THING THAT EVER SIDELINED MY RECRUITING EFFORTS WAS A FIRE ALARM.

charcoal kettle grills. These events became so popular that I often found myself scrambling for part-time demonstrators who could make a sales pitch while roasting a turkey. Equipped with my trusty Weber kettle, I came up with an unusual but highly effective way to recruit people with a good grip on barbecue basics, including fire safety.

Firefighters work several long days in a row, followed by a few days off. In their downtime,

many pick up odd jobs to supplement their income. I got the idea to drive up to a firehouse, remove a shiny, fire engine–red Weber charcoal kettle grill from my car, wheel it up to the door, and go find whoever was in charge (if someone hadn't already appeared to chase me off the property). After finding the usually suspicious watch commander, I would volunteer to cook a turkey for the crew and leave the grill behind for their use. I was generally regarded as insane, but the prospect of a tasty meal typically earned me a green light. After all, if any unintended flare-ups or worse resulted, this group could handle them.

As I lit the charcoal, I'd tell the firefighters stories about folks who didn't follow lighting instructions and some of the crazy things that could happen. I'd invariably hear about someone in their district who had used gasoline or another forbidden fire starter and unintentionally torched a lawn or deck. As we discussed ways of teaching fire safety, I could easily identify the natural storytellers and those comfortable speaking with a stranger—two important qualities for a grill demonstrator. While the briquettes developed their coating of gray ash, I'd prepare the turkey, usually by placing a stick of butter, a bay leaf or two, and some poultry seasoning in the cavity. Then, as the turkey roasted to a golden brown, I'd baste the outside of it with peanut oil.

While the turkey was cooking, someone would ask why Weber had sent me out to cook a turkey and give away a grill. I'd explain that we needed demonstrators who could set up a Weber charcoal grill for indirect cooking, safely light a fire, prepare a turkey for roasting, and then talk about the grill while the turkey was cooking. Because they had just witnessed a guy show up from nowhere and do all of this, they knew it was pretty easy. When I explained that they could earn a daily fee doing it, three or four firefighters usually applied for the job on the spot.

The only thing that ever sidelined my recruiting efforts was a fire alarm. One such time I was in Des Moines, Iowa, chatting up a firefighter who was a natural for the job. He could tell a story, he was the firehouse cook, and he needed some culinary help with his job. His name was Stewart Leathers, but his nickname was Shoe-Leather, obviously a jab at his firehouse steaks, which he cooked in a cast-iron skillet on the stove. Just as I was about to recruit Stu, bells went off, and the men—Stu included—scrambled into their gear, jumped onto fire trucks, and roared off.

About two hours later, they returned, grinning and looking mischievous. They had answered a call at a burning horse barn, and fortunately, no horses or people were injured. One of the firefighters returned with a badly scorched saddle horn, the rest of the saddle having been destroyed. The fire company presented the scorched saddle horn on a platter to Shoe-Leather. There was a raucous speech

about the saddle horn being more edible than Stu's firehouse cuisine, followed by plenty of laughter. That friendly ribbing lit a fire under poor Stu. The turkey was ready just as the "ceremony" ended. Everyone raved about how juicy and flavorful it was, and the bird was quickly reduced to bones. No one asked more questions about how to grill a turkey than Stu. Before my visit ended, Stu and two others had signed up to demonstrate our grills.

Over the next three months, I spoke to Stu by phone several times, instructing him on grilling steaks, hamburgers, chicken pieces, pork chops, and even fish fillets on the kettle grill I'd left behind. When I returned to Des Moines for the official demonstrator training session, Stu was there learning how to sell grills. After the session, he invited me back to the firehouse, where I was greeted with several air-horn blasts from the now happily fed company. Stu's former nickname of Shoe-Leather had been changed to Stupendous Griller.

If your cooking doesn't inspire the company around your house, maybe it's time to fire up the grill. You may never get to jump on a fire truck and put out a fire, but you just may earn yourself a nickname you'll be proud to add to an apron.

APPLE-BRINED,
HICKORY-SMOKED TURKEY

★

PREP TIME
15 MINUTES

BRINING TIME
24 HOURS

GRILLING TIME
2½ TO 3¼ HOURS

★

BRINE

2 quarts unsweetened apple juice

1 pound light brown sugar (2 cups packed)

1 cup kosher salt

3 quarts water

3 oranges, quartered

4 ounces fresh ginger, thinly sliced

15 whole cloves

6 bay leaves

6 large garlic cloves, crushed

1 turkey, 12 to 14 pounds, thawed if frozen

Vegetable oil

This juicy, amber-colored turkey imbued with wood smoke is a benchmark of pride every Thanksgiving. If the bird darkens too quickly, loosely cover with foil, then remove the foil in the final minutes of cooking.

SERVES 12 TO 14

1. In a saucepan over high heat, combine the juice, sugar, and salt and bring to a boil, stirring to dissolve the sugar and salt. Cook for 1 minute, remove from the heat, and skim off the foam. Let cool to room temperature.

2. In a 5-gallon food-grade plastic bucket or other large container, combine the water, oranges, ginger, cloves, bay leaves, and garlic. Add the apple juice mixture and stir well. Remove the neck and giblets from the cavity of the turkey and reserve for another use, then remove and discard any fat from the cavity. Submerge the turkey in the brine, topping it with a heavy weight if needed to keep it completely immersed. Refrigerate for 24 hours.

3. Soak 4 large handfuls hickory chips in water for at least 30 minutes. Prepare the grill for indirect cooking over medium-low heat (350°F).

4. Brush the cooking grates clean. Set a roasting rack in a large, heavy-gauge disposable foil pan. Remove the turkey from the brine and discard the brine. Pat the turkey dry with paper towels. Tie the legs together with butcher's twine. Brush the turkey all over with oil and place it on the roasting rack. Brush the cooking grates clean. Drain 2 handfuls of the wood chips, add to the charcoal or the smoker box of a gas grill, and close the lid. When smoke appears, place the pan with the turkey on the cooking grates and cook over **indirect medium-low heat**, with the lid closed. When the wings are golden brown, after about 40 minutes, wrap them with aluminum foil to prevent them from burning. Brush the rest of the turkey with more oil. If using a charcoal grill, replenish the charcoal as needed to maintain a steady temperature of 350°F. When the turkey breasts are golden brown, after about 1 hour, cover the turkey with aluminum foil to prevent the skin from overbrowning. Drain the remaining wood chips, add to the charcoal or the smoker box, and close the lid. Cook the turkey until the internal temperature of the thickest part of the thighs away from bone is about 165°F, 12 to 14 minutes per pound.

5. Transfer the turkey to a cutting board, cover loosely with aluminum foil, and let rest for 20 minutes before carving. Use the drippings to make gravy.

BRINED TURKEY
WITH HERBED PAN GRAVY

PREP TIME
15 MINUTES,
PLUS **1 HOUR
10 MINUTES**
FOR THE STOCK
AND **30 MINUTES**
FOR THE GRAVY

BRINING TIME
12 TO 14 HOURS

GRILLING TIME
ABOUT 2¾ HOURS

BRINE

1¼ cups kosher salt

1 cup packed light brown sugar

1 tablespoon black peppercorns

3 quarts cold water

6 quarts ice water

1 turkey, 12 to 14 pounds, thawed if frozen

2 5-pound bags ice cubes

2 yellow onions, chopped

1 tablespoon vegetable oil

2 quarts low-sodium chicken broth

3 tablespoons unsalted butter, melted, if needed

½ cup unbleached all-purpose flour

2 teaspoons chopped fresh herbs, such as rosemary, thyme, or sage, or a combination

Kosher salt and freshly ground black pepper

Just about anyone who has ever grilled a turkey for the holidays will say there is no turning back. It is a surprisingly simple way to prepare the centerpiece of the meal, with the only tricky part being keeping the temperature at a steady 350°F, and it frees up your oven for cooking other things. This recipe also includes an all-out delicious gravy.

SERVES 12 TO 14

1. The night before grilling, brine the turkey: In 10-quart nonreactive stockpot over high heat, combine the salt, brown sugar, peppercorns, and cold water and bring to a boil, stirring to dissolve the salt. Remove the brine from the heat and let cool until tepid. Add the ice water and stir. (If your stockpot is not large enough to hold 10 quarts liquid, pour the brine and the ice water into a clean bucket.) The brine should be very cold.

2. Remove and reserve the neck, giblets, and lumps of fat from the cavity of the turkey. Place them in a bowl, cover, and refrigerate. Remove and discard the pop-up timer from the bird if there is one. Put the turkey inside a large, sturdy, food-grade plastic bag. Arrange a thin layer of ice cubes on the bottom of an ice chest and set the turkey on top of it. Pour enough of the cold brine into the bag to cover the turkey completely when the bag is closed and tightly tied. Discard any extra brine. Tie the bag securely closed with butcher's twine. Add ice cubes and/or thermal ice packs to cover and surround the turkey to keep it cold. Close the ice chest and brine the turkey for 12 to 14 hours, no longer.

3. Remove the turkey from the bag and discard the brine. Pat the turkey dry inside and outside with paper towels. Fold the wing tips behind the back. Add half of the onion to the body cavity. Tie the legs together with butcher's twine. Set a roasting rack in a large, heavy-gauge disposable foil pan. Place the turkey on the rack and let stand at room temperature for 1 hour before grilling.

4. Prepare the grill for indirect cooking over medium-low heat (about 350°F).

(continued on next page)

BRINED TURKEY
WITH HERBED PAN GRAVY
(CONTINUED)

5. Brush the cooking grates clean. Place the reserved lumps of fat in the pan alongside the bird. Grill the turkey in the pan over **indirect medium-low heat**, with the lid closed and keeping the temperature of the grill as close to 350°F as possible, until an instant-read thermometer inserted in the thickest part of the thigh (not touching the bone) reaches 165°F, about 2¾ hours. If using a charcoal grill, replenish the charcoal as needed to maintain a steady temperature of 350°F. During grilling, occasionally tilt the bird so the juices run out of the cavity into the pan. The juices will reduce and turn dark brown, adding color and rich flavor for the gravy.

6. Meanwhile, in a large saucepan over medium-high heat on the stove, warm the oil. Using a heavy knife or cleaver, chop the reserved neck into 2-inch chunks. Add the neck and giblets to the saucepan and cook until well browned, 5 to 6 minutes, turning occasionally. Add the remaining onion and cook until softened, about 3 minutes, stirring often. Add the broth and bring the mixture to a low boil. Turn down the heat to low and simmer gently until the liquid is reduced by half, about 1 hour. Strain the liquid through a fine-mesh strainer set over a bowl. Discard the solids.

7. When the turkey is done, transfer it to a platter and let it rest for 20 to 30 minutes (the internal temperature will rise 5 to 10 degrees during this time). While the turkey is resting, strain the pan juices into a fat separator. Let stand for about 3 minutes to allow the fat to separate from the juices. Pour the juices into a 1-quart measuring cup; reserve the fat. Add some of the stock, if needed, to total 1 quart. Reserve the foil pan.

8. Measure the fat. You should have ½ cup; if now, add butter to total ½ cup. In a medium saucepan over medium heat on the stove, warm the fat. Whisk in the flour and let bubble for 1 minute, stirring constantly. Gradually whisk in the pan juices and bring to a boil. Turn down the heat to medium-low and simmer until you have a good gravy consistency, about 5 minutes, stirring often. Remove the simmering gravy from the heat and immediately pour it into the foil pan. Scrape up any browned bits with a rubber spatula, taking care not to pierce the pan, then return the gravy to the saucepan and add the herbs. Simmer for 5 minutes to blend the flavors, whisking often. Taste and season with salt and pepper (the brine may have seasoned the gravy enough).

9. Carve the turkey and serve with the gravy.

05

FISH & SHELLFISH

VIETNAMESE SHRIMP POPS
WITH PEANUT SAUCE

PREP TIME
30 MINUTES

CHILLING TIME
**30 MINUTES
TO 1 HOUR**

GRILLING TIME
4 TO 6 MINUTES

SAUCE

1 cup coconut milk

⅓ cup well-stirred natural peanut butter

1 teaspoon finely grated lime zest

3 tablespoons lime juice

1 tablespoon soy sauce

1 tablespoon packed light brown sugar

1 teaspoon hot chile-garlic sauce, such as Sriracha

½ teaspoon peeled, grated fresh ginger

SHRIMP POPS

1 pound lean ground pork

12 ounces shrimp, peeled and deveined

½ cup coarsely chopped fresh basil leaves

¼ cup panko (Japanese-style bread crumbs)

2 large garlic cloves

1 tablespoon soy sauce

½ teaspoon freshly ground black pepper

¼ cup vegetable oil

Once you have combined the shrimp, pork, and other "pop" ingredients and shaped the mixture into ovals, chill the ovals for at least 30 minutes. This makes the pops firmer and easier to turn on the grill. To prevent the exposed part of the bamboo skewers from burning, place a folded piece of foil directly on the cooking grate and set the exposed sections on the foil.

SERVES 4 TO 6 (MAKES 12 TO 15 POPS)

1. In a heavy-bottomed saucepan combine all the sauce ingredients. Place over medium heat and cook, without simmering, just until the sauce is smooth and slightly thickened, 2 to 3 minutes, whisking constantly. The sauce will thicken further as it cools. Remove from the heat.

2. In a food processor or blender pulse the shrimp pop ingredients, except the oil, until a chunky paste is formed. Pour the oil onto a sheet pan and brush it evenly over the bottom and sides. Using two tablespoons, shape the shrimp pop mixture into quenelles (small ovals), placing them on the oiled sheet pan as you make them. Turn them, making sure they are well coated with oil. Refrigerate for 30 minutes to 1 hour to firm up the texture.

3. Have ready 12 to 15 small metal or bamboo skewers. If using bamboo, soak in water for at least 30 minutes.

4. Prepare the grill for direct cooking over high heat (450° to 550°F).

5. Brush the cooking grates clean. Slide a quenelle onto the end of each skewer. Grill the quenelles over **direct high heat**, with the lid closed, until opaque throughout, 4 to 6 minutes, turning once or twice (cut one open with a sharp knife to test for doneness). Remove from the grill.

6. Arrange the shrimp pops on a serving platter. Serve warm with the dipping sauce.

JUICY SHRIMP
WITH AVOCADO-CHILE SAUCE

PREP TIME
25 MINUTES

GRILLING TIME
10 TO 16 MINUTES

One clever technique for ensuring great-tasting grilled shrimp is to nestle them closely together on skewers—so closely they almost appear to be a single piece. The shrimp will remain particularly juicy and will be easier to turn. The accompanying creamy chile sauce carries only mild heat but lots of flavor.

SERVES 4 TO 6

SAUCE

3 Anaheim chile peppers, each about 6 inches long

1 Hass avocado

1 large garlic clove

¼ cup sour cream

¼ cup mayonnaise

2 tablespoons roughly chopped fresh dill

½ teaspoon kosher salt

¼ teaspoon freshly ground black pepper

RUB

1 teaspoon garlic powder

1 teaspoon paprika

¾ teaspoon kosher salt

½ teaspoon ground cumin

¼ teaspoon freshly ground black pepper

2 pounds large shrimp (21/30 count), peeled and deveined, tails left on

Extra-virgin olive oil

1. Have ready 8 to 10 metal or bamboo skewers. If using bamboo, soak in water for at least 30 minutes.

2. Prepare the grill for direct cooking over medium heat (350° to 450°F).

3. Brush the cooking grates clean. Grill the chile peppers over **direct medium heat**, with the lid closed, until blackened and blistered all over, 8 to 12 minutes, turning occasionally. Place the chiles in a bowl and cover with plastic wrap to trap the steam. Let stand for 10 minutes. Remove and discard the charred skin, stems, and seeds. Drop the chiles into a food processor or blender. Add all the remaining sauce ingredients and process until a smooth sauce forms. If the sauce seems too thick, add a little water. Transfer the sauce to a serving bowl.

4. In a small bowl combine all the rub ingredients and mix well. Lay 5 to 7 of the shrimp on a work surface, arranging them so the single shrimp on one end lies one way and all the rest of the shrimp lie in the same way. Choose shrimp that are the same size so you can nestle them together with no empty spaces between them. This will help to keep the shrimp from spinning on the skewer and will prevent them from drying out on the grill. Pick up and slide each shrimp onto a skewer, piercing it through the middle and pushing the shrimp together as they are added to the skewer. Repeat the process with the remaining shrimp and skewers. Lightly brush the shrimp on both sides with oil and then season evenly with the rub.

5. Increase the temperature of the grill to high heat (450° to 550°F). Grill the shrimp over **direct high heat**, with the lid closed, until firm to the touch and just turning opaque in the center, 2 to 4 minutes, turning once. Remove from the grill.

6. Serve the shrimp warm with the dipping sauce.

GREEK SEAFOOD SALAD

★

PREP TIME
20 MINUTES

MARINATING TIME
20 TO 30 MINUTES

GRILLING TIME
3 TO 5 MINUTES

★

DRESSING

¼ cup plus 2 tablespoons extra-virgin olive oil

3 tablespoons red wine vinegar

½ teaspoon minced garlic

½ teaspoon kosher salt

½ teaspoon dried oregano

¼ teaspoon crushed red pepper flakes

1 pound small shrimp (36/45 count), peeled and deveined

1 pound bay scallops

5 medium tomatoes, cut into ½-inch-thick slices

½ cup pitted green olives, cut into halves or quarters

½ cup thinly sliced celery

¼ cup finely diced red onion

2 tablespoons roughly chopped fresh Italian parsley leaves

A perforated grill pan is like a large sheet pan with little holes all over the surface. It allows you to cook small foods, such as green beans, tiny tomatoes, broccoli, or shellfish like shrimp and bay scallops, without losing them through the bars of the cooking grate. To ensure beautifully browned food, always preheat a grill pan, just as you do a cooking grate.

SERVES 6

1. In a small bowl whisk together the dressing ingredients. In a large bowl combine the shrimp and scallops. Add ¼ cup of the dressing to the seafood and mix well. Cover and refrigerate for 20 to 30 minutes. Reserve the remaining dressing.

2. Prepare the grill for direct cooking over high heat (450° to 550°F).

3. Arrange the tomato slices on a serving platter. In a small bowl combine the olives, celery, and onion and mix well. Set aside.

4. Brush the cooking grates clean. Preheat a perforated grill pan over high heat. Drain the seafood in a fine-mesh strainer and discard the marinade. Spread the seafood in a single layer on the preheated grill pan and cook over **direct high heat**, with the lid closed, until slightly firm to the touch and just turning opaque in the center, 3 to 5 minutes, turning once or twice. Remove the pan from the grill and place it on a heatproof surface. Transfer the seafood to a large bowl to stop the cooking.

5. Spoon the seafood over the tomatoes. Scatter the olive mixture on top. Spoon the reserved dressing over the entire salad, coating it lightly (you may not need all of it). Garnish with the parsley. Serve at room temperature.

GRILLED SHRIMP RISOTTO
WITH ASPARAGUS

★

PREP TIME
20 MINUTES, PLUS
30 TO 40 MINUTES
FOR THE RISOTTO

GRILLING TIME
6 TO 8 MINUTES

★

1 pound asparagus

Extra-virgin olive oil

Kosher salt

18 extra-large shrimp
(16/20 count), peeled and
deveined

1 tablespoon lemon juice

RISOTTO

6 cups low-sodium
chicken broth

3 tablespoons unsalted
butter

2 tablespoons extra-virgin
olive oil

½ cup finely chopped
yellow onion

1 teaspoon kosher salt

2 cups Arborio rice

½ cup dry white wine

½ cup freshly grated
Parmigiano-Reggiano®
cheese (about 2 ounces)

1 tablespoon finely grated
lemon zest

¼ cup fresh lemon juice

2 tablespoons finely
chopped fresh Italian
parsley leaves

1 tablespoon finely
chopped fresh mint leaves

Freshly ground pepper

Asparagus is one of our favorite grilled vegetables, especially with lemon and Parmigiano-Reggiano cheese on top. Here we add creamy risotto and briny shrimp to that winning combination.

SERVES 6 TO 8

1. Prepare the grill for direct cooking over medium heat (350° to 450°F).

2. Snap the asparagus spears and discard the tough bases. Place the asparagus on a plate, drizzle with oil, and turn to coat. Season with salt. On another plate, brush the shrimp with oil and season lightly with salt.

3. Brush the cooking grates clean. Grill the asparagus over **direct medium heat**, with the lid closed, until browned in spots and crisp-tender, 6 to 8 minutes, turning occasionally. At the same time, grill the shrimp over **direct medium heat** until firm to the touch and just turning opaque in the center, 3 to 5 minutes, turning once. Remove the shrimp from the grill as they are ready and place in a medium bowl. Add the lemon juice and toss to coat evenly. When the asparagus and shrimp are cool enough to handle, cut them into 1-inch pieces. Set aside.

4. In a medium saucepan over high heat on the stove, bring the broth to a simmer. Keep warm over the lowest heat setting.

5. In a medium saucepan over medium heat on the stove, melt 2 tablespoons of the butter with the oil. Add the onion and ½ teaspoon of the salt and sauté until the onion is softened but not browned, 3 to 4 minutes. Add the rice and cook until the grains are coated with the butter mixture and turn opaque, about 2 minutes, stirring frequently. Add the wine and stir until evaporated, about 1 minute. Add 1 cup of the warm broth and simmer until the rice has absorbed nearly all of the liquid, stirring occasionally. Add all the remaining broth, ½ cup at a time, stirring until nearly all the liquid is absorbed before adding the next addition, 25 to 30 minutes. At this point, the risotto should be creamy and the grains should be plump and tender, yet still firm to the bite.

6. Remove the risotto from the heat and stir in the remaining 1 tablespoon butter, ¼ cup of the cheese, the lemon zest and juice, and the remaining ½ teaspoon salt. Fold in the asparagus, shrimp, parsley, and mint and season with pepper. Divide the risotto among individual bowls, garnish with the remaining ¼ cup cheese, dividing it evenly, and serve at once.

LEMON-DILL SHRIMP
WITH ORZO SALAD

PREP TIME
20 MINUTES

MARINATING TIME
30 MINUTES

GRILLING TIME
2 TO 4 MINUTES

VINAIGRETTE

½ cup extra-virgin olive oil

1 teaspoon grated
lemon zest

¼ cup fresh lemon juice

1 tablespoon finely
chopped fresh dill

1 teaspoon minced garlic

½ teaspoon kosher salt

¼ teaspoon freshly ground
black pepper

16 extra-large shrimp
(16/20 count), peeled and
deveined, tails left on

1 cup dried orzo pasta

⅓ cup plus 1 tablespoon
crumbled feta cheese
(about 2 ounces)

¾ cup finely diced red
bell pepper

⅓ cup pitted Kalamata
olives, cut into quarters

2 tablespoons thinly sliced
scallions (white and light
green parts only)

1½ tablespoons finely
chopped fresh oregano
leaves

This dish gets much of its character from the smoky flavor that only a grill can deliver to shrimp. The recipe works best with extra-large shrimp because they are typically more succulent than the smaller ones. If you prefer tangy vinaigrettes, start with just ¼ cup olive oil and taste the result, then add more oil to suit your palate.

SERVES 4

1. Have ready 4 metal or bamboo skewers. If using bamboo, soak in water for at least 30 minutes.

2. In a large serving bowl whisk together all the vinaigrette ingredients. Place the shrimp in a medium bowl, pour ¼ cup of the vinaigrette over the shrimp, and toss to coat evenly. Cover and marinate in the refrigerator for about 30 minutes. Set the serving bowl with the remaining vinaigrette aside.

3. Prepare the grill for direct cooking over high heat (450° to 550°F).

4. Bring a medium saucepan three-fourths full of salted water to a boil on the stove. Add the pasta and cook until al dente, according to package directions. Drain the pasta and add it to the vinaigrette in the serving bowl. Add the feta, bell pepper, olives, scallions, and oregano and toss to combine. Set aside at room temperature.

5. Thread 4 shrimp onto each skewer, bending each shrimp almost in half so the skewer passes through it twice, near the head and near the tail. Brush the cooking grates clean. Grill the shrimp over **direct high heat**, with the lid closed, until firm to the touch and just turning opaque in the center, 2 to 4 minutes, turning once. Remove from the grill and serve right away with the pasta.

SEAFOOD PAELLA

★

PREP TIME
40 MINUTES

MUSSELS
**30 MINUTES
TO 1 HOUR**

GRILLING TIME
35 TO 37 MINUTES

★

**8 ounces large shrimp
(21/30 count), peeled and
deveined, tails left on,
shells reserved for broth**

Extra-virgin olive oil

**Kosher salt and freshly
ground black pepper**

BROTH

Reserved shrimp shells

**4 cups low-sodium
chicken broth**

¾ cup dry white wine

2 bay leaves

**1½ teaspoons smoked
paprika**

1 teaspoon kosher salt

**½ teaspoon crushed red
pepper flakes**

¼ teaspoon saffron threads

**4 ounces thickly sliced
prosciutto, diced**

**1 cup finely chopped
red onion**

**¾ cup finely chopped
red bell pepper**

1 tablespoon minced garlic

2 cups Arborio rice

1 cup frozen baby peas

**12 live mussels, scrubbed
and beards removed**

Briefly grilling the shrimp gives this Spanish classic extra flavor. If you are using wild mussels, soak them in salted cold water for 30 minutes to 1 hour to expel any sand trapped in the shells. Our favorite part of this recipe just might be the crispy layer of rice—the *socarrat*—that forms on the bottom of the pan.

SERVES 6 TO 8

1. In a large bowl toss the shrimp with 2 teaspoons oil and season with salt and pepper. Cover and refrigerate until ready to grill.

2. In a medium saucepan bring the broth ingredients to a simmer over high heat. Simmer for 5 minutes. Pour the broth through a fine-mesh strainer placed over a bowl and discard the shells and bay leaves. Set aside. (The broth can be made up to 2 hours ahead.)

3. Prepare the grill for direct cooking over high heat (450° to 550°F) on one side of the grill and over medium heat (350° to 450°F) on the other side.

4. Brush the cooking grates clean. Grill the shrimp over **direct high heat**, with the lid closed, until cooked halfway, about 2 minutes, turning once (the shrimp will finish cooking in the broth). Remove from the grill and set aside to cool.

5. Place a deep 12-inch cast-iron skillet or paella pan over **direct high heat**. Warm 3 tablespoons oil in the skillet, add the prosciutto, and cook, stirring occasionally, until it begins to crisp, about 3 minutes. Add the onion, bell pepper, and garlic and cook until the onion is translucent, about 5 minutes, stirring occasionally and rotating the skillet for even cooking. Slide the skillet over **direct medium heat**, stir in the rice, and cook until well coated with the pan juices, about 2 minutes. Stir in the shrimp broth and peas. Close the grill lid and let the rice cook at a brisk simmer until al dente, about 15 minutes. Nestle the shrimp into the rice, then add the mussels, hinged side down. Cook over **direct medium heat**, with the lid closed, until the mussels open, 8 to 10 minutes.

6. Remove the skillet from the grill, cover with aluminum foil, and let stand for 5 minutes. Serve the paella hot directly from the skillet.

FOR PARTY MENUS, SEE PAGE 320

SALMON SKEWERS
WITH RED CURRY–COCONUT SAUCE

PREP TIME
25 MINUTES,
PLUS ABOUT
15 MINUTES
FOR COOKING
THE SAUCE

GRILLING TIME
3 TO 6 MINUTES

1 can (14 ounces) coconut milk, unopened, divided

3½ tablespoons Thai red curry paste, divided

1 tablespoon fish sauce

1 tablespoon soy sauce

1½ teaspoons packed light brown sugar

1 skinless whole salmon fillet, about 2 pounds, any pin bones removed

2 tablespoons vegetable oil

2 tablespoons finely chopped scallion (white and light green parts only)

This is the kind of soul-satisfying dish you might find in Southeast Asia at a beachside restaurant. A few tablespoons of red curry paste transform canned coconut milk into a rich, flavorful sauce that complements the salmon. The fish sauce and soy sauce provide a salty finish.

SERVES 4 TO 6

1. Have ready 12 metal or bamboo skewers. If using bamboo, soak in water for at least 30 minutes.

2. Open the coconut milk without shaking the can. Scoop ¼ cup coconut cream from the top of the coconut milk and transfer it to a small saucepan. Stir the remaining contents of the can, then pour off 1 cup of the milk and set aside for later. Reserve the remaining milk for another use. Place the pan over medium heat and bring to a boil. Add 2 tablespoons of the curry paste and cook until very fragrant, 3 to 5 minutes, stirring constantly. Gradually add the 1 cup coconut milk to the curry paste mixture, stirring constantly. Add the fish sauce, soy sauce, and sugar, stir well, and bring to a boil, stirring constantly. Adjust the heat to maintain a simmer and cook until thickened to a thin sauce consistency, 5 to 10 minutes, stirring frequently. Set aside off the heat.

3. Prepare the grill for direct cooking over high heat (450° to 550°F).

4. Cut the fillet into ¾-inch-thick slices. Thread the fish slices onto the skewers lengthwise, keeping the skewers inside the fish as much as possible.

5. In a small bowl combine the remaining 1½ tablespoons curry paste and the oil. Generously brush the salmon all over with the mixture. Brush the cooking grates clean. Grill the skewers over **direct high heat**, with the lid closed, until you can lift them off the cooking grates with tongs without sticking, 2 to 4 minutes. Turn the skewers over and cook, with the lid closed, to desired doneness, 1 to 2 minutes more for medium rare. Remove from the grill.

6. Reheat the sauce and pour it onto a shallow serving plate, creating a pool. Arrange the skewers on the sauce and garnish with the scallion. Serve warm.

SALMON FILLETS
WITH ROASTED CORN, TOMATO, AND AVOCADO SALSA

PREP TIME
30 MINUTES

GRILLING TIME
16 TO 24 MINUTES

2 ears corn, husked

Extra-virgin olive oil

Kosher salt

Freshly ground black pepper

¼ teaspoon prepared chili powder

2 cups cherry tomatoes, red, yellow, or a mixture, cut into quarters

1 cup roughly chopped arugula

2 scallions (white and light green parts only), finely chopped

2 tablespoons fresh lime juice

1 large Hass avocado, finely diced

6 skin-on salmon fillets, each 6 to 8 ounces and about 1 inch thick, any pin bones removed

1 lime, cut into 6 wedges

Flag this recipe for easy summertime entertaining. You can make the salsa a few hours before the party so you can focus on the salmon when it's time to eat. Oil the fish (not the grate) well and resolve not to turn the fillets too soon. They will stick initially, but after 6 to 8 minutes, they should release their grip, allowing you to flip them with a spatula.

SERVES 6

1. Prepare the grill for direct cooking over high heat (450° to 550°F).

2. Lightly brush the corn with oil and season evenly with ¼ teaspoon salt, ¼ teaspoon pepper, and the chili powder.

3. Brush the cooking grates clean. Grill the corn over **direct high heat**, with the lid closed, until browned in spots and tender, 8 to 12 minutes, turning occasionally. Remove from the grill and let cool.

4. Cut the corn kernels off the cobs and transfer them to a medium serving bowl. Add the tomatoes, arugula, scallions, 2 tablespoons oil, the lime juice, ½ teaspoon salt, and ¼ teaspoon pepper to the corn and stir gently to mix. Fold in the avocado. Set aside.

5. Generously coat the flesh side of the salmon fillets with oil and season evenly with salt and pepper. Grill the fillets, flesh side down first, over **direct high heat**, with the lid closed, until you can lift the fillets off the cooking grates without them sticking, 6 to 8 minutes. Turn the fillets over and continue to cook, with the lid closed, to desired doneness, 2 to 4 minutes more for medium rare. Slip a spatula between the skin and the flesh and transfer the fillets to individual serving plates.

6. Serve the salmon warm with the salsa and lime wedges.

HALIBUT
WITH ROASTED PEPPER VINAIGRETTE

PREP TIME
20 MINUTES

GRILLING TIME
15 TO 22 MINUTES

VINAIGRETTE

**3 bell peppers, preferably
1 red, 1 yellow, and 1 orange**

**3 tablespoons extra-virgin
olive oil**

**2 tablespoons fresh
orange juice**

**2 tablespoons finely
chopped fresh Italian
parsley leaves**

**1 tablespoon fresh lemon
juice**

½ teaspoon minced garlic

½ teaspoon ground cumin

¼ teaspoon kosher salt

**¼ teaspoon freshly ground
black pepper**

**¼ teaspoon hot-pepper
sauce**

**4 skinless halibut fillets,
each about 6 ounces and
1 inch thick, any pin bones
removed**

Extra-virgin olive oil

**Kosher salt and freshly
ground black pepper**

When we first published this recipe in 2005, it called for Chilean sea bass, which was wonderful and abundant. Since then, it has been overfished, so nowadays we recommend pairing thick, meaty halibut with the brightly colored and flavored vinaigrette. Take care not to overcook the fillets, which can go quickly from moist to dry.

SERVES 4

1. Prepare the grill for direct cooking over high heat (450° to 550°F).

2. Brush the cooking grates clean. Grill the bell peppers over **direct high heat**, with the lid closed, until blackened and blistered all over, 10 to 12 minutes, turning occasionally. Place the peppers in a bowl and cover with plastic wrap to trap the steam. Let stand for about 10 minutes. Remove and discard the charred skin, stems, and seeds, then cut each pepper lengthwise into ¼-inch-wide strips. In a medium bowl whisk together the remaining vinaigrette ingredients. Add the peppers to the vinaigrette, stir to coat evenly, cover, and set aside for up to 1 day.

3. Lightly brush the fillets on both sides with oil and then season on both sides with salt and pepper. Grill over **direct high heat**, with the lid closed, until the flesh is opaque in the center but still moist, 5 to 7 minutes, carefully turning once. Remove from the grill.

4. Serve the fish warm with the vinaigrette spooned on top.

A BOUT WITH A GIANT TROUT

BY MIKE KEMPSTER

I grew up in Kansas City, where the smell of hickory smoke is in the air and pork ribs and beef brisket were the quintessential—and most difficult—meals to master on a grill. Kansas City is also in the middle of the United States, which means it's a long way from fresh-caught ocean or gulf seafood.

Here's another fact about me: I'm the second-born child in a big Catholic family, and eating fish on Friday was an obligation when I was a kid. My mother was a good cook, but she didn't have a clue about how to prepare fish—

...IT WAS WAY TOO LONG TO FIT ON ANY OF OUR GRILLS. AT THAT MOMENT, I WAS STRUCK BY TERROR!

even freshwater fish—and my dad wasn't a bit interested in grilling fish. When your whole experience with seafood consists of overcooked, oily fish sticks and sandpaper-dry tuna casseroles, you're not likely to be enthusiastic about grilling fish.

Early in my career at Weber, I discovered that I wasn't alone in my aversion to preparing seafood. Like many grilling enthusiasts, I was afraid to cook fish because I didn't want to risk embarrassing results. But one day I found myself in a situation that forced me to take the plunge into mastering grilled lake trout.

As a young Weber salesman, I worked a lot of trade shows attended by hardware distributors. To gain retail distribution, we hosted combination grilling demonstrations and cocktail parties after the show hours. My unexpected course in lake trout grilling took place at a cocktail party held in the rooftop dining room of the Minneapolis Athletic Club. We knew the invitation would be quite a draw because, from the lofty eighth story, the dealers could enjoy a view of the Twin Cities as they sipped cocktails and ate grilled delicacies, all at Weber's expense.

While I was working the show on the morning of the party, my boss, Art, announced he was taking off to play golf with an important customer. Just after he left, the president of a major hardware wholesaler stopped by our exhibit. In the exchange of small talk, he boasted of the sixteen-pound trout he had caught on Lake Superior the day before. He had once seen Art demonstrate how to grill a lake trout, and he asked if we would grill his prized trout and serve it at our party. Although I had never laid eyes on a lake trout, I immediately volunteered that Art would be pleased to grill it to perfection.

That afternoon, as we prepared for the party, the trophy trout arrived covered in ice in a very large cooler. I was becoming more nervous by the minute because it was getting close to party time and Art was still off chasing a golf ball. I scooped off the ice for my first look ever at a lake trout. Fortunately, it had been cleaned. That was the good news. The bad news was that it was way too long to fit on any of our grills. At that moment, I was struck by terror!

A chef working at the club had experience

cooking lake trout, and he offered up a recipe for stuffing the scary thing. But he wisely withdrew from helping me possibly ruin the trophy catch on my grill. I wished for the same wisdom sometime in the future.

With the clock ticking, I plunged into the deep end. I cut off the tail and the head, leaving the meaty center in one piece. I prepared two grills for indirect grilling, and I placed the head and tail on one and the stuffed center portion on the other. My plan was to reassemble the fish parts on a huge serving tray and hide the wounds with garnishes.

I actually started to relax a bit as the aroma from the stuffing wafted into the air. But then I discovered a new problem. The head and tail would be grilled to a crisp before the meatier center was done! I wrapped the head and tail in foil to keep them from burning, shut down the air dampers so the fire would die down, and crossed my fingers.

The chef who had helped me stuff the fish came out to witness what he knew would be a cooking disaster. He found my colleagues chatting up early arrivals. I had moved my grill into an alley to avoid public embarrassment.

Ah, but the grilling gods were kind to me that day. The center portion cooked faster than I expected, and by some miracle, the head and tail were not incinerated. We transferred the fish pieces to a serving tray, and we performed the final touches of cosmetic surgery by covering the cuts with sautéed lemon slices and lots of fresh parsley. To my compete surprise, the fish parts looked like a perfectly grilled whole lake trout.

Just as we finished, Art arrived, placed the chef's toque on his head, grabbed a knife and spatula, and marched into the dining room. Two of us junior sales guys followed, carrying the trout beautifully displayed and ready to serve. The president beamed with pride and thanked Art for cooking his fish to perfection. Raising his glass in a toast, Art proclaimed that he owed the perfect results to his Weber grill. I bit my tongue, the chef winked knowingly at me, and our guests gave the fish rave reviews.

And that's how I overcame my fear of grilling fish and went on to learn how to grill a wide variety of seafood.

CARIBBEAN
SWORDFISH STEAKS
WITH MANGO SALSA

★

PREP TIME
20 MINUTES

MARINATING TIME
**30 MINUTES
TO 4 HOURS**

GRILLING TIME
10 TO 12 MINUTES

★

MARINADE

¼ cup extra-virgin olive oil

Juice of 4 limes

2 tablespoons light rum

2 tablespoons soy sauce

¼ teaspoon ground cloves

¼ teaspoon freshly ground
black pepper

4 swordfish steaks, each
7 to 8 ounces and about
1 inch thick

SALSA

1 mango, about 1 pound,
peeled and cut into
½-inch dice

2 teaspoons thinly sliced
scallions (white part only)

1 jalapeño chile pepper,
seeded and finely chopped

1 tablespoon finely
chopped fresh basil leaves

1 teaspoon fresh lime juice

Rum, lime juice, and mangoes are key players in this laid-back recipe, conjuring up festive cocktails on a sultry late afternoon in the West Indies. Swordfish fits the feeling just right because its firm flesh makes it perhaps the easiest of all fish to grill. Here, the Caribbean marinade works twice: first to flavor the raw fish and then to keep it moist as it grills.

SERVES 4

1. In a large, wide bowl whisk together the marinade ingredients. Add the swordfish steaks to the bowl and turn to coat evenly with the marinade. Cover and refrigerate for at least 30 minutes or up to 4 hours, turning the swordfish once.

2. Prepare the grill for direct cooking over medium heat (350° to 450°F).

3. In a medium bowl combine all the salsa ingredients and mix gently. Set aside.

4. Remove the steaks from the bowl and pour the marinade into a small saucepan. Place the pan over medium-high heat on the stove, bring to a rolling boil, then remove from the heat.

5. Brush the cooking grates clean. Grill the steaks over **direct medium heat**, with the lid closed, until just opaque in the center but still juicy, 10 to 12 minutes, turning and brushing once with the boiled marinade. Remove from the grill.

6. Serve the steaks warm with the salsa spooned over the top.

CEDAR-PLANKED SALMON
WITH HOISIN-MUSTARD GLAZE

PREP TIME
15 MINUTES

GRILLING TIME
15 TO 25 MINUTES

GLAZE

1 tablespoon hoisin sauce

1 tablespoon Dijon mustard

1 tablespoon fresh
lemon juice

1 tablespoon unsalted
butter, melted

½ teaspoon toasted
sesame oil

1 skin-on whole salmon
fillet, 2 to 2½ pounds and
about ¾ inch thick, any pin
bones removed

½ teaspoon kosher salt

¼ teaspoon freshly ground
black pepper

The simplest route to an impressive seafood main may be this one, in which a whole salmon fillet is roasted on a cedar plank. The smoldering wood fills the inside of the grill with aromatic smoke, flavoring the fish as it gently cooks, and the dark, tangy glaze of mustard-spiked hoisin sauce adds a perfect layer of complex flavors.

SERVES 6 TO 8

1. Soak an untreated cedar plank, about 16 by 8 inches, in water for at least 1 hour.

2. Prepare the grill for direct cooking over medium heat (350° to 450°F).

3. In a small bowl combine all the glaze ingredients and mix well. Place the salmon, skin side down, on a large cutting board. Cut the salmon in half lengthwise but do not cut through the skin. Then cut the salmon crosswise to make six to eight servings, again being careful not to cut through the skin. Brush the glaze evenly over the salmon flesh, brushing some of the glaze between the individual servings. Season evenly with the salt and pepper.

4. Brush the cooking grates clean. Place the soaked plank over **direct medium heat** and close the lid. After 5 to 10 minutes, when the plank begins to smoke and char, turn the plank over. Place the salmon pieces, skin side down, on the plank. Close the lid and cook until the salmon is lightly browned on the surface and opaque in the center but still moist, 15 to 25 minutes. Using sturdy tongs or spatulas, transfer the plank, with the salmon still on it, to a heatproof surface.

5. Serve the salmon on the plank, or plate individual servings by slipping a spatula between the skin and flesh. Serve warm or at room temperature.

SALMON
WITH BROWN SUGAR AND MUSTARD GLAZE

PREP TIME
15 MINUTES

GRILLING TIME
25 TO 30 MINUTES

1 tablespoon packed light brown sugar

2 teaspoons unsalted butter

1 teaspoon honey

2 tablespoons Dijon mustard

1 tablespoon soy sauce

1 tablespoon extra-virgin olive oil

2 teaspoons peeled, grated fresh ginger

1 skin-on whole salmon fillet, about 2½ pounds and ¾ to 1 inch thick, any pin bones removed

Grilling salmon on a sheet of aluminum foil eliminates any chance the fish will stick to the grate. Plus, you can close the lid knowing you don't even need to flip the salmon over. Then, once the fish is opaque and the sweet-and-sour glaze has caramelized, you can easily lift the fish from the foil, leaving the skin behind.

SERVES 6 TO 8

1. Prepare the grill for indirect cooking over medium heat (350˚ to 450˚F).

2. In a sauté pan combine the sugar, butter, and honey and warm over medium heat on the stove until melted. Remove from the heat and whisk in the mustard, soy sauce, oil, and ginger. Let cool to room temperature.

3. Place the salmon, skin side down, on a large sheet of aluminum foil. Trim the foil to leave a border of ¼ to ½ inch around the edge of the salmon. Brush the top of the salmon with the brown sugar mixture.

4. Brush the cooking grates clean. Place the salmon on the foil over **indirect medium heat**, close the lid, and cook until the edges begin to brown and the inside is opaque, 25 to 30 minutes. Transfer the salmon with the foil to a cutting board.

5. Cut crosswise into six to eight pieces but do not cut through the skin. Slip a spatula between the skin and the flesh, transfer the pieces to individual plates, and serve right away.

06

SIDES

SUMMER CORN, TOMATO, AND
AVOCADO SALAD

PREP TIME
15 MINUTES

GRILLING TIME
10 TO 15 MINUTES

2 ears corn, husked

3 tablespoons extra-virgin olive oil, plus more for brushing corn

Kosher salt

2 tablespoons fresh lime juice

½ teaspoon ground cumin

¼ teaspoon freshly ground black pepper

1 large Hass avocado, cut into ½-inch dice

1½ cups halved cherry or grape tomatoes

½ cup finely chopped red onion

¼ cup chopped fresh Italian parsley leaves

The versatility of this salad is one of its charms. You can replace the parsley with cilantro and serve it as a salsa alongside chicken or fish. If you like minced shallots, swap out the red onions for them. For a more substantial dish, spoon the mixture over a bed of salad greens. Choose a ripe but firm avocado, so the pieces hold their shape when the salad is tossed.

SERVES 4

1. Prepare the grill for direct cooking over medium heat (350° to 450°F).

2. Brush the cooking grates clean. Brush the corn with oil and lightly season with salt. Grill over **direct medium heat**, with the lid closed, until browned in spots and tender, 10 to 15 minutes, turning occasionally. Remove from the grill. When the corn is cool enough to handle, cut the kernels off the cobs. Transfer the kernels to a medium serving bowl.

3. In a small bowl whisk together the 3 tablespoons oil, lime juice, cumin, ½ teaspoon salt, and the pepper to make a dressing.

4. Add the avocado, tomatoes, onion, and parsley to the corn, then pour the dressing on top. Toss and stir gently to mix well. Taste and adjust the seasoning with salt and pepper if needed. Serve right away.

CORN ON THE COB
WITH BASIL-PARMESAN BUTTER

PREP TIME
10 MINUTES

GRILLING TIME
10 TO 15 MINUTES

BUTTER

¼ cup (½ stick) unsalted butter, softened

¼ cup freshly grated Parmigiano-Reggiano® cheese (scant 1 ounce)

2 tablespoons finely chopped fresh basil leaves

½ teaspoon kosher salt

¼ teaspoon freshly ground black pepper

¼ teaspoon garlic powder

4 ears corn, husked

Go easy when you first brush the butter on the corn. You don't want to use so much that it drips into the fire and causes flare-ups. Once the corn is on a platter, add as much of the flavored butter as you like. For a variation with lime butter, stir together 5 tablespoons melted unsalted butter with 1 tablespoon fresh lime juice, then follow the directions in this recipe.

SERVES 4

1. Prepare the grill for direct cooking over medium heat (350° to 450°F).

2. In a small bowl mash together all the butter ingredients with the back of a fork and then stir to distribute the seasonings evenly throughout the butter.

3. Brush the cooking grates clean. Spread about 1 tablespoon of the seasoned butter all over each ear of corn. Grill the corn over **direct medium heat**, with the lid closed, until browned in spots and tender, 10 to 15 minutes, turning occasionally. Remove from the grill.

4. Spread the remaining butter on the corn. Serve warm.

MEXICAN-STYLE
CORN ON THE COB

PREP TIME
10 MINUTES

GRILLING TIME
10 TO 15 MINUTES

SPREAD

3 tablespoons mayonnaise

2 tablespoons sour cream

1 tablespoon fresh
lime juice

TOPPING

3 tablespoons grated Cotija
or Parmigiano-Reggiano®
cheese

¾ teaspoon prepared
chili powder

¼ teaspoon chipotle
chile powder

4 ears corn, husked

We borrowed this brilliant idea from the street vendors in Mexico City who roast corn over live coals and then sell the ears coated in *crema*, cheese, and chili powder. For a decorative touch, peel the husks back (like a banana peel) but leave them attached, then tie them into a bundle with a narrow strip of husk.

SERVES 4

1. Prepare the grill for direct cooking over medium heat (350° to 450°F).

2. In a small bowl combine all the spread ingredients and mix well. In a second small bowl combine all the topping ingredients and mix well.

3. Brush the cooking grates clean. Grill the corn over **direct medium heat**, with the lid closed, until the kernels are browned in spots and tender, 10 to 15 minutes, turning occasionally. Remove from the grill.

4. Smear the spread all over the corn and then season evenly with the topping. Serve right away.

GRILLED BROCCOLI
WITH TOASTED BREAD CRUMBS AND PARMESAN

1 pound broccoli

2 tablespoons extra-virgin olive oil

3 medium garlic cloves

¼ teaspoon kosher salt

1 teaspoon fresh lemon juice

BREAD CRUMBS

¼ cup panko (Japanese-style bread crumbs)

1 tablespoon extra-virgin olive oil

½ teaspoon crushed red pepper flakes

¼ teaspoon kosher salt

¼ teaspoon freshly ground black pepper

2 tablespoons freshly grated Parmigiano-Reggiano® cheese

Broccoli is a great choice for grilling with just a few smart moves. First, tenderize it by blanching, then finish it on a perforated grill pan, making sure the edges of the florets are nicely browned. Garlic and lemon add flavor, and bread crumbs deliver crunch.

SERVES 6

1. Cut off the broccoli crowns from the stalks, then cut the crowns into florets and cut any large florets into bite-sized pieces. Trim off the tough ends from the stalks and cut the stalks crosswise into ½-inch-thick slices. You should have about 6 cups broccoli.

2. Have ready a large bowl of ice water. Bring a large saucepan of salted water to a rolling boil, add the broccoli, and parboil until barely tender, 2 to 3 minutes. Drain the broccoli and then plunge it into the ice water to stop the cooking. When the broccoli is cool, drain it well. If desired, set aside at room temperature for up to 30 minutes or cover and refrigerate for up to 1 hour.

3. Prepare the grill for direct cooking over medium heat (350° to 450°F).

4. In a large bowl combine the broccoli and oil and toss to coat evenly. Roughly chop the garlic with a chef's knife. Sprinkle the salt over the garlic, mince the garlic with the salt, and then use the side of the knife to crush the garlic with the salt to a smooth paste. Add the garlic paste and lemon juice to the broccoli and toss to coat evenly.

5. In a small bowl combine all the bread crumb ingredients and mix well.

6. Brush the cooking grates clean. Preheat a perforated grill pan over medium heat. Spread the broccoli in a single layer on the preheated grill pan and grill over **direct medium heat**, with the lid closed, for 3 minutes, turning the broccoli once or twice. Scatter the bread crumb mixture evenly over the broccoli and continue to grill, with the lid closed, until the broccoli is golden brown in parts but still mostly bright green and crisp-tender, 3 to 4 minutes more. Remove the pan from the grill.

7. Transfer the broccoli to a serving dish. Top with the cheese and serve warm.

HOW A REINDEER BROUGHT GRILLING TO NORWAY

BY MIKE KEMPSTER

Let's say you arrive in a country that has no tradition of grilling or of barbecue parties. How do you go about building a culture that enjoys barbecuing at home? Many people figure that you need to understand the differences between Americans and the people living wherever your plane has landed. Early on, I discovered the opposite was true: the key to success is to understand the similarities.

I made a sales call on a prospective distributor in Norway at a time when barbecuing was almost nonexistent there. I had been to Oslo a couple of times, and I had noticed that Norwegians enjoyed their food

AS I LEFT HIS OFFICE, A FEW BARS OF "RUDOLF THE RED-NOSED REINDEER" FILLED MY HEAD...

and drink. They also liked outdoor sporting activities, despite the climate. Houses had garden areas, and multistory housing had generous balconies. As I expected, the owner of the company listened to my sales presentation and then pointed out that the weather was cold and wet for about nine months of the year. He was convinced that few Norwegians would invest in

a pricey grill for a short summer of grilling.

Sometimes you get lucky, though if you like summertime weather, you probably won't call this luck. It was February, it was cold, and the snow was piled high around Oslo. I had a classic Weber kettle, charcoal, sausages, and barbecue tools with me, so I offered to cook my prospective customer lunch out in the company parking lot. He was a busy guy with no time for lunch, but he invited me to his home for a cookout. He said he had a saddle of reindeer on hand that he had intended to roast in his oven that evening and that his brother and sister-in-law were coming for dinner. As I left his office, a few bars of "Rudolf the Red-Nosed Reindeer" filled my head, and I was plenty anxious about grilling a reindeer roast in subzero weather.

It was a slippery and snowy drive to my host's home overlooking Oslo, but on my arrival, the skies cleared and the city lights shimmered in the frosty air—a beautiful view.

A saddle of reindeer looks like a saddle of venison but smaller. My host's wife had already made a delicious sauce from red currants and apples and was about to prepare potato pancakes with homemade applesauce, as well as steamed carrots. My job came down to roasting the reindeer in bitter-cold conditions, a failure of which would result in a disastrous dinner party and no chance for a business relationship. I knew this was a test, and my host figured this foolish American would fail. He hoped, of course, that I would not freeze in the process and that the reindeer roast would not burn to a

pile of ash, so it could be salvaged in the oven. Like many others, he assumed that grilling could only be done in nice weather and the person doing the grilling had to stand at the grill for the duration of the cooking time.

I used a chimney starter to ignite the charcoal, configured the glowing coals for indirect grilling, placed the roast on the cooking grate, and put the lid on the grill.

The dinner foursome was sipping aquavit inside the warm house and looking through large, sliding glass doors at the grilling spectacle, expecting disaster. Much to their surprise, I joined them and enjoyed their hospitality while the grill did the work.

I've often seen what happened next. After we finished one drink inside, the guys threw on their coats and, to their surprise, enjoyed more aquavit while standing around the grill, urging me to lift the lid occasionally so they could see the progress. They were actually having fun

outside on a frigid February night!

We didn't stand outside for the entire ninety minutes it took for the roast to reach the right internal temperature. When it emerged from the grill, it was just a bit pink at the center, was juicy, and had a hint of charcoal flavor—in other words, it was perfect. The sauce was delicious, the wine flowed, and the dinner conversation was lively and filled with laughter.

This event was strikingly similar to wintertime cookouts I have regularly hosted at my home near Chicago, with folks socializing around the grill and at the dinner table. The fact that it was winter and the main dish was grilled outdoors made it special. From this single evening, our prospective customer was able to envision his fellow Norwegians grilling year-round, and that was the start of a terrific business relationship. Norway is now one of our best markets, and Norwegians love grilling on their Weber grills in all kinds of weather.

EGGPLANT
WITH SPICY ASIAN DRESSING

PREP TIME
10 MINUTES

GRILLING TIME
8 TO 10 MINUTES

DRESSING

1 to 2 serrano chile peppers, seeded and minced

3 tablespoons soy sauce

2 tablespoons fresh lemon juice

2 tablespoons minced yellow onion

1 tablespoon water

2 globe eggplants, each about 12 ounces

¼ cup vegetable oil

1 teaspoon garlic powder

When firm slices of oiled eggplant hit a hot cooking grate, they soften and develop a touch of bitterness that calls for a sauce to balance the flavor. Here, a bold blend of chile, soy sauce, onion, and lemon juice does that perfectly. If the sauce seems a bit thick, thin it with water, a tablespoon at a time, until the consistency suits you.

SERVES 4

1. Prepare the grill for direct cooking over medium heat (350° to 450°F).

2. In a small bowl whisk together all the dressing ingredients. Set aside.

3. Remove about ½ inch from both ends of each eggplant. Cut the eggplants crosswise into ½-inch-thick slices. Lightly brush both sides of the slices with the oil and sprinkle evenly with the garlic powder.

4. Brush the cooking grates clean. Grill the eggplant slices over **direct medium heat**, with the lid closed, until well marked and tender, 8 to 10 minutes, turning once. Remove from the grill.

5. Arrange the eggplant slices in a single layer on a platter and immediately spoon the dressing evenly over the top. Serve warm.

CHARRED ASPARAGUS
WITH BASIL-LIME DIPPING SAUCE

PREP TIME
15 MINUTES

GRILLING TIME
6 TO 8 MINUTES

You can grill all sizes of asparagus with success, but the skinny spears are more prone to burning. Thicker spears have a richer, juicier texture and are easier to maneuver on the grill. Whatever size you choose, arrange the spears on the cooking grate perpendicular to the bars so they won't slip into the fire.

SAUCE

1 cup mayonnaise

2 tablespoons minced fresh basil leaves

Finely grated zest of 1 lime

2 teaspoons fresh lime juice

1 garlic clove, minced

⅛ teaspoon cayenne pepper

2 pounds asparagus

2 tablespoons extra-virgin olive oil

½ teaspoon kosher salt

½ teaspoon freshly ground black pepper

SERVES 4 TO 6

1. In a small serving bowl whisk together all the sauce ingredients. Cover and refrigerate until ready to serve.

2. Prepare the grill for direct cooking over medium heat (350° to 450°F).

3. One at a time grasp the end of each asparagus spear and bend it gently until it snaps at its natural point of tenderness, usually about two-thirds of the way down the spear. Discard the tough ends. Brush the asparagus spears on all sides with the oil and season with the salt and pepper.

4. Brush the cooking grates clean. Grill the asparagus over **direct medium heat**, with the lid closed, until nicely marked and crisp-tender, 6 to 8 minutes, rolling the spears occasionally. Remove from the grill.

5. Serve the asparagus warm with the sauce.

GRILLED CARROTS
WITH SPICED BUTTER

PREP TIME
10 MINUTES

GRILLING TIME
3 TO 5 MINUTES

8 medium carrots, each 6 to 8 inches long and about 1 inch wide at the stem, peeled

¼ cup (½ stick) unsalted butter

½ teaspoon red wine vinegar

¼ teaspoon freshly ground nutmeg

½ teaspoon kosher salt, divided

¼ teaspoon freshly ground black pepper, divided

1 teaspoon minced fresh Italian parsley leaves

This is an ideal accompaniment to steaks, chops, or other mains grilled over high heat. If you have room on the grate, cook the carrots at the same time, rolling them over the fire just until they are warm and striped like tigers. For an especially colorful dish, grill yellow and purple heirloom carrots along with conventional orange ones.

SERVES 4

1. Have a large bowl of ice water ready. Bring a large pot of salted water to a rolling boil. Add the carrots and cook until partially cooked but still crisp, 4 to 6 minutes. Drain the carrots and then plunge them into the ice water to stop the cooking. When the carrots are cool, drain well and set aside in a single layer on a large platter.

2. Prepare the grill for direct cooking over high heat (450° to 550°F).

3. In a small saucepan over medium heat on the stove, melt the butter with the vinegar and nutmeg and stir to mix. Remove from the heat and brush about half of the mixture on the carrots, coating evenly. Season the carrots with half of the salt and pepper.

4. Brush the cooking grates clean. Grill the carrots over **direct high heat**, with the lid open, until lightly charred with spots and stripes, 3 to 5 minutes, turning occasionally. Transfer the carrots to a clean platter.

5. Brush the carrots with the remaining butter mixture and season with the remaining salt and pepper. Garnish with the parsley and serve warm.

NEW POTATO SALAD
WITH BACON AND ONIONS

PREP TIME
20 MINUTES

GRILLING TIME
30 TO 37 MINUTES

STANDING TIME
1 HOUR (OPTIONAL)

⅓ cup plus 2 tablespoons
extra-virgin olive oil

Kosher salt

**Freshly ground black
pepper**

2½ pounds new potatoes,
about 1½ inches in
diameter, cut in half

8 ounces thick-cut bacon,
cut into ¼-inch dice

2 medium sweet onions,
cut crosswise into ½-inch-
thick slices

6 scallions (white part
only), thinly sliced

3 tablespoons finely
chopped fresh Italian
parsley leaves

1 tablespoon finely
chopped fresh thyme
leaves

3 tablespoons sherry
vinegar

3 tablespoons low-sodium
chicken broth or water

Here we elevate the ho-hum potato salad of backyard
barbecues by roasting the potatoes on the grill. Crisp
diced bacon and fresh herbs do their part to deliver
big flavors, as do the sweet onions, which are brushed
with bacon fat before they hit the grill.

SERVES 8

1. Prepare the grill for direct cooking over medium heat (350° to 450°F).

2. In a large bowl whisk together the 2 tablespoons oil, ½ teaspoon salt,
and ½ teaspoon pepper. Add the potatoes and toss to coat.

3. Brush the cooking grates clean. Grill the potatoes over **direct
medium heat**, with the lid closed, until golden brown and tender,
20 to 25 minutes, turning occasionally. Remove from the grill and let
cool until they can be handled. Cut each potato half into two pieces
and place in a large bowl. Cover and set aside at room temperature.

4. In a skillet over medium heat on the stove, fry the bacon until crisp,
10 to 12 minutes, stirring occasionally. With a slotted spoon, transfer
the bacon to the bowl of potatoes; reserve the bacon fat.

5. Brush the onion slices on both sides with some of the reserved bacon
fat and season on both sides with salt and pepper. Grill the onion slices
over **direct medium heat**, with the lid closed, until lightly browned and
tender, 10 to 12 minutes, turning the slices and basting with more of the
reserved bacon fat once. Transfer the slices to a cutting board and cut
each slice into quarters. Add to the potatoes along with the scallions,
parsley, and thyme.

6. In a small bowl combine the vinegar, broth, ¼ teaspoon salt, and
¼ teaspoon pepper. Slowly whisk in the remaining ⅓ cup oil. Pour the
dressing over the potatoes and toss gently. Serve right away, or, to blend
the flavors more fully, cover and let stand at room temperature for
about 1 hour before serving.

TWICE-GRILLED POTATOES

PREP TIME
25 MINUTES

GRILLING TIME
40 TO 45 MINUTES

4 russet potatoes, about 2½ pounds total, cut in half lengthwise

Vegetable oil

STUFFING

¾ cup sour cream

½ cup whole milk

½ cup minced cooked ham

1½ cups grated Gruyère cheese (about 6 ounces), divided

2 teaspoons Dijon mustard

Kosher salt and freshly ground black pepper

2 tablespoons finely chopped chives and/or fresh flat-leaf parsley (optional)

This version of an old-school side dish ups the ante with Gruyère cheese and Dijon mustard. The ingredients are very French, but the stuffed potatoes are likely a little bolder—and maybe more memorable—than what you might find in a traditional bistro.

SERVES 8

1. Prepare the grill for direct cooking over medium heat (350° to 450°F).

2. Brush the cooking grates clean. Brush the potato halves with oil. Grill over **direct medium heat**, with the lid closed, until tender when pierced with a fork, 30 to 35 minutes, turning three or four times. Remove from the grill and let cool slightly.

3. When the potatoes are cool enough to handle, use a small knife to cut around the cut side of each potato half to within ¼ inch of the skin. Then, using a small pointed spoon, carefully scoop out the potato flesh, placing it in a large bowl and leaving a ¼-inch-thick shell. As you work, be careful not to puncture the shell. Set the potato shells aside.

4. Using a potato masher, mash the potato flesh until smooth. Add the sour cream and milk and mix well. Stir in the ham, half of the cheese, and the mustard and season with salt and pepper. Taste and adjust the seasoning with more mustard if needed. Divide the stuffing evenly among the potato shells, mounding it slightly. Top the stuffed potatoes with the remaining cheese.

5. Grill the stuffed potatoes over **direct medium heat**, with the lid closed, until the cheese melts and the potatoes are heated through, about 10 minutes. Garnish with the herbs, if desired, and serve immediately.

ASPARAGUS, TOMATO, AND FETA
FRITTATA

PREP TIME
20 MINUTES

GRILLING TIME
ABOUT 17 MINUTES

8 ounces asparagus

6 large eggs

¼ cup half-and-half

¼ cup freshly grated
Parmigiano-Reggiano®
cheese (scant 1 ounce)

¼ teaspoon kosher salt

¼ teaspoon freshly ground
black pepper

1 tablespoon extra-virgin
olive oil

2 garlic cloves, finely
chopped

1 cup ripe cherry tomatoes,
cut in half crosswise

6 ounces feta cheese,
crumbled (scant 1¼ cups)

This recipe illustrates how your grill has the flexibility of an outdoor kitchen. First, you use it like a stove top to sauté the asparagus in a skillet and then you add the tomatoes, cheese, and beaten eggs and it becomes an oven for baking the frittata.

SERVES 6

1. One at a time grasp the end of each asparagus spear and bend it gently until it snaps at its natural point of tenderness, usually about two-thirds of the way down the spear. Discard the tough ends. Cut the spears on the diagonal into 1-inch pieces. Set aside.

2. In a blender combine the eggs, half-and-half, Parmigiano-Reggiano®, salt, and pepper and process for 10 seconds to blend thoroughly. Set aside.

3. Prepare the grill for direct cooking over medium heat (350° to 450°F).

4. Brush the cooking grates clean. Preheat a 10-inch grill-proof skillet, preferably nonstick, over **direct medium heat**, with the lid closed, for 3 minutes. Add the oil to the skillet and then add the asparagus and stir briefly to coat with the oil. Cook over **direct medium heat**, with the lid closed, for 2 minutes. Remove the skillet from the grill and roll the asparagus around in the skillet so the oil coats the bottom and sides of the pan evenly. Place the skillet back on the cooking grate, arrange the asparagus in an even layer, and then scatter the garlic, tomatoes, and feta evenly over the asparagus. Pour the egg mixture into the skillet. Grill the frittata over **direct medium heat**, with the lid closed, until the eggs are puffed, browned, and firm in the center, about 15 minutes. Remove from the grill.

5. Slide the frittata out of the skillet onto a serving plate. Cut into wedges and serve immediately.

GRILLED POLENTA
WITH TOMATILLO SAUCE

PREP TIME
40 MINUTES

COOLING TIME
2 HOURS

GRILLING TIME
18 TO 22 MINUTES

POLENTA

1 tablespoon extra-virgin olive oil

2 tablespoons unsalted butter

½ cup finely chopped yellow onion

4 cups whole milk

1 cup polenta

1 teaspoon chili powder

¾ teaspoon kosher salt

SAUCE

2 slices yellow onion, each about ½ inch thick

8 ounces tomatillos, husks removed and rinsed

1 poblano chile pepper

Extra-virgin olive oil

¼ cup tightly packed fresh cilantro leaves, plus more for garnish

½ teaspoon packed light brown sugar

¼ teaspoon kosher salt

4 ounces queso fresco, crumbled

1 Hass avocado, sliced

Fire-roasted slices of polenta provide heft, while melted cheese, avocado, and a sauce of smoky grilled vegetables give this vegetarian dish its Latin accent. Oil the polenta pieces well before they go on the grill or their bumpy surface might stick to the grate.

SERVES 4

1. Brush an 8-inch-square pan with the oil. In a large saucepan over medium heat, melt the butter. Add the onion and cook until lightly browned, 3 to 5 minutes, stirring occasionally. Add the remaining polenta ingredients and whisk until the mixture begins to boil. Turn the heat to very low and cook, stirring with a wooden spoon constantly to prevent burning, until the polenta is thick and no longer gritty to the bite, 15 to 20 minutes. Remove from the heat, pour into the pan, and spread into an even layer. Let cool at room temperature for 2 hours.

2. Prepare the grill for direct and indirect cooking over medium heat (350° to 450°F).

3. Brush the cooking grates clean. Brush the onion, tomatillos, and chile all over with oil. Grill over **direct medium heat**, with the lid closed, until the onion slices are lightly charred, the tomatillos are blistered, and the chile is blackened but holds its shape, turning as needed. The onion slices will take 8 to 10 minutes, the tomatillos about 10 minutes, and the poblano 10 to 12 minutes. Remove the vegetables from the grill as they are done. Place the poblano in a bowl and cover with plastic wrap to trap the steam. Let stand for about 10 minutes. Remove and discard the charred skin, stem, and seeds. Put the chile, onion, tomatillos, cilantro, sugar, and salt in a food processor or blender and whirl until evenly pureed. Taste and adjust the seasoning with sugar and salt if needed. Set aside.

4. Invert the pan of cooled polenta onto a cutting board. Cut the polenta into four to eight pieces of whatever size and shape you like. Place the polenta pieces, smooth, oiled side down, over **indirect medium heat**. Divide the cheese evenly among the pieces, carefully piling it on top. Grill, with the lid closed, until the polenta is warm and the cheese begins to melt, 8 to 10 minutes, without turning.

5. Transfer the polenta to individual plates. Spoon the tomatillo sauce over the polenta and top with avocado slices and cilantro. Serve right away.

MAC AND CHEESE
WITH HAM AND POBLANOS

PREP TIME
30 MINUTES

GRILLING TIME
33 TO 40 MINUTES

3 or 4 medium poblano chile peppers, about 12 ounces total

1 baked ham steak, about 8 ounces and ⅓ inch thick

6 scallions (white and green parts)

Extra-virgin olive oil

¼ cup (½ stick) unsalted butter, plus more for greasing the baking dish

¼ cup unbleached all-purpose flour

4 cups whole milk

4 cups shredded Monterey Jack cheese (about 1 pound), divided

¼ cup freshly grated Parmigiano-Reggiano® cheese (scant 1 ounce)

¾ teaspoon kosher salt

¼ teaspoon freshly ground black pepper

10 ounces dried large elbow macaroni

½ cup fresh bread crumbs

2 teaspoons finely chopped fresh thyme leaves

We've seen decent mac and cheese embellished with everything from beer (interesting) to ranch dressing (not so interesting). But what makes this version the best are bits of smoky meat and vegetables.

SERVES 6 TO 8

1. Prepare the grill for direct and indirect cooking over medium heat (350° to 450°F).

2. Brush the cooking grates clean. Brush the poblanos, ham, and scallions with oil and then grill over **direct medium heat**, with the lid closed, until the poblanos are blackened all over, turning as needed, and the ham and scallions are lightly charred, turning once or twice. The poblanos will take 8 to 10 minutes, and the ham and scallions will take 4 to 5 minutes. Remove the vegetables and ham from the grill as they are done. Place the poblanos in a bowl and cover with plastic wrap to steam. Let stand for 10 minutes. Remove and discard the charred skin, stems, and seeds, then roughly chop them. Cut the ham into ⅓-inch cubes. Cut the scallions crosswise into thin slices and discard the root ends. Reserve the vegetables and ham.

3. Grease a 3-quart grill-proof pan with butter. In a saucepan over medium heat on the stove, melt the butter. Whisk in the flour to form a paste and then cook until it starts to brown, 3 to 4 minutes, stirring occasionally. Slowly add the milk while whisking. Raise the heat to medium-high and gradually add 3 cups of the Monterey Jack, all of the Parmigiano-Reggiano®, the salt, and the pepper. As the cheese melts into the sauce and the sauce begins to boil, lower the heat to a simmer and cook, stirring often, for 4 to 5 minutes. Remove from the heat and set aside.

4. Bring a large pot filled with water to a rolling boil. Add the macaroni, stir well, and cook for 3 minutes less than the cooking time recommended on the package. Drain the macaroni well. Add the macaroni to the cheese sauce in the saucepan and mix well. Add the poblanos, ham, and scallions and again mix well. Transfer to the prepared baking pan.

5. In a bowl, combine the bread crumbs, the remaining 1 cup Monterey Jack, and the thyme and stir well. Sprinkle the bread crumb mixture over the pasta and press it into the surface. Place the baking dish over **indirect medium heat** and cook, with the lid closed, until the mac and cheese is golden brown on top, 25 to 30 minutes. Let cool slightly before serving.

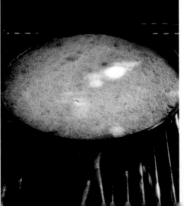

07

DESSERTS

FIRE-ROASTED
STRAWBERRIES

**PREP TIME
10 MINUTES**

**GRILLING TIME
8 TO 12 MINUTES**

**2 pints large strawberries
(20 to 24 berries)**

¼ cup granulated sugar

**¼ cup orange-flavored
liqueur, or 2 tablespoons
water and 1 tablespoon
fresh lemon juice**

½ teaspoon vanilla extract

**1 tablespoon unsalted
butter, softened**

Vanilla ice cream

Some desserts benefit from the woodsy smoke of charcoal, but this is not one of them. This recipe is all about the concentrated taste of ripe strawberries that have bubbled in their own natural juices—a heavenly topping for scoops of vanilla ice cream. We recommend a small baking pan on a gas grill for this one.

SERVES 6 TO 8

1. Hull the strawberries, then trim the stem end of each berry so it is flat. In a medium bowl combine the berries, sugar, liqueur, and vanilla and toss to coat evenly.

2. Generously coat the bottom and sides of a grill-proof 8-inch-square baking pan (or disposable foil pan) with the butter. The pan should be just large enough to hold the berries in a single layer with their sides almost touching (this allows the berries to support one another gently as they begin to soften).

3. Prepare the grill for direct cooking over high heat (450° to 550°F).

4. Remove the berries from the bowl and stand them in a single layer, flat side down and almost touching, in the prepared pan. Pour any liquid remaining in the bottom of the bowl evenly over the berries. Brush the cooking grates clean. Place the pan over **direct high heat** and grill, with the lid closed, until the liquid in the pan is bubbling and the berries are beginning to slump, 8 to 12 minutes. Cooking times will vary depending on the variety, size, and ripeness of the strawberries. Watch closely to catch the berries before they collapse.

5. Remove the pan from the grill and spoon the pan juices over the berries to moisten them. Let cool for 5 minutes, then carefully cut the berries into quarters or leave whole. Scoop ice cream into individual dessert bowls and spoon the berries and juices over the ice cream. Serve right away.

SKILLET BLUEBERRY
COBBLER

★

PREP TIME
20 MINUTES

GRILLING TIME
45 TO 50 MINUTES

★

Even cooks intimidated by the thought of making a pie crust or baking a cake will declare this dessert a slam dunk, especially if it's made midsummer when blueberries are at their best. Serve the cobbler heaped into bowls and topped with whipped cream as suggested—or with ice cream if you prefer. It's as easy as summer ought to be.

SERVES 8 TO 10

FILLING

¼ cup (½ stick) unsalted butter

8 cups fresh or thawed frozen blueberries, divided

1 cup granulated sugar, divided

2 tablespoons all-purpose flour

2 teaspoons finely grated lemon zest

2 tablespoons fresh lemon juice

½ teaspoon freshly grated nutmeg

BATTER

2½ cups unbleached all-purpose flour

1 cup granulated sugar

3 teaspoons baking powder

1 teaspoon ground cinnamon

½ teaspoon kosher salt

1 cup whole milk

½ cup (1 stick) unsalted butter, melted and cooled

2 teaspoons vanilla extract

Whipped cream for serving

1. Prepare the grill for indirect cooking over medium heat (ideally 350°F).

2. In a large skillet over medium heat on the stove, melt the butter. Add 4 cups of the blueberries and ½ cup of the sugar and heat until the mixture is the consistency of jam, about 10 minutes, stirring frequently. Remove from the heat. Add the remaining 4 cups berries, the remaining ½ cup sugar, the flour, the lemon zest and juice, and the nutmeg and stir to combine, making sure all the whole berries are evenly coated. Transfer to a grill-proof 2-quart shallow baking pan.

3. In a large bowl sift together the flour, sugar, baking powder, cinnamon, and salt. In a small bowl whisk together the milk, melted butter, and vanilla. Add the milk mixture to the flour and stir until until well mixed, scraping down the sides of the bowl as needed. There may still be some lumps. Drop the batter onto the fruit in large spoonfuls, starting in the center of the skillet and working toward the edge and leaving a 1-inch border of exposed fruit around the edge. It will seem like too little batter, but it will expand as it bakes.

4. Brush the cooking grates clean. Bake the cobbler over **indirect medium heat**, with the lid closed, for 20 minutes. Carefully rotate the pan 90 degrees, being careful as the fruit mixture will be bubbling up, then continue to bake, with the lid closed, until a skewer inserted into the center of the crust comes out clean, 25 to 30 minutes more.

5. Carefully transfer the pan to a wire rack and let cool for at least 10 minutes. Serve warm or at room temperature topped with whipped cream.

GRILLED PEACHES
WITH FRESH CHERRY SAUCE

PREP TIME
15 MINUTES

GRILLING TIME
10 TO 12 MINUTES

SAUCE

1 pound dark cherries, pitted

1 tablespoon sugar

½ cup dry red wine

1 teaspoon balsamic vinegar

1 teaspoon kirsch (cherry liqueur)

4 medium peaches

2 tablespoons unsalted butter

2 tablespoons packed light brown sugar

4 scoops vanilla ice cream

4 cookies, any kind (optional)

The ideal fruits for grilling are ripe yet still firm enough to move around the grate easily. A fruit as soft as melon or mango slices is a little tricky, but halved peaches are a breeze, with the flat sides caramelizing beautifully and the interiors turning warm, soft, and sweet—the perfect accompaniment to ice cream and a red wine–cherry sauce.

SERVES 4

1. In a sauté pan over medium-high heat, combine the cherries, sugar, wine, and vinegar and bring to a simmer. Cook until the cherries are soft, 6 to 8 minutes, stirring occasionally. Transfer the mixture to a food processor and puree until completely smooth. Return the mixture to the sauté pan over medium-high heat. Add the kirsch and simmer until reduced to about ¼ cup, stirring often. Remove from the heat and set aside.

2. Prepare the grill for direct cooking over medium heat (350° to 450°F).

3. Cut the peaches in half through the stem end and remove and discard the pits. Place the halves in a medium bowl. In a small saucepan over low heat on the stove, melt together the butter and sugar. Remove from the heat, drizzle over the peaches, and toss gently to coat evenly.

4. Brush the cooking grates clean. Grill the peaches over **direct medium heat**, with the lid closed, until grill marks are clearly visible and the peaches are soft, 10 to 12 minutes, turning once. Remove from the grill.

5. While the peaches are still warm, arrange 2 peach halves in the bottom of each individual serving dish, top with a scoop of ice cream and then with 1 tablespoon of the sauce. Tuck a cookie into each serving, if you like. Serve immediately.

PARADISE
GRILLED PINEAPPLE

PREP TIME
20 MINUTES

GRILLING TIME
6 TO 8 MINUTES

GLAZE

¾ cup fresh orange juice

1 tablespoon honey

1 tablespoon fresh
lime juice

2 teaspoons cornstarch

4 slices peeled, cored
fresh pineapple, each
about ½ inch thick

1 teaspoon freshly cracked
dried green peppercorns
or black peppercorns, plus
½ teaspoon for garnish
(optional)

4 scoops vanilla ice cream

Do you like easy? We've got easy . . . and glorious.
Grilled pineapple with ice cream is a pleasure that
reaches the level of greatness when it's drizzled with
an orange juice glaze and seasoned with pepper. Yes,
we said pepper, which brings a nice undertone of
spice to the acidic pineapple and sweet citrus glaze.

SERVES 4

1. In a small saucepan whisk together all the glaze ingredients until
smooth. Place over medium-high heat, bring to a boil, and cook until
thickened, 1 to 2 minutes, stirring occasionally. Remove from the heat
and keep warm or reheat gently before serving.

2. Prepare the grill for indirect cooking over medium heat (350° to 450°F).

3. Brush the cooking grates clean. Season the pineapple slices on both
sides with the peppercorns. Grill over **indirect medium heat**, with
the lid closed, until well marked, 6 to 8 minutes, turning once halfway
through the grilling time. Remove from the grill.

4. Place each pineapple slice on a dessert plate and set a scoop of
ice cream on top. Drizzle the glaze over the top, sprinkle with the
additional cracked pepper if you like, and serve right away.

SPICED BANANA CHOCOLATE
SUNDAES

PREP TIME
15 MINUTES

GRILLING TIME
2 TO 3 MINUTES

SAUCE

½ cup heavy whipping cream

3 ounces semisweet chocolate, finely chopped

¼ cup (½ stick) unsalted butter

½ teaspoon ground cinnamon

¼ teaspoon ground ginger

⅛ teaspoon ground cloves

4 ripe but firm bananas, peeled

1 pint vanilla ice cream

If you think regular chocolate sundaes are good, wait until you try one with buttery, spice-dusted grilled bananas. Be sure to start with ripe but fairly firm bananas so they are easy to maneuver on the grill, and buy the best chocolate your budget will allow for a top-notch sauce.

SERVES 4 TO 6

1. Prepare the grill for direct cooking over medium heat (350° to 450°F).

2. In a small saucepan over medium-high heat on the stove, bring the cream to a simmer. Remove the pan from the heat and immediately add the chocolate. Stir until the chocolate melts and the mixture is dark and smooth. Set aside.

3. In a large skillet over medium heat on the stove, melt the butter. Add the cinnamon, ginger, and cloves and stir to mix. Remove from the heat, place the bananas in the skillet, and brush them on all sides with the butter mixture.

4. Brush the cooking grates clean. Gently pick the bananas out of the skillet and place over **direct medium heat**. Grill, with the lid closed, until warm and well marked but not too soft, 2 to 3 minutes, gently turning once. Transfer the bananas to a cutting board and cut crosswise on the diagonal into ½-inch-thick slices.

5. Reheat the chocolate sauce over medium heat on the stove. In dessert bowls or sundae glasses, layer the ice cream, warm banana slices and chocolate sauce. Serve immediately.

PINEAPPLE
UPSIDE-DOWN CAKE

**PREP TIME
30 MINUTES**

**GRILLING TIME
46 TO 58 MINUTES**

This recipe has received rave reviews since it appeared in *Weber's Way to Grill* in 2008. Not surprisingly, folks often mention that flipping the cake upside down onto a platter is always a dramatic—and tense—moment. Nine times out of ten, though, it works just perfectly.

SERVES 6 TO 8

TOPPING

6 slices peeled, cored fresh pineapple, each ½ inch thick

2 tablespoons unsalted butter, melted

½ cup packed dark brown sugar

¼ cup heavy whipping cream

½ teaspoon ground cinnamon

BATTER

1 cup unbleached all-purpose flour

1 teaspoon baking powder

½ teaspoon kosher salt

¼ teaspoon baking soda

⅔ cup buttermilk

2 large eggs

1 teaspoon vanilla extract

½ cup (1 stick) unsalted butter, softened

¾ cup granulated sugar

1. Prepare the grill for direct and indirect cooking over medium heat (350° to 450°F). Brush the cooking grates clean. Brush the pineapple rings on both sides with the butter and then grill over **direct medium heat**, with the lid open, until nicely marked, 4 to 6 minutes, turning once. Remove from the grill and let cool. Leave one ring whole and cut the others in half.

2. Have a sheet pan nearby. In a 12-inch cast-iron skillet, combine the brown sugar, cream, cinnamon and any butter remaining from brushing the pineapple slices and place over **direct medium heat**. Cook, with the lid open, until the sugar has melted and the liquid starts to bubble around the outer edge of the pan, about 2 minutes. Remove the skillet from the grill and place on the sheet pan. Place the whole pineapple slice in the center of the skillet and arrange the halved pineapple slices around it. Set aside.

3. In a bowl stir together the flour, baking powder, salt, and baking soda. In a second bowl whisk together the buttermilk, eggs, and vanilla. In a medium bowl, using an electric mixer, cream the butter and sugar on medium-high speed until lightened, 2 to 4 minutes. On low speed, add the buttermilk mixture and beat until mixed. Gradually add the flour mixture and beat until smooth, scraping down the sides of the bowl as needed. Spread the batter evenly over the pineapple slices.

4. Place the skillet over **indirect medium heat** and close the lid. Bake the cake, keeping the temperature of the grill at 350°F, until the top is golden brown and a skewer inserted into the center comes out clean, 40 to 50 minutes. Remove from the grill and let cool for about 10 minutes.

5. Run a paring knife around the inside edge of the skillet, then carefully invert the skillet and cake onto a platter. Slowly lift off the skillet and dislodge any pineapple slices that have stuck to the bottom of the skillet, replacing them on the cake top. Let the cake cool briefly before slicing into wedges and serving. The cake is best served warm or at room temperature the day it is made.

WARM MOLTEN
CHOCOLATE CAKES
WITH FRESH BERRIES

1½ cups (1½ sticks) unsalted butter, plus 1 tablespoon for greasing

8 ounces bittersweet chocolate, chopped

4 large eggs

½ cup sugar

2 tablespoons all-purpose flour

Whipped cream for serving (optional)

2 cups fresh raspberries for serving

In the 1990s, restaurant-goers ordered warm chocolate cakes with molten chocolate centers every chance they got. We're still crazy about these little cakes, which is why this recipe made the cut. The list of ingredients is short and the method is easy, but make sure each muffin cup holds about ½ cup batter.

SERVES 10

1. Use the 1 tablespoon butter to grease ten cups of a grill-proof 12-cup standard muffin pan (cups 2¾ inches in diameter and 1¼ inches deep).

2. Select a heatproof bowl and a saucepan with a rim in which the bowl will rest. Fill the pan with water to a depth of 3 or 4 inches and bring the water to a bare simmer. Combine the remaining butter and the chocolate in the heatproof bowl. Set the bowl over (not touching) the simmering water and melt the chocolate and butter, stirring occasionally, until smooth. Remove the bowl from the pan. In a medium bowl whisk together the eggs and sugar until light and fluffy, about 20 seconds. Add the warm chocolate mixture to the egg mixture and whisk until smooth. Add the flour and mix until specks of white are no longer visible.

3. Divide the batter evenly among the prepared muffin cups, filling each cup almost to the rim (about ½ cup batter per cup). (If you are not ready to bake the cakes, the batter can be refrigerated for up to 3 hours.)

4. Prepare the grill for indirect cooking over medium heat (ideally 400°F).

5. Brush the cooking grates clean. Place the muffin pan over **indirect medium heat** and bake, with the lid closed, until the cake tops no longer jiggle when you shake the pan, about 10 minutes if the batter has not been refrigerated and up to 14 minutes if it has been refrigerated. Remove from the grill and let rest for 5 to 10 minutes.

6. Run a knife around the inside edge of each muffin cup to loosen the cake sides. Invert a platter on top of the muffin pan, then carefully invert the pan and platter together and set them on a work surface. Slowly lift off the pan. Carefully transfer the cakes to individual dessert plates and serve immediately with whipped cream, if using, and raspberries.

PANTRY RECIPES

HONEY-MUSTARD DRESSING

1 cup mayonnaise

¼ cup plus 2 tablespoons Dijon mustard

¼ cup honey

2 tablespoons fresh lemon juice

Kosher salt

Freshly ground black pepper

In a small bowl combine all the ingredients, including salt and pepper to taste, and mix well. (The dressing can be made up to 2 days ahead. Cover and refrigerate, then bring to room temperature before serving.)

MAKES ENOUGH FOR 6 SERVINGS

LEMON-PARSLEY DRESSING

¼ cup plus 2 tablespoons extra-virgin olive oil

2 tablespoons fresh lemon juice

2 tablespoons cold water

2 tablespoons finely chopped fresh Italian parsley leaves

½ teaspoon kosher salt

¼ teaspoon freshly ground black pepper

In a medium bowl whisk together all the ingredients. Taste and adjust the seasoning if needed. (The dressing can be made up to 2 hours ahead and kept at room temperature.)

MAKES ENOUGH FOR 6 TO 8 SERVINGS

TAHINI-YOGURT DRESSING

½ cup plain whole-milk Greek yogurt

½ cup tahini, well stirred before measuring

¼ cup finely chopped fresh cilantro or mint leaves, or a combination

3 tablespoons fresh lemon juice

2 tablespoons extra-virgin olive oil

½ teaspoon kosher salt

In a small bowl combine all the ingredients and mix well. If the dressing is too thick, whisk in up to 3 tablespoons water to achieve a good consistency. Cover and refrigerate until needed. (The dressing can be made up to 2 hours ahead.)

MAKES ENOUGH FOR 6 SERVINGS

HONEY-LIME CREAM

½ cup sour cream

½ teaspoon finely grated lime zest

1 tablespoon fresh lime juice

1 tablespoon extra-virgin olive oil

2 teaspoons honey

¼ teaspoon kosher salt

⅛ teaspoon freshly ground black pepper

In a small bowl whisk together all the ingredients. Cover and refrigerate until ready to serve. Let the sauce stand at room temperature for about 30 minutes before serving. (The sauce can be made up to 2 days ahead. Cover and refrigerate, then bring to room temperature before serving.)

MAKES ENOUGH FOR 4 TO 6 SERVINGS

LEMON YOGURT SAUCE

2 cups plain whole-milk Greek yogurt

1 teaspoon finely grated lemon zest

½ cup fresh lemon juice

¼ cup finely chopped fresh mint leaves

2 medium garlic cloves, minced

1 teaspoon kosher salt

In a medium bowl whisk together all the ingredients. Cover and refrigerate until ready to serve. (The sauce can be made up to 2 hours ahead.)

MAKES ENOUGH FOR 4 SERVINGS

BALINESE PEANUT SAUCE

½ cup creamy peanut butter

½ cup stirred coconut milk

2 tablespoons fresh lime juice

2 teaspoons hot chile-garlic sauce, such as Sriracha

2 teaspoons fish sauce

In a small saucepan combine all the ingredients. Cook over very low heat until smooth, 3 to 5 minutes, whisking occasionally (do not let the sauce simmer). If the sauce seems too thick, whisk in 1 to 2 tablespoons water. Remove from the heat. (The sauce can be made up to 4 days ahead. Let cool completely, then cover and refrigerate. Warm gently before serving.)

MAKES ENOUGH FOR 4 SERVINGS

TOMATO-AVOCADO SALSA

3 plum tomatoes, diced

2 Hass avocados, diced

⅓ cup minced red onion

⅓ cup finely chopped fresh cilantro leaves

2 to 3 pickled jalapeño chile peppers, minced

3 tablespoons fresh lime juice

1 tablespoon minced garlic

Kosher salt

In a medium bowl combine all the ingredients except the salt. Mix well, and season with salt. Let the salsa sit at room temperature for about 30 minutes to allow the flavors to blend. (The salsa can be made up to 2 hours ahead. Cover and refrigerate, then bring to room temperature before serving.)

MAKES ENOUGH FOR 12 TO 15 SERVINGS

PINEAPPLE-RUM SALSA

2 cups (about 12 ounces) finely diced fresh pineapple

¼ cup finely diced red bell pepper

¼ cup finely diced white onion

2 tablespoons roughly chopped fresh cilantro leaves

1 teaspoon kosher salt

½ to 1 teaspoon hot-pepper sauce, or to taste

1 tablespoon fresh lime juice

1 tablespoon dark or spiced rum

In a medium nonreactive bowl combine the pineapple, bell pepper, onion, cilantro, salt, and hot sauce and mix well. Cover and refrigerate. Just before serving, stir in the lime juice and rum. (The salsa can be made up to 1 day ahead.)

MAKES ENOUGH FOR 4 TO 6 SERVINGS

PICO DE GALLO 1

3 plum tomatoes, cored, seeded, and cut into ¼-inch dice

¼ cup roughly chopped fresh cilantro leaves

3 tablespoons finely diced red onion

2 tablespoons seeded and minced jalapeño chile peppers

1½ tablespoons fresh lime juice

½ teaspoon kosher salt

¼ teaspoon freshly ground black pepper

In a medium bowl combine all the ingredients and mix well. Set aside. (The pico de gallo can be made up to 2 hours ahead and kept at room temperature.)

MAKES ENOUGH FOR 4 SERVINGS

GUACAMOLE

2 Hass avocados

1 tablespoon fresh lime juice

2 medium garlic cloves

¼ teaspoon kosher salt

1 tablespoon finely chopped fresh cilantro leaves

⅛ teaspoon freshly ground black pepper

In a medium bowl mash the avocados with the back of a fork and immediately mix in the lime juice. Roughly chop the garlic with a chef's knife. Sprinkle the salt over the garlic, mince the garlic with the salt, and then use the side of the knife to crush the garlic with the salt to a smooth paste. Add the garlic mixture, cilantro, and pepper to the avocado and mix well. Serve at once or refrigerate, covered with plastic wrap, until ready to serve. (The guacamole can be made up to 2 hours ahead. Cover and refrigerate, then bring to room temperature before serving.)

MAKES ENOUGH FOR 4 TO 6 SERVINGS

PICO DE GALLO 2

2 cups finely diced tomato

1 cup finely diced red onion

1 tablespoon extra-virgin olive oil

1 tablespoon fresh lime juice

2 tablespoons finely chopped fresh cilantro leaves

1 to 2 teaspoons minced serrano chile pepper, including seeds

1 teaspoon kosher salt

In a medium bowl combine all the ingredients and mix well. Cover and let stand at room temperature for about 1 hour to allow the flavors to blend.

MAKES ENOUGH FOR 4 SERVINGS

TRI-TIP BARBECUE SAUCE

1 tablespoon olive oil

½ cup finely diced red onion

1 teaspoon minced garlic

½ cup low-sodium chicken broth

½ cup steak sauce

¼ cup ketchup

1 tablespoon finely chopped fresh Italian parsley leaves

1 tablespoon Worcestershire sauce

1½ teaspoons ground coffee

¼ teaspoon freshly ground black pepper

In a medium saucepan over medium-high heat, warm the oil. Add the onion and garlic and cook until soft, about 5 minutes, stirring occasionally. Add all the remaining ingredients, stir well, and bring to a boil. Turn down the heat to a simmer and cook until reduced to ½ cup, about 10 minutes, stirring occasionally. Remove from the heat, let cool slightly, transfer to a blender or food processor, and puree until smooth. Let cool, transfer to an airtight container, and refrigerate until ready to use. Bring to room temperature before serving.

MAKES ENOUGH FOR 6 SERVINGS

TANGY BARBECUE SAUCE

1½ cups ketchup

¾ cup unsweetened apple juice

¾ cup cider vinegar

3 tablespoons packed light brown sugar

3 tablespoons tomato paste

1½ tablespoons unsulfured molasses (not blackstrap)

1 tablespoon Worcestershire sauce

1½ teaspoons mustard powder

¾ teaspoon hot-pepper sauce

¾ teaspoon kosher salt

½ teaspoon freshly ground black pepper

In a medium, heavy saucepan whisk together all the ingredients. Place over medium heat on the stove and bring to a simmer. Cook for about 5 minutes, stirring occasionally. Set aside. (The sauce can be made up to 4 days ahead. Let cool completely, then cover and refrigerate. Warm gently before serving.)

MAKES ENOUGH FOR 12 SERVINGS

SASSY BARBECUE SAUCE

½ cup ketchup

½ cup water

2 tablespoons unsulfured molasses (not blackstrap)

1 tablespoon white wine vinegar

1 tablespoon Dijon mustard

1 tablespoon packed light brown sugar

2 teaspoons Worcestershire sauce

½ teaspoon kosher salt

¼ teaspoon hot-pepper sauce

¼ teaspoon garlic powder

¼ teaspoon freshly ground black pepper

In a small heavy saucepan whisk together all the ingredients. Place over medium heat and bring to a boil, stirring occasionally. Turn down the heat to a simmer and cook for 10 minutes, stirring occasionally. Remove from the heat, cover, and set aside. (The sauce can be made up to 4 days ahead. Let cool completely, then cover and refrigerate. Warm gently before serving.)

MAKES ENOUGH FOR 6 SERVINGS

GORGONZOLA-TOMATO SAUCE

1 tablespoon unsalted butter

1 tablespoon minced shallot

1 teaspoon minced garlic

½ cup vegetable juice

2 teaspoons prepared horseradish

½ teaspoon kosher salt

¼ cup crumbled Gorgonzola cheese (about 1 ounce)

In a small saucepan over medium heat, melt the butter and sauté the shallot and garlic until softened, about 2 minutes. Add the vegetable juice, horseradish, and salt, stir well, and bring to a simmer, then remove from the heat. If serving with oysters, spoon some sauce onto each oyster before grilling, top with a sprinkle of the cheese, and then grill the oysters as directed.

MAKES ENOUGH FOR 4 TO 6 SERVINGS

PIZZA SAUCE

1 can (8 ounces) tomato sauce

¼ cup freshly grated Parmigiano-Reggiano® cheese (scant 1 ounce)

2 tablespoons tomato paste

1 tablespoon extra-virgin olive oil

1 garlic clove, minced

½ teaspoon dried oregano

½ teaspoon dried basil

½ teaspoon dried thyme

In a small bowl, combine all the ingredients and mix well. Set aside until ready to use. (The sauce can be made up to 4 days ahead. Cover and refrigerate, then bring to room temperature before serving.)

MAKES ENOUGH FOR 6 TO 8 SERVINGS

SPICY TOMATO SAUCE

1 tablespoon extra-virgin olive oil

1 cup finely chopped yellow onion

2 medium garlic cloves, minced

1 teaspoon crushed red pepper flakes

½ teaspoon dried oregano

1 can (28 ounces) crushed Italian plum tomatoes in juice

2 tablespoons tomato paste

1 teaspoon kosher salt

In a large, deep skillet over medium heat, warm the oil. Add the onion and sauté until tender but not golden, about 3 minutes. Add the garlic, pepper flakes, and oregano and cook until fragrant, about 1 minute, stirring often. Add the tomatoes and their juice, tomato paste, and salt and stir well. Cover partially and simmer until slightly thickened, about 30 minutes. Remove from the heat and cover to keep warm. (The sauce can be made up to 4 days ahead. Let cool completely, then cover and refrigerate. Warm gently before serving.)

MAKES ENOUGH FOR 6 SERVINGS

RED CURRY SAUCE

1 tablespoon vegetable oil

1 tablespoon tomato paste

1 teaspoon minced garlic

½ teaspoon Thai red curry paste

1½ cups coconut milk

1 tablespoon fresh lime juice

1 teaspoon packed dark brown sugar

½ teaspoon ground turmeric

¼ teaspoon kosher salt

¼ teaspoon freshly ground black pepper

1 tablespoon finely chopped fresh basil or mint

In a saucepan over medium heat, warm the oil. Add the tomato paste, garlic, and curry paste and stir for 1 minute. Add the remaining ingredients except the basil and stir. Bring to a simmer and cook until the consistency of a cream sauce, 5 to 10 minutes, stirring occasionally. Add the basil during the last minute, then remove from the heat and set aside until ready to use.

MAKES ENOUGH FOR 4 TO 6 SERVINGS

GARLIC-THYME BUTTER

4 tablespoons (½ stick) unsalted butter, divided

1 tablespoon minced garlic

¼ cup white wine

2 teaspoons sherry vinegar

2 teaspoons minced fresh thyme leaves

¼ teaspoon kosher salt

In a skillet over medium heat, melt 1 tablespoon of the butter. Sauté the garlic until it starts to brown, about 2 minutes. Add the wine and vinegar and simmer until the sauce reduces by half, about 2 minutes. Remove from the heat. Cut the remaining butter into chunks and whisk into the wine mixture, a few chunks at a time. Stir in the thyme and salt and use right away.

MAKES ENOUGH FOR 4 TO 6 SERVINGS

ASIAN BUTTER SAUCE

1 tablespoon toasted sesame oil

2 teaspoons peeled, minced fresh ginger

2 tablespoons oyster sauce

1 teaspoon soy sauce

¼ teaspoon mustard powder

¼ cup (½ stick) unsalted butter, cut into cubes

In a small skillet over medium heat, combine the oil and ginger and heat until the oil foams. Remove from the heat and stir in the oyster sauce, soy sauce, and mustard. Whisk in the butter, a few cubes at a time, until incorporated.

MAKES ENOUGH FOR 4 TO 6 SERVINGS

GRAPEFRUIT-BASIL AIOLI

¼ cup mayonnaise

1 tablespoon chopped fresh basil

1½ teaspoons finely grated grapefruit zest

2 teaspoons fresh grapefruit juice

1 teaspoon minced garlic

¼ teaspoon kosher salt

In a small bowl combine all the ingredients and mix thoroughly.

MAKES ENOUGH FOR 4 TO 6 SERVINGS

JALAPEÑO MAYO

½ cup mayonnaise

1 jalapeño chile pepper, seeded and minced

1 tablespoon finely grated lime zest

1 tablespoon fresh lime juice

1 garlic clove, minced

¼ teaspoon ground cumin

¼ teaspoon kosher salt

¼ teaspoon freshly ground black pepper

In a small bowl whisk together all the ingredients. Cover and refrigerate until needed.

MAKES ENOUGH FOR 4 SERVINGS

APPLE-TARRAGON RELISH

2 tablespoons extra-virgin olive oil

1 large yellow or red onion, finely chopped (about 2 cups)

2 medium Fuji apples, cored and cut into ¼-inch cubes (about 2 cups)

1 teaspoon finely grated lemon zest

1 tablespoon fresh lemon juice

1 tablespoon finely chopped fresh tarragon leaves

½ teaspoon kosher salt

¼ teaspoon freshly ground black pepper

In a 12-inch skillet over medium heat, warm the oil. Add the onion and sauté until tender and slightly golden, about 10 minutes, stirring often. Stir in the apples and cook for 2 minutes more, stirring occasionally. Remove from the heat, stir in all the remaining relish ingredients, and cover to keep warm. (The relish can be made up to 1 day ahead. Let cool completely, then cover and refrigerate. Warm gently before serving.)

MAKES ENOUGH FOR 6 SERVINGS

BALSAMIC ONION JAM

2 tablespoons unsalted butter

2 tablespoons extra-virgin olive oil

2 large sweet yellow onions, each about 12 ounces, thinly sliced

½ teaspoon kosher salt

½ cup balsamic vinegar

½ cup packed light brown sugar

¼ cup dried currants or raisins

In a large skillet over medium-high heat, warm the butter and olive oil. Add the onions and salt and cook until translucent and reduced in volume by half, about 10 minutes, stirring frequently to prevent browning. Stir in the vinegar, sugar, and currants. Reduce the heat to medium-low and cook until the onions become jam-like and most of the liquid has evaporated, about 35 minutes, stirring occasionally to prevent scorching. Remove from the heat and let cool to room temperature. The jam will thicken as it cools. (The jam can be made up to 2 days ahead. Cover and refrigerate, then bring to room temperature before serving.)

MAKES ENOUGH FOR 10 TO 12 SERVINGS

CASHEW JASMINE RICE

1½ cups jasmine rice

2¼ cups water

¾ teaspoon kosher salt

½ cup coarsely chopped roasted cashews

⅓ cup thinly sliced scallions (white and light green parts only)

Put the rice in a fine-mesh strainer and rinse well under cold running water. Drain well, transfer the rice to a medium saucepan, add the water and salt, and bring to a boil over high heat. Turn down the heat to medium-low, cover, and cook until the water has been absorbed and the rice is tender, 17 to 20 minutes. Remove from the heat and scatter the cashews and scallions over the top but do not stir. Re-cover the pan and let stand for 5 to 10 minutes. Uncover the pan, fold in the cashews and scallions, and fluff the rice.

MAKES ENOUGH FOR 6 SERVINGS

GRILLING BEEF

CUT	THICKNESS/WEIGHT	APPROXIMATE GRILLING TIME
Steak: New York strip, porterhouse, rib eye, T-bone, and filet mignon (tenderloin)	¾ inch thick	**4–6 minutes** direct high heat
	1 inch thick	**6–8 minutes** direct high heat
	1¼ inches thick	**8–10 minutes** direct high heat
	1½ inches thick	**10–14 minutes:** sear 6–8 minutes direct high heat, grill 4–6 minutes indirect high heat
Beef, ground	¾ inch thick	**8–10 minutes** direct medium-high heat
Flank steak	1½–2 pounds, ¾ inch thick	**8–10 minutes** direct medium heat
Flat iron steak	1 inch thick	**8–10 minutes** direct medium heat
Hanger steak	1 inch thick	**8–10 minutes** direct medium heat
Kabob	1-inch cubes	**4–6 minutes** direct high heat
	1½-inch cubes	**6–7 minutes** direct high heat
Rib roast (prime rib), boneless	5–6 pounds	**1¼–1¾ hours** indirect medium heat
Rib roast (prime rib), with bone	8 pounds	**2–3 hours:** sear 10 minutes direct medium heat, grill 2–3 hours indirect low heat
Skirt steak	¼–½ inch thick	**4–6 minutes** direct high heat
Strip loin roast, boneless	4–5 pounds	**50 minutes–1 hour:** sear 10 minutes direct medium heat, grill 40–50 minutes indirect medium heat
Tenderloin, whole	3½–4 pounds	**35–45 minutes:** sear 15 minutes direct medium heat, grill 20–30 minutes indirect medium heat
Top sirloin	1½ inches thick	**10–14 minutes:** sear 6–8 minutes direct high heat, grill 4–6 minutes indirect high heat
Tri-tip	2–2½ pounds	**30–40 minutes:** sear 10 minutes direct medium heat, grill 20–30 minutes indirect medium heat
Veal loin chop	1 inch thick	**6–8 minutes** direct high heat

All cooking times are for medium-rare doneness, except ground beef (medium). The cuts, thicknesses, weights, and grilling times are guidelines rather than rules. Cooking times are affected by such factors as altitude, wind, outside temperature, and desired doneness. Rules of thumb: Grill steaks, chops, and kabobs using the direct method for the time given on the chart or to your desired doneness, turning once. Grill roasts and thicker cuts using the indirect method for the time given on the chart or until an instant-read thermometer reaches the desired internal temperature. Let larger cuts of meat rest for 5 to 10 minutes before carving; the internal temperature will rise 5 to 10 degrees during this time.

TYPES OF RED MEAT FOR THE GRILL

TENDER CUTS FOR GRILLING
- Beef New York strip steak
- Beef porterhouse steak
- Beef rib steak/rib eye steak
- Beef T-bone steak
- Beef tenderloin (filet mignon) steak
- Lamb loin chop
- Lamb sirloin chop
- Veal loin chop

MODERATELY TENDER CUTS FOR GRILLING
- Beef flank steak
- Beef flat iron steak
- Beef hanger steak
- Beef skirt steak
- Beef top sirloin steak
- Lamb shoulder blade chop
- Lamb sirloin chop
- Veal shoulder blade chop

BIGGER CUTS FOR SEARING AND GRILL-ROASTING
- Beef standing rib roast (prime rib)
- Beef strip loin roast
- Beef tri-tip roast
- Beef whole tenderloin
- Leg of lamb
- Rack of lamb
- Rack of veal

TOUGHER CUTS FOR BARBECUING
- Beef ribs
- Brisket

GRILLING LAMB

CUT	THICKNESS/ WEIGHT	APPROXIMATE GRILLING TIME
Chop: loin or rib	¾ inch thick	**4–6 minutes** direct high heat
	1 inch thick	**6–8 minutes** direct high heat
	1½ inches thick	**8–10 minutes** direct high heat
Lamb, ground	¾ inch thick	**8–10 minutes** direct medium-high heat
Leg of lamb, boneless, rolled	2½–3 pounds	**30–45 minutes:** sear 10–15 minutes direct medium heat, grill 20–30 minutes indirect medium heat
Leg of lamb, butterflied	3–3½ pounds	**30–45 minutes:** sear 10–15 minutes direct medium heat, grill 20–30 minutes indirect medium heat
Rack of lamb	1–1½ pounds	**15–20 minutes:** sear 5 minutes direct medium heat, grill 10–15 minutes indirect medium heat
Rib crown roast	3–4 pounds	**1–1¼ hours** indirect medium heat

All cooking times are for medium-rare doneness, except ground lamb (medium).

GRILLING PORK

CUT	THICKNESS/WEIGHT	APPROXIMATE GRILLING TIME
Bratwurst, fresh	3-ounce link	**20–25 minutes** direct medium heat
Bratwurst, precooked	3-ounce link	**10–12 minutes** direct medium heat
Chop, boneless or bone-in	¾ inch thick	**6–8 minutes** direct medium heat
	1 inch thick	**8–10 minutes** direct medium heat
	1¼–1½ inches thick	**10–12 minutes:** sear 6 minutes direct medium heat, grill 4–6 minutes indirect medium heat
Loin roast, boneless	3½ pounds	**28–40 minutes:** sear 8–10 minutes direct high heat, grill 20–30 minutes indirect high heat
Loin roast, bone-in	3–5 pounds	**1¼–1¾ hours** indirect medium heat
Pork shoulder (Boston butt), boneless	5–6 pounds	**5–7 hours** indirect low heat
Pork, ground	½ inch thick	**8–10 minutes** direct medium heat
Ribs, baby back	1½–2 pounds	**3–4 hours** indirect low heat
Ribs, spareribs	2½–3½ pounds	**3–4 hours** indirect low heat
Ribs, country-style, boneless	1 inch thick	**12–15 minutes** direct medium heat
Ribs, country-style, bone-in	1 inch thick	**45–50 minutes** indirect medium heat
Tenderloin	1 pound	**15–20 minutes** direct medium heat

The USDA recommends that pork is cooked to 160°F, but most chefs today cook it to 145°F or 150°F, when it still has some pink in the center and all the juices haven't been driven out. Of course, the doneness you choose is entirely up to you. Let roasts, larger cuts of meat, and thick chops rest for 5 to 10 minutes before carving. The internal temperature of the meat will rise 5 to 10 degrees during this time.

TYPES OF PORK FOR THE GRILL

TENDER CUTS FOR GRILLING
- Center-cut chop
- Loin or rib chop
- Tenderloin

MODERATELY TENDER CUTS FOR GRILLING
- Ham steak
- Shoulder blade steak
- Sirloin chop

BIGGER CUTS FOR GRILL-ROASTING
- Center loin roast
- Center rib roast
- Country-style ribs
- Cured ham
- Rack of pork

TOUGHER CUTS FOR BARBECUING
- Baby back ribs
- Shoulder (Boston butt)
- Spareribs

GRILLING POULTRY

CUT	THICKNESS/WEIGHT	APPROXIMATE GRILLING TIME
Chicken breast, bone-in	10–12 ounces	**23–35 minutes:** 3–5 minutes direct medium heat, 20–30 minutes indirect medium heat
Chicken breast, boneless, skinless	6–8 ounces	**8–12 minutes** direct medium heat
Chicken drumstick	3–4 ounces	**26–40 minutes:** 6–10 minutes direct medium heat, 20–30 minutes indirect medium heat
Chicken thigh, bone-in	5–6 ounces	**36–40 minutes:** 6–10 minutes direct medium heat, 30 minutes indirect medium heat
Chicken thigh, boneless, skinless	4 ounces	**8–10 minutes** direct medium heat
Chicken thigh, ground	¾ inch thick	**12–14 minutes** direct medium heat
Chicken, whole	4–5 pounds	**1¼–1½ hours** indirect medium heat
Chicken, whole leg	10–12 ounces	**48 minutes–1 hour:** 40–50 minutes indirect medium heat, 8–10 minutes direct medium heat
Chicken wing	2–3 ounces	**35–43 minutes:** 30–35 minutes indirect medium heat, 5–8 minutes direct medium heat
Cornish game hen	1½–2 pounds	**50 minutes–1 hour** indirect high heat
Duck breast, boneless	10–12 ounces	**9–12 minutes:** 3–4 minutes direct low heat, 6–8 minutes indirect high heat
Duck, whole	5½–6 pounds	**40 minutes** indirect high heat
Turkey breast, boneless	2½ pounds	**1–1¼ hours** indirect medium heat
Turkey, whole, not stuffed	10–12 pounds	**2½–3½ hours** indirect medium-low heat

The cuts, thicknesses, weights, and grilling times are meant to be guidelines rather than rules. Cooking times are affected by such factors as altitude, wind, and outside temperature. Cooking times are for the USDA's recommendation of 165°F. Let whole poultry rest for 10 to 15 minutes before carving. The internal temperature of the meat will rise 5 to 10 degrees during this time.

GRILLING SEAFOOD

TYPE	THICKNESS/WEIGHT	APPROXIMATE GRILLING TIME
Fish, fillet or steak: halibut, red snapper, salmon, sea bass, swordfish, and tuna	½ inch thick	**6–8 minutes** direct high heat
	1 inch thick	**8–10 minutes** direct high heat
	1–1¼ inches thick	**10–12 minutes** direct high heat
Fish, whole	1 pound	**15–20 minutes** indirect medium heat
	2–2½ pounds	**20–30 minutes** indirect medium heat
	3 pounds	**30–45 minutes** indirect medium heat
Clam (discard any that do not open)	2–3 ounces	**6–8 minutes** direct high heat
Lobster tail	6 ounces	**7–11 minutes** direct medium heat
Mussel (discard any that do not open)	1–2 ounces	**5–6 minutes** direct high heat
Oyster	3–4 ounces	**5–7 minutes** direct high heat
Scallop	1½ ounces	**4–6 minutes** direct high heat
Shrimp	1½ ounces	**2–4 minutes** direct high heat

The types, thicknesses, weights, and grilling times are meant to be guidelines rather than rules. Cooking times are affected by such factors as altitude, wind, outside temperature, and desired doneness.

The general rule of thumb for grilling fish: 8 to 10 minutes per 1-inch thickness.

TYPES OF SEAFOOD FOR THE GRILL

FIRM FILLETS AND STEAKS
- Arctic char
- Grouper
- Salmon
- Swordfish
- Tuna

MEDIUM-FIRM FILLETS AND STEAKS
- Halibut
- Mahimahi
- Monkfish
- Red snapper

TENDER FILLETS
- Cod
- Striped bass
- Trout

WHOLE FISH
- Branzino
- Grouper
- Red snapper
- Striped bass
- Trout

SHELLFISH
- Clam
- Lobster
- Mussel
- Oyster
- Scallop
- Shrimp
- Squid

GRILLING VEGETABLES

TYPE	THICKNESS/SIZE	APPROXIMATE GRILLING TIME
Artichoke hearts	whole	**14–18 minutes:** boil 10–12 minutes; cut in half and grill 4–6 minutes direct medium heat
Asparagus	½-inch diameter	**6–8 minutes** direct medium heat
Beet (6 ounces)	whole	**1–1½ hours** indirect medium heat
Bell pepper	whole	**10–12 minutes** direct medium heat
Carrot	1-inch diameter	**7–11 minutes:** boil 4–6 minutes, grill 3–5 minutes direct high heat
Corn, husked		**10–15 minutes** direct medium heat
Corn, in husk		**20–30 minutes** direct medium heat
Eggplant	½-inch slices	**8–10 minutes** direct medium heat
Garlic	whole	**45 minutes–1 hour** indirect medium heat
Mushroom, button or shiitake		**8–10 minutes** direct medium heat
Mushroom, portabello		**8–12 minutes** direct medium heat
Onion	halved	**35–40 minutes** indirect medium heat
	½-inch slices	**8–12 minutes** direct medium heat
Potato, new	halved	**15–20 minutes** direct medium heat
Potato, russet	whole	**45 minutes–1 hour** indirect medium heat
	½-inch slices	**9–11 minutes** direct medium heat
Potato, sweet	whole	**45 minutes–1 hour** indirect high heat
	½-inch slices	**12–15 minutes** direct medium heat
Scallion	whole	**3–4 minutes** direct medium heat
Squash, acorn (1½ pounds)	halved	**40 minutes–1 hour** indirect medium heat
Tomato, garden or plum	whole	**8–10 minutes** direct medium heat
	halved	**6–8 minutes** direct medium heat
Zucchini	½-inch slices	**4–6 minutes** direct medium heat

Just about everything from artichoke hearts to zucchini tends to cook best over direct medium heat.
The temperature on the grill's thermometer should be somewhere between 350° and 450°F.

GRILLING FRUIT

TYPE	THICKNESS/SIZE	APPROXIMATE GRILLING TIME
Apple	whole	**35–40 minutes** indirect medium heat
	½-inch slices	**4–6 minutes** direct medium heat
Apricot	halved lengthwise	**4–6 minutes** direct medium heat
Banana	halved lengthwise	**3–5 minutes** direct medium heat
Nectarine	halved lengthwise	**6–8 minutes** direct medium heat
Peach	halved lengthwise	**6–8 minutes** direct medium heat
Pear	halved lengthwise	**6–8 minutes** direct medium heat
Pineapple	½-inch slices or 1-inch wedges	**5–10 minutes** direct medium heat
Plum	halved lengthwise	**6–8 minutes** direct medium heat
Strawberry	whole	**4–5 minutes** direct medium heat

Just about everything from apples to strawberries tends to cook best over direct medium heat. The temperature on the grill's thermometer should be somewhere between 350° and 450°F.

USDA AND CHEF STANDARDS FOR DONENESS

For optimal safety, the United States Department of Agriculture (USDA) recommends cooking red meat to 145°F (final temperature) and ground red meat to 160°F. The USDA believes that 145°F is medium rare, but virtually all chefs today believe medium rare is closer to 130°F. This chart compares chef standards with USDA recommendations. Ultimately, doneness decisions are your choice.

DONENESS	CHEF STANDARDS	USDA
PORK	145°F	145°F
RED MEAT: Rare	120° to 125°F	n/a
RED MEAT: Medium rare	125° to 135°F	145°F
RED MEAT: Medium	135° to 145°F	160°F
RED MEAT: Medium well	145° to 155°F	n/a
RED MEAT: Well done	155°F +	170°F
POULTRY	160° to 165°F	165°F

METRIC EQUIVALENTS

METRIC EQUIVALENTS FOR DIFFERENT TYPES OF INGREDIENT

A standard cup measure of a dry or solid ingredient will vary in weight depending on the type of ingredient. A standard cup of liquid is the same volume for any type of liquid. Use the following chart when converting standard cup measures to grams (weight) or milliliters (volume).

Standard Cup	Fine Powder (e.g., flour)	Grain (e.g., rice)	Granular (e.g., sugar)	Liquid Solids (e.g., butter)	Liquid (e.g., milk)
1/8	18 g	19 g	24 g	25 g	30 ml
1/4	35 g	38 g	48 g	50 g	60 ml
1/3	47 g	50 g	63 g	67 g	80 ml
1/2	70 g	75 g	95 g	100 g	120 ml
2/3	93 g	100 g	125 g	133 g	160 ml
3/4	105 g	113 g	143 g	150 g	180 ml
1	140 g	150 g	190 g	200 g	240 ml

USEFUL EQUIVALENTS FOR LIQUID INGREDIENTS BY VOLUME

1/4 tsp						=	1 ml		
1/2 tsp						=	2 ml		
1 tsp						=	5 ml		
3 tsp	=	1 tbs			=	1/2 fl oz	=	15 ml	
		2 tbs	=	1/8 cup	=	1 fl oz	=	30 ml	
		4 tbs	=	1/4 cup	=	2 fl oz	=	60 ml	
		5 1/3 tbs	=	1/3 cup	=	3 fl oz	=	80 ml	
		8 tbs	=	1/2 cup	=	4 fl oz	=	120 ml	
		10 2/3 tbs	–	2/3 cup	=	5 fl oz	=	160 ml	
		12 tbs	=	3/4 cup	=	6 fl oz	=	180 ml	
		16 tbs	=	1 cup	=	8 fl oz	=	240 ml	
		1 pt	=	2 cups	=	16 fl oz	=	480 ml	
		1 qt	=	4 cups	=	32 fl oz	=	960 ml	
						33 fl oz	=	1000 ml	= 1 L

USEFUL EQUIVALENTS FOR COOKING/OVEN TEMPERATURES

	Fahrenheit	Celsius	Gas Mark
Freezing point	32°F	0°C	
Room temperature	68°F	20°C	
Boiling point	212°F	100°C	
Bake	325°F	160°C	3
	350°F	180°C	4
	375°F	190°C	5
	400°F	200°C	6
	425°F	220°C	7
	450°F	230°C	8

USEFUL EQUIVALENTS FOR DRY INGREDIENTS BY WEIGHT

To convert ounces to grams, multiply the number of ounces by 30.

1 oz	=	1/16 lb	=	30 g
4 oz	=	1/4 lb	=	120 g
8 oz	=	1/2 lb	=	240 g
12 oz	=	3/4 lb	=	360 g
16 oz	=	1 lb	=	480 g

USEFUL EQUIVALENTS FOR LENGTH

To convert inches to centimeters, multiply the number of inches by 2.5.

1 in			=	2.5 cm			
6 in	=	1/2 ft	=	15 cm			
12 in	=	1 ft	=	30 cm			
36 in	=	3 ft	=	1 yd	=	90 cm	
40 in			–	100 cm	=	1 m	

INDEX

ACKNOWLEDGMENTS

I feel fortunate that many years ago Mike Kempster at Weber decided to build a publishing program and welcome me into it. Mike continues to run the publishing program enthusiastically, along with Brooke Jones and Susan Maruyama, and I can't thank them enough for their help with this book. Brooke held everyone involved to high standards and Susan led us strategically through every phase of development.

At Weber, I relied on many other wonderful people as well. I raise a glass of gratitude to all of them, including Jim Stephen, Kim Lefko, Suzanne Brown, Deanna Budnick, Katy Davis, Kim Durk, Melissa Enos, Lexy Fricano, Kelsey Heidkamp, Heather Herriges, Melanie Hill, Kevin Kolman, Jennie Lussow, Stig Pedersen, and the main man with the big vision, Tom Koos.

Houghton Mifflin Harcourt (HMH) has proven once again to be an excellent partner in bringing Weber books to the market. I want to thank Bruce Nichols and Deb Brody for their total commitment to success. Cindy Kitchel is an angel of an editor with enviable smarts. I appreciate the hard work of all my HMH colleagues, including Tai Blanche, Jessica Gilo, Maire Gorman, Mike Harrigan, Tom Hyland, Marina Lowry, Brad Parsons, James Phirman, Rebecca Liss, Colleen Murphy, and Adriana Rizzo.

Kim Laidlaw arrived on the Weber cookbook scene in 2016 to help us create a new interpretation of our best recipes. Thank you, Kim, for bringing such an uplifting attitude along with amazing attention to detail. One of Kim's many accomplishments was gathering a world-class team of creative people to produce the book's photography and design. I am thrilled to see how brilliantly Ray Kachatorian refreshed and reimagined the recipes in the photographs, and I want to send a special shout-out to Ray's awesome assistants, Toven Stith and Mario Kroes. Thank you, Valerie Aikman-Smith, for styling the food so beautifully. We were all lucky to work with you and your assistants, Alyse Sakai, Amanda Frederickson, and Alicia Deal. For the props, we received great help from Jennifer Barguiarena and Christine Wolheim as well as prop assistants Ian Hartman and Laura Riegler.

I owe loads of appreciation to Ali Zeigler for the gorgeous design of this book. Your art directing is totally consistent with your personality. Both are spectacular, even in the oppressive heat of some photo shoots. Thank goodness for Nixon (Ray's dog), who made us laugh in sun-blasted Burbank. Special thanks go out to Keith Laidlaw, who assembled countless grills for us, and also to Nicole Moore Perullo, who made us feel right at home on location in Petaluma.

I also want to thank the many grillers who have reached out to me in person and via social media through the years about their experiences with my recipes. While cooking up ideas in my California backyard, I sometimes wonder how they will be received throughout the United States and the rest of the world. Just who are the people making my recipes and what do they think of them? Thanks to all of you who let me know. You helped to create this book.

AUTHOR

Jamie Purviance

CREATIVE TEAM

Producer and Managing Editor: Kim Laidlaw

Art Director and Lead Designer: Ali Zeigler

Senior Production Designer: Diana Heom

Photographer: Ray Kachatorian

Illustrator: Patrick Long

Food Stylist: Valerie Aikman-Smith

Prop Stylists: Jennifer Barguiarena
and Christine Wolheim

Photo Assistants: Toven Stith and Mario Kroes

Food Stylist Assistants: Alyse Sakai,
Amanda Frederickson, and Alicia Deal

Prop Stylists Assistants: Ian Hartman
and Laura Riegler

Copyeditor: Sharon Silva

Proofreader: Rachel Markowitz

Indexer: Elizabeth Parson

Color Imaging and In-House Prepress

Weber Creative Services:
Amy O'Brien
Mike Chavez
Neal Conner

Round Mountain Media

Consulting Global Publishing Director:
Susan J. Maruyama

Weber-Stephen Products LLC

Executive Board Member and Brand Godfather:
Mike Kempster

Chief Marketing Officer: Kim Lefko

VP Marketing, Global Marketing: Brooke Jones

Houghton Mifflin Harcourt

Editorial Director, Culinary and Lifestyle:
Deb Brody

Editorial Director: Cindy Kitchel

Art Director: Tai Blanche

Managing Editor: Marina Padakis Lowry

Production Director: Thomas Hyland

The following stories first appeared in *Weber's Big Book
of Grilling* ©2001: "Extreme Grilling," "A First-Class Luau,"
"A Firehouse Turkey Tale," and "A Bout with a Trout"

www.hmhco.com
www.weber.com®

Library of Congress Cataloging-in-Publication
Data is available.

ISBN 978-0-54495-237-9 (pbk)
ISBN 978-0-54495-163-1 (ebk)
ISBN 978-1-328-85713-2 (Weber edition)

Printed in the United States of America

DOW 10 9 8 7 6 5 4 3 2 1

WEBER'S GREATEST PARTIES

Tailgate Party (pages 54–55)

Hot, Sweet, and Sticky Chicken Wings (page 52),
Best-on-the-Block Babyback Ribs (page 170),
Corn on the Cob with Basil-Parmesan Butter
(page 258), New Potato Salad with Bacon and
Onions (page 272)

Dinner Party (pages 126–127)

Grilled Oysters with Four Sauces (page 33), Peach
and Blue Cheese Bruschetta Drizzled with Honey
(page 42), Lamb Loin Chops with Lemon-Mint
Salsa Verde (page 125), Salmon Fillets with Roasted
Corn, Tomato, and Avocado Salsa (page 242),
Grilled Carrots with Spiced Butter (page 271)

Mexican Fiesta (pages 160–161)

Chicken and Poblano Quesadillas (page 61),
T-Bones with Avocado Salsa (page 103),
Disappearing Pork Tenderloins with Pico
de Gallo (page 158), Mexican-Style Corn on
the Cob (page 261)

Paella Party (page 238–239)

Zesty Garlic Shrimp (page 38), Grilled
Romaine Salad with Caesar Dressing (page 48),
Seafood Paella (page 236), Charred Asparagus
with Basil-Lime Dipping Sauce (page 268)